W9-AVJ-822

Customer Satisfaction Measurement Simplified:

A Step-by-Step Guide for ISO 9001:2000 Certification

Also Available from ASQ Quality Press:

Improving Your Measurement of Customer Satisfaction: A Guide to Creating, Conducting, Analyzing, and Reporting Customer Satisfaction Measurement Programs
Terry G. Vavra

Analysis of Customer Satisfaction Data
Derek R. Allen and Tanniru R. Rao

Measuring Customer Satisfaction: Survey Design, Use, and Statistical Analysis Methods, Second Edition
Bob E. Hayes

Customer Centered Six Sigma: Linking Customer, Process Improvement, and Financial Results
Earl Naumann and Steven H. Hoisington

Customer Satisfaction Measurement and Management
Earl Naumann and Kathleen Giel

ISO 9001:2000 Explained, Second Edition
Joseph J. Tsiakals, Charles A. Cianfrani, and John E. (Jack) West

Value Leadership: Winning Competitive Advantage in the Information Age
Michael C. Harris

Improving Performance through Statistical Thinking
ASQ Statistics Division

To request a complimentary catalog of ASQ Quality Press publications, call 800-248-1946, or visit our Web site at www.qualitypress.asq.org .

Customer Satisfaction Measurement Simplified:

A Step-by-Step Guide for ISO 9001:2000 Certification

Terry G. Vavra, Ph.D.

ASQ Quality Press
Milwaukee, Wisconsin

Customer Satisfaction Measurement Simplified: A Step-by-Step Guide for ISO 9001:2000 Certification
Terry G. Vavra, Ph.D.

Library of Congress Cataloging-in-Publication Data

Vavra, Terry G.
    Customer satisfaction measurement simplified : a step-by-step guide for
ISO 9001:2000 certification / by Terry G. Vavra.
        p. cm.
    Includes bibliographical references and index.
    ISBN 0-87389-500-2 (alk. paper)
    1. Consumer satisfaction—Statistical methods. 2. Questionnaires. 3. ISO 9000
Series Standards—Handbooks, manuals, etc. I. Title.

HF5415.335 .V378 2001
658.5'62—dc21   2001040046

10 9 8 7 6 5 4 3 2 1

ISBN 0-87389-500-2

Acquisitions Editor: Annemieke Koudstaal
Production Editor: Craig S. Powell
Production Administrator: Gretchen Trautman
Special Marketing Representative: David Luth

ASQ Mission: The American Society for Quality advances individual and
organizational performance excellence worldwide by providing opportunities for
learning, quality improvement, and knowledge exchange.

Attention Bookstores, Wholesalers, Schools, and Corporations: ASQ Quality
Press books, videotapes, audiotapes, and software are available at quantity
discounts with bulk purchases for business, educational, or instructional use.
For information, please contact ASQ Quality Press at 800-248-1946, or write to
ASQ Quality Press, P.O. Box 3005, Milwaukee, WI 53201-3005.

To place orders or to request a free copy of the ASQ Quality Press Publications
Catalog, including ASQ membership information, call 800-248-1946. Visit our
Web site at www.asq.org or http://qualitypress.asq.org .

Printed in the United States of America

∞ Printed on acid-free paper

American Society for Quality

Quality Press
600 N. Plankinton Avenue
Milwaukee, Wisconsin 53203
Call toll free 800-248-1946
Fax 414-272-1734
www.asq.org
http://qualitypress.asq.org
http://standardsgroup.asq.org
E-mail: authors@asq.org

Dedication

My father, Marvin Joseph Vavra, believed there was only one way to do things—the *right* way! While he was living, he inspired me by example to investigate, understand, learn, and then to reciprocate by passing newly acquired knowledge along to others. I have tried to respect all of his principles in my personal conduct and career. I trust he would be proud of this book.

Table of Contents

Part I   Discovery ●◉◉◉◉

What Are Your Customers' Requirements?

Part II   Design and Deployment

How Should You Measure Your Customers' Satisfaction?

Part III   Deduction ⚫⚫●⚫⚫

How Will You Analyze the Information You Collect?

Part IV   Discourse ⚫⚫⚫●⚫

How Will You Report Your Findings?

Part V   Development ●●●●●

How Will You Stimulate Continual Improvement?

Introduction

Welcome! I've been studying, measuring, and helping to improve customer satisfaction for the past 15 years. I find it an extremely interesting and rewarding profession. Imagine, I get to monitor whether customers are really getting what they want, how they want it, and when they want it. If not, my work helps identify the necessary modifications my client should make to its products, processes, or procedures to increase the satisfaction it's delivering to its customers.

I've written an earlier book for the American Society for Quality, *Improving Your Measurement of Customer Satisfaction*. But it's quite thick and rather theory oriented. I was pleased when Ken Zielske of the ASQ asked me if I'd be interested in creating a new book, more oriented to the practical questions of quality and to satisfaction professionals who need quick answers to specific issues. I liked the idea. I've extended this basic premise to many of you who are adopting customer satisfaction procedures to comply with the newly revised International Organization for Standardization (ISO) 9000 series standards. But no matter the reason you're building (or revising) a customer satisfaction program, my intention is to provide you with a sourcebook directed specifically at the decisions you have to make. I hope you'll find it well organized and relevant for your day-in, day-out needs.

THE ISO STANDARDS

The family of ISO 9000 quality requirements has been tremendously successful in the 17 years since it was introduced. Today, more than a quarter of a million organizations worldwide have gained certification through the program. Yet the program hasn't been without its detractors. In the early 1990s, I was surprised as my firm began a relationship with a division of Motorola to find that Motorola, an acknowledged leader of the quality movement, had some reservations concerning the ISO requirements. In a 1992 conversation with Olga Striltschuk (now corporate vice president and director, GTSS Performance Excellence, Motorola) I asked why Motorola wasn't more supportive of the ISO process, having created its own QSR evaluation instead. Olga replied:

> *ISO 9001 requires that all business processes are documented and that there is evidence that a company performs according to the documented process. That is a basic requirement for any sound quality system and defines the "approach." However, we find "deployment" (pervasive use of the process) and "results" (benefits from executing the process) to be equally important. In our Quality System Review (QSR) System (developed in 1987), we require rigid documentation of process, but we've also specified that, in order to be best in class, the entire organization must use the process, drive continuous improvement and demonstrate its effectiveness through increasing comparative results. A critical aspect of the results is that they are customer-focused and that is why Motorola has always been committed to the measurement and improvement of customer satisfaction.*

I was struck with this core belief: *processes and process control are most valuable when their use is pervasive and ultimate contribution or consequence is also considered.*

ISO has enjoyed a phenomenal acceptance worldwide. Initially a good portion of that acceptance has been motivated by the basic belief that to produce quality products and services on a consistent basis, tested, established, and accepted processes are absolutely necessary.

In part, processes speak to the conformance (or technical) definition of quality. Processes help us keep our products and services conforming to a set of specifications. The other side of quality, recognized by even someone as process oriented as W. Edwards Deming, is the expectational side. The satisfaction of customers' expectations is necessarily measured, Deming said, "through consumer research . . . by which the manufacturer . . . is able to redesign his product to make it better as measured by the quality and uniformity that are best suited to the end users of the product and to the price that the consumer can pay" (1986, 178).

THE EVOLUTION OF ISO

After a two-year process of international planning sessions, improvements to the ISO 9000 standards have been identified for the rollout of ANSI/ISO/ASQ Q9001-2000. In this author's opinion, two of the more significant improvements are:

- Identifying customers' requirements (to ensure that an organization's processes are properly aligned to those requirements)

- Specifying that consequences of the established processes ought to be productive of customer satisfaction

These additions align the ANSI/ISO/ASQ Q9001-2000 process orientation with the customer satisfaction measurement movement.

This monograph is dedicated to helping all quality and customer service professionals gain comfort with the world of CSM (customer satisfaction measurement). It is also adapted specifically for the ISO 9000 professional who is charged with helping his or her organization recertify for ANSI/ISO/ASQ Q9001-2000. For some, CSM will be a frightening world of subjectivity—quite different from the very objective nature of specifying and observing processes. Yet when one learns how to properly process and interpret customers' subjective views, the potential value is substantial because in customers' subjectivity can be found insights for understanding, suggestions for modification, and actions for improvement. This subjectivity elevates ANSI/ISO/ASQ Q9001-2000 from a closed process to an open process whose elements are based on feedback from customers.

ISO registrants may typically be involved in business-to-business (B2B) customer situations; other readers of this book may be engaged in business-to-consumer (B2C) situations. My comments are intended to be useful to both constituencies.

WRITING CONVENTIONS

Throughout the book, when referring to the reader's company, business, organization, or other for-profit or not-for-profit entity, I will defer to the global term *organization*. I do this to make my comments as applicable as possible to a wide range of institutions. I will adopt the ISO convention of using *product* to represent *any output from a process* (be it hardware, software, or services). One of my pet peeves is the emerging confusion between the process, a *survey,* and the means by which answers are collected, a *questionnaire.* With increasing regularity I hear my colleagues speak of a new survey returned in the mail or of the responses of a customer on a survey. In this book I'll distinguish between the two terms.

All these conventions are not intended to offend, and I hope and trust no reader will take offense.

ORGANIZATION OF THIS BOOK

The book is organized using the following process model. The table of contents lists chapters according to the stage of the model they serve.

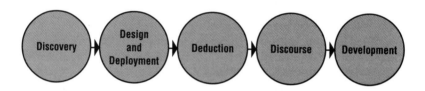

These five stages describe discrete phases of the development and execution of a customer satisfaction survey process. We'll investigate each further, on a chapter-by-chapter basis.

If you need assistance for only part of your survey process, use the model to guide you to the appropriate chapter (or chapters) for your questions or needs. If you're totally new to customer satisfaction measurement, you'll probably wish to read the entire book. The chapters are arranged in a logical, chronological order most useful to a reader new to CSM.

ORGANIZATION OF THE CHAPTERS

For convenience of use, each chapter contains at least four basic components:

- A *Step-by-Step* list of Issues. This list shows the reader the topics to be discussed and allows the reader to more appropriately use the content to suit his or her immediate needs.

- Discussions of each step, numbered to match the topic.

- *Checkpoints* at the end of each step's discussion.

- A reprise of the *Step-by-Step* list, this time with Answers for the Issues, at the conclusion of each chapter. Impatient readers who require a primer for immediate action can start at the end of the chapter and then draw selectively on the chapter contents.

Some chapters contain these additional sections:

- *Toolkits*. These contain very detailed descriptions of specific tools or procedures that might slow the chapter discussion down if left in the middle of a chapter. Reading these sections is completely optional.

- *Theory bites and personal observations*. The pragmatic reader may not have the time or interest in immersing himself/herself in a theoretical discussion, yet there are some valuable learnings to be made. Hopefully the author's own personal experiences will provide a bit of 'real world experience' to our discussions.

Lastly, the main Appendix discusses some general techniques that may be applied in the chapters. It also includes worksheets for several activities described in the chapters.

In addition to the material in the book, the accompanying CD-ROM contains many templates and graphs you may use in organizing, analyzing, and reporting your CSM process.

MY APPRECIATION

No effort of this sort is the work of a single person, even though my name is on the cover. I am indebted to many wonderful individuals. My thanks to my literary agent, Ms. Sally Wecksler of Inscom, for her constant nudgings. I appreciate the wonderful staff at ASQ: Annemieke Koudstaal, Craig Powell, and David Luth. With their efforts my work gets to press far faster than with any other publisher. Three superb peer reviewers—among them John J. Lanczycki, and Dr. Roy Richardson—offered thorough and helpful suggestions to an earlier version of the manuscript. While they inadvertently made me work all the harder, the value of their suggestions has made the book a better product! I am also indebted to the high level of involvement of the graphics house that designed and set type for this book, thanks Paul and Leayn Tabili of New Paradigm! My colleagues at Marketing Metrics—Tim Keiningham, Charles Patton, Ken Peterson, Jack Poon, and Doug Pruden—all gave me encouragement and labored through early drafts. My immense gratitude goes to Karen Liu who has programmed all the spreadsheets and graphs in the book. Thanks for your patience and assistance. Final thanks to my daily confidant, Trice Gately, who supervised numerous aspects of the project.

READY, SET, GO!

I hope you enjoy this exciting adventure you're about to start. There are thousands of professionals like you the world over who have already begun or who are just now initiating this fascinating journey. Keep your eyes and ears open—you'll derive a wealth of information from your organization's customers. And become a zealot for acceptance of those insights and an instigator of change. You can make a profound impact on your organization with this information and your responsibility for it.

In the words of an esteemed friend (and client), Ms. Melinda Goddard of Roche Laboratories:

> *Keep your customer satisfaction measurement as strategically focused as your marketing and sales efforts, and the customers whose loyalty you want most will lead you to success as long as you—and your leadership team—are really listening. Beware of ranking against one's competitors or setting unrealistic goals. Goals set to follow others can focus the organization on competitors, and goals set too high can focus it on attaining scores—instead of satisfying customers. When your customers come first, your competitors are more likely to follow you—and your goals will take care of themselves!*

Finally, as is said so frequently in the world of customer satisfaction, establishing measurement and improvement programs for customer satisfaction is best undertaken as a continuing journey, not as a destination. It should be always ongoing, never concluded, never finished. I wish you much success and satisfaction!

Terry G. Vavra
tvavra@marketingmetrics.com

I.

Discovery

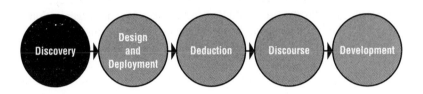

What Are Your Customer's Requirements?

*This is the stage at which you need to iden-
tify the requirements your customers have of
your organization, and the issues on which
they judge their satisfaction with your organization, and use to determine whether they'll
continue to do business with you. This is a
stage at which you momentarily set aside
your intuitions and assumptions, and question and listen to your customers directly.*

1

Understanding Customer Satisfaction Measurement and Its Role in the ANSI/ISO/ASQ Q9001-2000 Standard

The marketplace of our global economy has never been more competitive. Companies and organizations everywhere are striving to find any point of uniqueness with which to differentiate themselves from their competitors. Customers buying products and services are similarly seeking out suppliers whose products and services are noticeably better and using these perceived differences to guide their selection process and to justify any price premium they decide to pay. Because most customers have the option of buying from several suppliers who all offer products of near similar quality *(parity products)*, they generally must look beyond the physical product for other indications of quality. They seek any cues they can find to help identify the best vendor for their needs. In seeking cues, they are likely to observe vendors' internal practices as well as any external evidence of a vendor's quality focus. The practice of measuring customer satisfaction is one internal practice that signals a company's orientation to quality. ISO certification is another very respected cue. It's far from coincidence then, that the revised ANSI/ISO/ASQ Q9001-2000 standards emphasize the importance of measuring and striving to improve customer satisfaction.

Step-by-Step: The Issues of Understanding Customer Satisfaction Measurement and Its Role in the ANSI/ISO/ASQ Q9001-2000 Standard

1.1 Create a statement defining what customer satisfaction means to your organization.

1.2 Review the philosophical reasons for maximizing your customers' satisfaction.

1.3 Review the economic justification for maximizing your customers' satisfaction.

1.4 Review the ANSI/ISO/ASQ Q9001-2000 certification reasons for measuring your customers' satisfaction.

1.5 Review the ANSI/ISO/ASQ Q9001-2000 requirements for documentation and auditable items.

1.6 Achieve a basic understanding of the revisions to the ISO 9000 standards advanced by the ANSI/ISO/ASQ Q9001-2000 family of quality management standards.

1.7 Examine the basic theory underlying customer satisfaction.

SO WHAT'S THE PURPOSE?

Since this book is dedicated to the measurement of customer satisfaction, it probably makes good sense to tackle the issue of a definition and the value of the construct (satisfaction) before you create massive systems and before you begin to interview hundreds, even thousands of your customers. Recognize that as your organization's customer satisfaction measurement (CSM) professional, you may be asked at any time, by anyone in your organization (including your immediate boss or even your CEO), "Just why are we spending so much effort measuring satisfaction?" Or perhaps you'll be asked, "Exactly what will we be able to do with all this data you're collecting?" You'll want to have answers readily available.

STEP 1.1 DEFINING CUSTOMER SATISFACTION

While there is no intention of making this book a dry collection of definitions, rules, and theories, there is nevertheless good reason for establishing some basic building blocks. One such necessary understanding is how we intend to define satisfaction. In the literature on the topic, one finds two basic orientations to a definition of satisfaction:

- Satisfaction is defined as a customer's satisfaction with the end state resulting from having consumed a product or service.

- Satisfaction is defined as a customer's process of perceiving and evaluating a consumption experience (Yi 1991).

We will accept the latter perspective and suggest the following definition of satisfaction:

Satisfaction is a customer's emotional response to his or her evaluation of the perceived discrepancy between his or her prior experience with and expectations of our product and organization and the actual experienced performance as perceived after interacting with our organization and consuming our product. We believe that customers' satisfaction will influence their future reactions toward our organization (readiness to repurchase, willingness to recommend us, willingness to pay our price without haggling or seeking a lower-cost provider).

Furthermore, we accept that customers can experience satisfaction with:

- Our organization's products, overall

- Specific performance aspects of our organization's products

- Our organization's conduct of transactions (sales presentations, delivery of goods, repair visits, complaint handling, etc.)

- Our organization, representatives, and/or departments as entities

- The prepurchase relationship our organization creates with them

- The postpurchase relationship our organization creates with them

The quality control specialist will surely note how subjective this definition of customer satisfaction is. The quality control movement has accepted that there are two different approaches to satisfaction:

- *The conformance approach.* Frequently referred to as the engineer's perspective, essentially this perspective deems a product satisfactory if it meets the specifications to which it was produced. (If these specifications acknowledge all of the customers' requirements, an argument could be made that conformance also implies the second form of satisfaction, expectational.)

- *The expectational approach.* This perspective deems a product satisfactory if it meets the customer's expectations. The problem here is constantly tracking the evolving requirements of customers.

Checkpoint 1.1

1. Establish an operational definition in Worksheet 1.1 (located in the Appendix) of what you will consider customer satisfaction. Be explicit as to which of your products, transactions, and relationships it applies.

THE FAST-GROWING UBIQUITY OF CUSTOMER SATISFACTION

At the beginning of the new millennium, customer satisfaction seems to be everywhere:

- A 1994 survey conducted by the Juran Institute found 90 percent of the top managers of more than 200 of America's largest companies agreeing with the statement, "Maximizing customer satisfaction will maximize profitability and market share." About 90 percent of these companies evidenced their belief by funding some organized effort for systematically tracking and improving customer satisfaction scores (Fay 1994).

- In a 1994 survey of 124 large U.S. companies, Mentzer and colleagues (1995) found 75 percent of the companies surveyed mentioned customer satisfaction in their mission statements. Though the two are intricately related, satisfaction preempted product/service quality, which was specifically mentioned in only 65 percent of the statements. Almost half of the mission statements addressed customer service (56 percent) and a customer orientation (49 percent).

- Recent surveys have shown that more than 95 percent of all senior U.S. executives say that customer satisfaction is an important concern for their organizations.

In fact, one sees claims to a dedication to customer satisfaction everywhere:

- Amtrak boasts, "Satisfaction guaranteed."

- Lexus announces it is "No. 1 in customer satisfaction."

- L.L.Bean proclaims, "Our products are guaranteed to give 100% satisfaction in every way. Return anything purchased from us at any time if it proves otherwise. We will replace it, refund your purchase price or credit your credit card, as you wish. We do not want you to have anything from L.L.Bean that is not completely satisfactory."

- Popular recording artist Britney Spears starts her live performances by proclaiming, "Your satisfaction is guaranteed!"

And so, there is evidence of a widespread appreciation of the importance of satisfying customers. It probably exists in your organization, since you're reading this book. But beyond the simple "epidemic spread" of ensuring satisfaction, there is a wide range of justifications for managing for customer satisfaction. They can be conveniently grouped into three major reasons for being attentive to the satisfaction one's organization creates among its customers:

- The philosophical, or *core values,* reason

- The economic reason

- The reason of certification

STEP 1.2 THE PHILOSOPHICAL REASONS FOR MAXIMIZING CUSTOMER SATISFACTION

Win-Win-Win

Customer satisfaction has a far-reaching impact on the current and perhaps future viability of an organization. Schlesinger and Heskitt (1991) explained the relationship they believe exists between satisfied customers and satisfied employees in their construct called the Cycle of Good Service (see Figure 1.1). The cycle suggests that satisfied customers tolerate higher margins that can be used to pay employees higher salaries. The higher pay boosts employee morale, reducing employee turnover. With more tenured employees servicing customers, there is greater likelihood of better satisfying customers, and so on and so on. In the end, the organization following this philosophy ought to be more successful and ultimately more profitable, a truly win-win-win situation!

While some critics have called the Cycle of Good Service unrealistically idealistic, it is nevertheless a worthwhile objective to aim for. The primary criticism is the supposed link between employee and customer satisfaction. Most of us recognize that behaviors that maximize employee

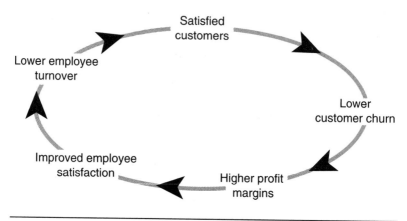

Figure 1.1   The cycle of good service.
Source: Schlesinger and Heskitt (1991)

satisfaction could be detrimental to satisfying customers. A reasonable compromise has been voiced by human resources professionals such as Dr. Ben Schneider (2000), who suggests that getting employees to understand and accept policies and practices (and to fully support them with enabling tools and procedures) may be as close as any company can get to aligning employee and customer satisfactions.

Core Company Values

The orientation to customer satisfaction is no recent phenomenon. Many very successful businesspeople over the years have identified the importance of focusing on customer satisfaction.

The Consumer-Oriented Marketing Movement

The perspective of *consumer-oriented* marketing championed in the early 1960s by academics McCarthy and Perreault (1960) and Kotler (1967) is based on determining what a target group of consumers wants and then maximizing that group's satisfaction with a product or service. In this perspective, satisfaction lies at the very heart of the practice of marketing. Unfortunately, marketers in the 1990s seem to have developed a form of satisfaction myopia, too often focusing on the physical characteristics of their product or service rather than on the benefits (or satisfaction) delivered to their consumers. Whenever such a misorientation is present, customer satisfaction is likely not to be a top priority.

- Sir Henry Royce, creator of the Rolls-Royce motorcar and whose name has become synonymous with quality, laid down the primary principles of customer satisfaction for his company in 1906 when he declared, "Our interest in the Rolls-Royce cars does not end at the moment when the owner pays for and takes delivery of the car. Our interest in the car never wanes. Our ambition is that every purchaser of a Rolls-Royce car shall continue to be more than satisfied" (Rolls-Royce).

- A similar appreciation for customer satisfaction is voiced by today's Toyota Motor Sales organization: "Total customer satisfaction is the cornerstone of Toyota's business plan in the United States. It is our fundamental corporate philosophy and part of everything we do!" (Gieszl 1995).

- Gordon Selfridge, an American retailer and onetime associate of Marshall Field, journeyed to London in the late 1800s to create his own department store empire. His founding principle was, "The customer is always right!" (Cohen and Cohen 1980). (Though often attributed to Field, this philosophy makes customer satisfaction the very heart of the business, the raison d'être.)

- The Connecticut dairy-store magnate Stew Leonard (showcased for American business by Tom Peters) has built on Selfridge's philosophy. He reminds retailers of the importance of customer satisfaction with the often-quoted rules of his dairy superstores:

  Rule #1: The customer is always right.

  Rule #2: If the customer is ever wrong, reread Rule #1!

- The Seattle-based department store chain Nordstrom has built a reputation for going to extreme lengths to create satisfied customers. This reputation alone seems to have secured for it a beachhead in U.S. markets previously believed to be impenetrable because of the strong presence of indigenous stores such as Bloomingdale's, Strawbridge and Clothier, Hecht's, and Neiman-Marcus. Nordstrom has redefined the nature of the department store business for these incumbent stores by making the satisfaction of its customers a top priority.

Checkpoint 1.2

1. Describe, if you can, why your organization has become interested in measuring (and improving) customer satisfaction.

STEP 1.3 THE ECONOMIC REASONS FOR COMMITTING TO CUSTOMER SATISFACTION

The performance of all businesses ultimately depends on their success in keeping customers—lengthening the *lifetimes* of their customers. (A customer's lifetime is the period of time, or the number of purchase cycles, a customer stays with an organization before taking his or her requirements to another supplier. Generally, the longer the lifetime, the more valuable the customer.)

Satisfied customers can be expected to:

- Remain as customers longer

- Spread positive word of mouth about an organization to other, potential customers, possibly causing them to try your products or services

- Increase their share of spending with the organization that best satisfies them

In addition, having a customer satisfaction monitoring process in place helps to identify current or potential problems before they become so threatening as to compromise an organization's entire business.

Global Level: Competition with Other Quality-Focused Economies

During the post–World War II decades, Japanese companies were anxious to change their reputation in the United States, where they were perceived as manufacturers of inferior-quality merchandise. They evolved processes for measuring customer satisfaction and for assessing the quality of competitive product offerings. They then incorporated information gathered on customer preferences in their decision making. Japanese business leaders studied and learned from American quality gurus W. Edwards Deming and Joseph Juran (whose messages were largely being disregarded in the states).

Even though the quality of U.S. goods was gradually improving, the rate of improvement of Japanese goods was much greater; ultimately the Japanese overtook U.S. manufacturers. It wasn't long before Japanese automobiles—once unsalable in the U.S.—were surpassing U.S. autos both in product quality and in sales. According to Juran, by 1975, although U.S. automakers didn't know it, the Japanese had already far surpassed them (this was true in other industries as well, most notably, consumer electronics).

To compete with other quality-oriented economies today, it is absolutely necessary to collect the right data, to be attuned to the appropriate market indicators. In a world oriented to quality improvement, customer satisfaction is the appropriate indicator.

Industry Level: Competition within One's Own Industry

Satisfaction is quickly becoming the key to competitive posture within categories and industries. Products or services initially establish themselves in the market by fulfilling a basic need. But offering only minimal functionality grants a product nothing more than commodity status. To ensure long-term market success, businesses have created brands. Brands allow businesses to develop and sustain a unique image, differentiating one's products in the eyes of consumers. Consider how Frank Perdue (entrepreneur-founder of Perdue Chicken, a northeast regional brand) was able to take a commodity—raw chicken—and elevate his brand of that commodity far above the category, commanding a higher price in exchange for his promise of better quality. Today most companies are leveraging branding to its maximum benefit. Product and service categories have become crowded with *parity brands*, each offering basic functionality and imbued with its own unique brand personality.

The author believes that customer satisfaction is quickly becoming the next competitive factor. Companies are recognizing that the brand that best satisfies its customers not only keeps them longer but also is likely to benefit from positive word of mouth. There are ample success stories to illustrate this strategy. Motorola and Federal Express are two companies that have focused on customer satisfaction as a competitive strategy. Motorola's commitment to quality and customer satisfaction not only won the company a Baldrige Award but allowed it to maintain premium pricing in categories given to price competition. Federal Express, another Baldrige winner, successfully adopted customer satisfaction as a competitive tool to achieve its dominant position in the package delivery category.

Improved Profitability

There is both an intuitive belief and mounting empirical evidence that improved customer satisfaction will increase organizational profitability.

- Accounting professor David Larcker of the Wharton Business School determined that companies in the top quartile of customer satisfaction (according to the American Customer Satisfaction Index [ACSI] model) experienced a higher appreciation in stock values than did the overall S&P 500 (5.3 percent in stock value against a much lower 2.7 percent). Even more compelling, the top 10 food, personal care, and tobacco companies in the ACSI model gained an impressive 15 percent in the same period—August 1994 to February 1995 (Fierman 1995).

- Fornell and Wernerfelt (1987) investigated the link between market share, servicing costs, and satisfaction as they examined the efficacy of complaint handling on customer retention. They conclude there is a positive relationship between effective complaint management and retention (and therefore derived revenue). Buzzell and Gale's (1987) monumental analysis of the profit impact of market strategy (PIMS) data provides irrefutable evidence of the relationship between service quality and profitability. Those firms delivering the highest returns on investment were those firms that also provided higher-quality service.

- Reichheld and Sasser's (1990) frequently quoted data on the profit impact of reducing customer defection or "churn" clearly show the value of retaining a greater proportion of customers in several service industries. Postulating a reduction in churn of just 5 percent, Reichheld and Sasser report an impact on bottom-line profitability of anywhere from +25 percent to +85 percent depending on the specific service industry tracked.

Customer satisfaction is a *threshold requirement* for achieving better customer retention although additional considerations help improve retention even further.

Improved Customer Retention

Satisfaction extends customers' lifetimes and their lifetime values (the net value contributed through a customer's purchases). In addition, focusing on satisfaction helps minimize or eliminate the negative word of mouth spread by dissatisfied customers.

It's been found that more than 90 percent of dissatisfied customers won't exert their own effort to contact a company to complain; they simply take their business to a competitor while voicing their dissatisfaction to other potential customers.

Losing one dissatisfied customer may be more severe than it sounds; one dissatisfied customer may speak to a multitude of others, multiplying his or her dissatisfaction manyfold! Moreover, in today's Internet-oriented business community, Melinda Goddard has identified "word of mouse" as spreading customers' feelings further and faster than ever before.

Most consumers, whether rational or simply hedonistic, are looking for manufacturers, suppliers, and retailers who offer them maximal satisfaction and a sense of value. By taking the time and effort to assess their current customers' satisfactions, organizations take a major step toward running a business that is customer oriented, both for their current customers and for future customers.

Improved Market Share

Traditionally market share has been identified as the result of conquest marketing activities (considered *offensive* marketing strategies). According to this perspective, market share is viewed as directly related to the level of advertising, sales promotion, and other outreach marketing efforts. The only recognition under such models of satisfaction and customer retention, Rust and Zahorik (1993) point out, is through "adjustment terms," which incorporate the influence of loyalty or "buyer inertia."

Retention marketing activities (*defensive* strategies) posit that marketing dollars may be more efficiently directed at retaining current customers than at attempting to win new ones.

Research conducted by numerous organizations has given us the maxim that *it is at least five times as costly to attract a new customer as to keep a current customer.*

This maxim has been voiced many times since. In 1999, the Sears department store chain announced that it was 12 times more costly for them to win a new customer than to keep a current customer satisfied. The fact of the matter is that each organization should know these economics for itself. How much does the organization typically invest in winning a new customer (advertising costs, direct mail contacts, new business presentations, conference participations, etc.)? This dollar amount should be compared with any activities directed at keeping current customers satisfied (such as the costs of your customer satisfaction survey). It will always be more efficient to spend to keep rather than to attract a customer.

 Checkpoint 1.3

1. How important is customer satisfaction as a competitive tool within your industry? How important is customer satisfaction for your customers in choosing suppliers? Complete Worksheet 1.2 (located in the Appendix).

2. Think about building a case for the economic value of maximizing customer satisfaction within your industry. Ideally you should isolate two comparable groups of customers: one with whom you practice satisfaction-improving tactics, the other whom you isolate from any special treatment. Then you would track the difference in spending and lifetimes between these two groups. In reality you can't deprive some of your customers of good service. So consider showing the impact of satisfaction by comparing the behaviors (repurchase, recommendation, share of spending) between your most satisfied customers and your least satisfied customers. The more favorable level of behavior (among your satisfied customers) is the evidence for committing to and investing in customer satisfaction. See Worksheet 1.3 (located in the Appendix).

STEP 1.4 THE CERTIFICATORY REASONS FOR MEASURING CUSTOMER SATISFACTION

Ultimately, the most pragmatic reason for measuring customer satisfaction is simply to comply with the new ISO guidelines. While the revised standards leave no doubt that customer satisfaction should be measured and tracked, they nevertheless leave the exact process open:

8.2 Monitoring and Measurement

8.2.1 Customer Satisfaction

As one of the measurements of the performance of the quality management system, the organization shall monitor information relating to customer perception as to whether the organization has met customer requirements. The methods for obtaining and using this information shall be determined.

Source: ANSI/ISO/ASQ Q9001-2000

It is notable that these provisions do not go so far as to define or explicate exactly how organizations should comply with this requirement. Considerable latitude is left for the organization. It is unusual, but realistic that the ISO committee has elsewhere (in the scope statement) made it clear that it is customer perceptions that are important. Also noteworthy is the acknowledged need for the organization to extend its customer measurement process beyond simply measuring conformance to requirements. The astute organization will use the ISO mandated dialogue with its customer-base to collect other useful information as well. This information could include, but is by no means limited to, the following:

- *Unstated needs.* These are needs that your customers may have but that are left unarticulated until you possibly ask the right, triggering question or provoke your customers to objectively assess why they are currently happy or unhappy.

- *Unmet expectations.* Your category and the world are undergoing constant change. Actions of one of your competitors that your customers become aware of affect the expectations of your customers. Even the actions of a company or organization completely outside your industry subtly affect how your customers perceive you should be servicing them.

- *Unsolved problems.* Sometimes customers will constrain their real needs because they recognize that no provider in a category is offering something they'd ideally like. In such cases they are undertaking sacrifice (they'd like something but think it's probably not attainable). A useful practice to elicit such hidden needs or problems is to ask, "Is there anything you need (related to our product or service) that neither we nor any other organization is

When banks finally gave customers access to their money "24×7," it created heightened expectations for the way all of us conduct all sorts of other business. If your customers can contact American Express and get an answer to a question on a Saturday evening at 10 PM, they may similarly begin to expect your organization to "be there for them" beyond standard business hours. What impact does FedEx's instant package-tracing system (on the Internet) have on the way your organization delivers goods or allows customers to track your progress on a project?

currently offering?" Another, possibly more direct, approach, is simply to ask, "Are you currently experiencing any problems with our product/service?"

- *Future needs and/or desires.* Getting ahead of the wave is something that we all instinctively know will help us succeed; yet few of us are able to see ahead into the future. While their vision will not be perfect, your customers can alert you to changes in their environments that may suggest imminent changes your organization will be forced to confront. And your customers are generally willing to alert you to changes in their requirements.

The ISO standard does specify that your process for collecting the information be "determined," that is, that you should document and establish it. This means one deliverable you must fulfill is to supply at least a process map of your CSM process. This probably should be prepared and documented in a manner similar to the way your auditor and registrar have required you to document other internal processes.

The revised ISO standard further implies that an advantage accrues to the organization from planning how the collected information will be used. The necessary planning to meet this requirement suggests a complete description of how your satisfaction information will be:

- Gathered

- Interpreted

- Used to improve the product and processes of your organization

We will discuss each of these points in detail in later chapters.

Checkpoint 1.4

1. If certification is the primary reason your organization is measuring (and improving) customer satisfaction, try to extend the commitment to deliver to other benefits, (i.e., philosophical or economic). Never stop "selling" the value of satisfying customers!

2. If you're not currently engaged in the ISO 9000 standards, consider suggesting applying for ISO certification. Your CSM will be an important element for application, and gaining certification will surely assist your business.

3. Even if you are not applying for or renewing ISO certification, consider the value of adhering to some of the requirements of these standards for their value to your organization's processes and programs.

STEP 1.5 THE REQUIRED DOCUMENTATION AND AUDITABLE ITEMS

Regarding the documentation specified by ANSI/ISO/ASQ Q9001-2000 for customer requirements and satisfaction, several requirements are detailed:

Document 1. Describe the requirements and satisfaction information you are collecting. This should probably take the form of several lists:

- An exhaustive listing of all the requirements you identified in your exploratory phase of requirements/needs evaluation. Next to each item you should probably indicate whether you have decided to currently measure it.

- A list of all the criteria and performance variables that you have included in your satisfaction questionnaires/interviews. In addition, you probably will wish to provide a brief rationale for why each element of information is important to monitor.

- If you develop a model of customer satisfaction, you can easily identify how your measured variables fit into this model. See chapters 3 and 5.

Document 2. Identify who will collect your satisfaction information and exactly how it will be gathered. See chapter 4.

Document 3. Describe in what form you will collect your satisfaction information. See chapter 4.

Document 4. Identify who will analyze your satisfaction information and how. See chapter 6.

Document 5. Describe exactly what you plan to do with your customer satisfaction information. See chapters 7 and 8.

There are fewer actual auditable items. Among them are the following:

Audit Item 1. Is registrant collecting customer satisfaction information?

Audit Item 2. Are the methods for gathering and using customer satisfaction information identified and deployed throughout the registrant's organization?

Audit Item 3. Are appropriate data analyzed to identify opportunities for improvement?

Audit Item 4. Does the organization analyze the information to determine levels of satisfaction among its customers?

Audit Item 5. Does the organization analyze the information to determine customers' requirements?

In addition, you should consider how your customer satisfaction process fits into your organization's overall quality processes. If you have responsibility for the general quality initiative then this interface will be easier for you to visualize and achieve. However, if the other quality initiatives are supervised out of other departments then you will want to create a relationship with your colleagues in those areas. Your joint resolve should be to integrate your customer input (requirements) and feedback (satisfaction) processes into your organization's overall quality programs.

Step-by-Step: The Answers for Understanding Customer Satisfaction Measurement and Its Role in the ANSI/ISO/ASQ Q9001-2000 Standard

1.1 Creating a definition of customer satisfaction for your organization will make the concept more easily understood for everyone involved. This book suggests a process-based definition of satisfaction focusing on the customer's evaluation of a consumption or interaction experience with your organization. Satisfaction becomes, then, a comparison between what your customer expected and what he or she believes was experienced. Ultimately, you may wish to create a model to show what impacts your various actions can have on your customers, increasing their satisfaction. See pages 25 and 26. Possible definition: *Customer satisfaction* is the result of your customer perceiving that your organization has met or exceeded his or her expectations regarding overall conduct and key performance criteria (which you have identified as being critical).

1.2 Philosophically, a goal of satisfying customers is consistent with several different aspects of modern businesses. First, the relationship between satisfied customers and satisfied employees continues to be discussed. While this relationship is probably not as simple as some have suggested, there are obvious complementary benefits. Second, many businesses have been founded on the core belief that they will offer satisfaction to their customers and thereby prosper and confirm their contribution to society. Third, marketing practice is shifting from a focus on conquest to a focus on retention. The only way customers will maintain their loyalty is if they are satisfied. See pages 7–10.

1.3 Build a case for the economic value of satisfying your customers. No matter how committed your organization currently is to satisfying customers, at some point in the future some manager is likely to

(continued)

ask, "What's the benefit to us of this substantial investment?" You must be ready with an answer. To collect the appropriate information, isolate two groups: your most and least satisfied customers. Then compare these groups in terms of some key behaviors (length of their average lifetimes; frequency and volume of repurchases; willingness to recommend you to others, share of their category requirements that your organization fulfills). You should be able to make a nice case for the return on investment your organization is deriving by satisfying customers. See pages 10–14.

1.4 ANSI/ISO/ASQ Q9001-2000 has recognized that a true and desirable consequence of a properly run business is satisfied customers. Because of this, the requirements for certification include evidence of a monitoring program to ensure that the organization is assessing its performance, in part through the satisfaction it is creating among its customers.

1.5 The list on pages 17–18 identifies all the necessary documentation to show that your organization is appropriately measuring customer satisfaction and that you are managing improvement, in part based on information you collect from your customers. Key components include:

- a description of the satisfaction information you are collecting

- who collects the information and how

- in what form your satisfaction information is collected

- who will analyze the information and how

- what you do with the information once it is analyzed

See pages 17–18.

(Answers for Steps 1.6 and 1.7 may be found in the sections following.)

Chapter 1 Deliverables

As a result of your work in this chapter, you will have prepared the following for your program:

1. A statement of how your organization defines satisfaction (use Worksheet 1.1)

2. An overview of the extent to which your competitors are using customer satisfaction as a business strategy (use Worksheet 1.2)

3. A statement of the role your customer satisfaction program will play in your overall quality process

4. A listing of the necessary ISO documents originating with your customer satisfaction program (see pages 17–18 in this chapter)

STEP 1.6 AN ANSI/ISO/ASQ Q9001-2000 PRIMER

The ISO 9000 family of quality standards was first issued in 1987. The standards underwent a modest revision in 1994. However, their rapid acceptance and the voicing of some concerns over their focus on process as distinct from results suggested they could benefit from a more thorough revision. To that end, a committee, Technical Committee 176, labored through the final years of the second millennium to identify more useful criteria that could become the substance for a major revision. The committee's first product was a set of eight guiding principles that are the cornerstones of the new ANSI/ISO/ASQ Q9001-2000 and ANSI/ISO/ASQ Q9004-2000 standards. They are as follows:

1. *Customer-focused organization.* Organizations depend on their customers and therefore should understand current and future customer needs, meet customer requirements, and strive to exceed customer expectations.

2. *Leadership.* Leaders establish unity of purpose and direction for an organization. They should create and maintain the internal environment in which people can become fully involved in achieving the organization's objectives.

3. *Involvement of people.* People at all levels are the essence of an organization, and their full involvement enables their abilities to be used for the organization's benefit.

4. *Process approach.* A desired result is achieved more efficiently when related resources and activities are managed as a process.

5. *System approach to management.* Identifying, understanding, and managing a system of interrelated processes for a given objective improves an organization's effectiveness and efficiency.

6. *Continual improvement.* Continual improvement should be a permanent objective of an organization.

7. *Factual approach to decision making.* Effective decisions are based on the analysis of data and information.

8. *Mutually beneficial supplier relationships.* An organization and its suppliers are interdependent, and a mutually beneficial relationship enhances the ability of both to create value.

These eight principles are said to have had a pervasive impact on the content of the new standards. The most basic improvements evident in ISO 9001 are the following ideas:

- The components of the standard are united by a process model that integrates customer inputs, business processes, products as the output, and satisfaction as an *outcome.*

- There is an ideological shift from mere documentation of processes (for documentation's sake itself) to the more valuable testing and improving of the effectiveness of an organization's products and processes.

- The customer is recognized as key to the survival and success of business enterprises. The standards therefore emphasize:

  - Understanding the customer's needs and requirements

  - Measuring and striving to improve the customer's satisfaction

- The standard asserts that all collected information should be oriented to stimulate continual improvement within the organization.

As to how relatively important these several themes are, in the opinion of three authors (Cianfrani, Tsiakals, and West 2001), "One of the most fundamental reasons for the existence of ISO 9001 (the revised standard) is *to achieve customer satisfaction*" (author's emphasis). One can substantiate this feeling by simply reading the introductory statement of scope for the revised standards:

---

1 Scope

1.1 General

This International Standard specifies requirements for a quality management system where an organization

a) needs to demonstrate its ability to consistently provide product that meets customer and applicable regulatory requirements, and

b) aims to enhance customer satisfaction through the effective application of the system, including processes for continual improvement of the system and the assurance of conformity to customer and applicable regulatory requirements.

Source: ANSI/ISO/ASQ Q9001-2000

The prominence given to customer satisfaction in the new standard is considered significant in the opinions of Cianfrani, Tsiakals, and West (two of whom served on the ISO Technical Committee 176). The placement of customer satisfaction in the General Scope section illustrates the strong belief of the internal committee in the critical importance of customer satisfaction and the committee's belief that organizations should institute a robust process to assess and track their customers' satisfaction. It is this belief to which this book is oriented.

The importance of communication is also much more obvious in the revised standards. Improving customer satisfaction almost always depends upon educating the entire organization about the importance of customer satisfaction, and how to help improve it. From Section 5 of ANSI/ISO/ASQ Q9001-2000:

5.6 Management Review

5.6.1. General

Top management shall review the organization's quality management system, at planned intervals, to ensure its continuing suitability, adequacy and effectiveness. This review shall include assessing opportunities for improvement and the need for changes to the quality management system, including the quality policy and quality objectives.

Records from management reviews shall be maintained. (See 4.2.4).

5.6.2 Review Input

The input to management review shall include information on:

a) results of audits,

b) customer feedback,

c) process performance and product conformity,

d) status of preventive and corrective actions,

e) follow-up actions from previous management reviews,

f) changes that could affect the quality management system, and

g) recommendations for improvement.

Source: ANSI/ISO/ASQ Q9001-2000

The Process Model of ANSI/ISO/ASQ Q9001-2000

The spirit of the new standard is evident in the process chart shown in Figure 1.2.

STEP 1.7 THE THEORETICAL SIDE OF SATISFACTION

No CSM program should be undertaken in the absence of an underlying theoretical construct. You'll need this in case you ever get asked why you are measuring the things you're measuring, the way you're measuring them. It won't hurt to develop your own version of the following model, adapted to fit your particular business.

A basic satisfaction model will contain the elements shown in Figure 1.3.

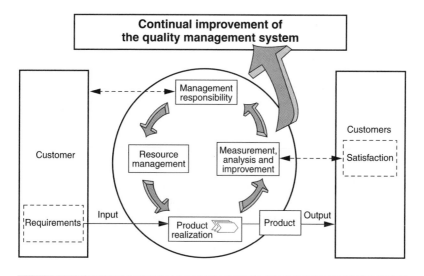

Figure 1.2   A process chart for ANSI/ISO/ASQ Q9001-2000.
Source: ANSI/ISO/ASQ Q9001-2000

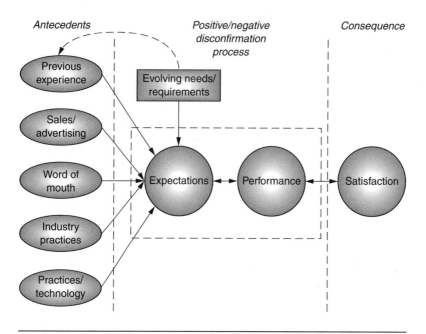

Figure 1.3   A "generic" satisfaction-dissatisfaction model.

   Consider the model as being divided into three sections: inputs (or antecedents), the confirmation/disconfirmation process, and outputs (satisfaction). You can enlarge upon the model by extending it to encompass other constructs such as customer loyalty. But be advised, this author considers loyalty to be more of an emotional bond, while satisfaction deals more with functional performance, as illustrated in Figure 1.4.

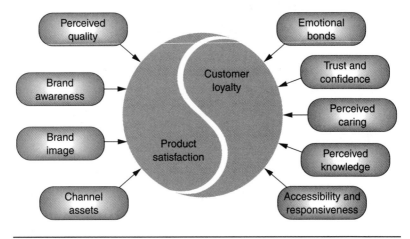

Figure 1.4   How customer satisfaction and loyalty interrelate.

2

Identifying Your Customers

The seemingly most trivial aspect of measuring customer satisfaction, yet perhaps the most problematic, is knowing who your customers are! Most customer satisfaction books don't even bother to mention that one first has to identify one's customers before their satisfaction can be measured. It seems an inconsequential issue, and yet it becomes the Achilles' heel of many a satisfaction program.

Most companies possess databases their accounting, billing, and shipping departments use to interact with customers. But rarely do these databases have actual addressee names—and if they do, one still needs to question whether the identified individuals are actually decision makers. Far too many customer satisfaction measurement (CSM) programs have gotten into trouble by asking all of the *right questions* of the *wrong people!* In this chapter, we consider some of the hurdles you'll have to overcome to build an all-inclusive listing of your company's actual customers.

THE CONSEQUENCES OF NOT KNOWING YOUR CUSTOMERS

Sad though it is, many customer satisfaction programs are conducted whose findings (overall satisfaction ratings, willingness-to-repurchase scores, etc.) show little or no correlation with the state of the sponsoring organization's business situation (when the attitudinal data are compared with the behavior of customers). In such cases, satisfaction scores could be steadily trending upward, but sales might be headed south. Could it be such programs are measuring the wrong things? Possibly. *But the more likely answer is that they are asking the wrong people!* The reason for this seems evident: in most CSM builds, the majority of developmental effort is focused on *what to ask.* Scant time or effort is ever devoted to determining *whom to ask.* And even if that important question were asked, all too often, there wouldn't be a list readily available to identify the customers who were truly *key decision makers.* It is these people whose satisfaction really counts!

> *Mandate:* Don't create a CSM initiative if you can't be sure you'll be able to interview the *right* people!

The term *customer* turns out to be a fairly ambiguous term. To assure your management you know whom you interviewed and why you chose them, you'll need to establish a tight definition of what you mean by *customer.*

Step-by-Step: The Issues of Identifying Your Customers

To create an appropriate listing of your customers you'll need to:

2.1 Define who you mean by *customer*, understanding that there can be multiple customers in each buying unit that purchases your products or services.

2.2 Locate sources for your customers' names.

2.3 Select the database software you will use to create a storage area for your customers.

2.4 Plan ahead! Establish a database and fields for deposit of your customers and their contact information.

2.5 Decide whether you will interview a sample of your customers or conduct a census.

2.6 Determine the appropriate sampling method (if you'll be sampling).

2.7 Determine how many customers should be in your sample.

2.8 Consider the response rate you're likely to get and how to maximize it. (Not all of the customers you identify will cooperate.)

STEP 2.1 RECOGNIZE THE DIFFERENT TYPES OF CUSTOMERS YOU MAY HAVE

Satisfaction surveys can be conducted among a wide range of *stakeholders*. Stakeholders can be defined as anyone manifesting impact on your organization's ability to survive and conduct business. When you consider this definition, you will realize there are numerous groups whose attitudes, opinions, and behavior affect your organization's day-to-day success:

- *External customers.* External customers exist outside your organization. The type that comes immediately to mind is your "end-use" customers, the ones who use or consume your product for their own purposes or production. But you may also have other external customers who exist in your channel of distribution between your organization and your end users. Such intermediate, external customers include distributors, manufacturers' representatives, and so on. The satisfaction of these other external customers may be as critical to your long-term success as the satisfaction of your end-use customers.

- *Internal customers.* We all have colleagues and neighboring departments to whom we provide products, services, or servicing. (You may be an information technology department that distributes and maintains PC hardware and software applications. You could be the human resources department supplying recruiting and training services.) In each of these cases your ultimate customer is internal, within your organization.

- *Employees.* Employees are a category of stakeholder whose importance is only recently being fully appreciated. As skilled labor becomes more and more important, the balance of power is shifting toward employees. They will begin to have sufficient value to companies that the companies must be alert to their satisfaction and be mindful of how to increase that satisfaction or lose them.

- *Stockholders.* Profitability is surely one of the most important satisfiers an organization can offer to stockholders. In most industries one finds numerous corporations who all offer about the same degree of profitability, and yet investors may prefer one corporation above others. Corporations are becoming aware that the sentiments and perceptions of stockholders should be monitored.

- *Influential community leaders, etc.* The failure of many American companies in other countries attests to our naïveté concerning the importance of governmental and civic leaders as stakeholders in our organizations. Acknowledged or not, these individuals can exert tremendous power over an organization's ability to operate and succeed. Their satisfaction should also be considered.

External customers are the most likely and most frequent target of CSM programs. But having said that, you'll still have a number of more specific issues to address:

- How do you define a *current* customer—what purchase recency makes someone a current or *past* customer? As you will notice, even the class *current customers* will challenge you. When is a customer no longer current? Invariably you will have to establish certain definitions. Currency will depend, in large part, on the purchase cycle or frequency in your industry. With a good database you can identify all those customers who may be considered current but have missed the last three purchase cycles. Such customers probably should not be considered current; they're probably *lost* or *at risk*. Try the following definition:

    A customer will be considered a current customer *if it has either (1) made a purchase within the last six months, or (2) not missed consecutively more than two of its expected three most recent purchase occasions.*

- You should present your definition of *current customer* to your management to make sure they understand your need to qualify customers as current and that they agree with the criteria you have selected.

- Should you necessarily focus on all of your current customers? When your resources are extremely precious, you may wish to narrow your focus and interview only your high-value customers (those 20 percent or so [according to the Pareto Principle] who account for the lion's share of your sales).

- You may also need to account for *special interest customers* (these could be segments of your customers that you know represent special needs—the armed forces, municipalities, airports, and so on).

- Consider vocal/conspicuous customers (perhaps those customers who are active in a user group, and so forth).

- Is it useful to attempt to interview some past customers? They can be a good source of insight about your failures.

- Many of your past customers are currently customers of your competitors. Sometimes it's useful to attempt to interview a certain number of customers of each of your key competitors.

- Potential customers, those who may ultimately require your products and services, may often be looked to for guiding input.

 Checkpoint 2.1

1. Determine which of your customers (external and possibly internal) you intend to interview.

2. Your list of target customers will most certainly include current customers. How are you defining a *current customer*? Make sure the criteria you specify are knowable (measurable or observable).

3. Establish similar definitions for any other customer types or segments you plan to include in your survey process.

STEP 2.2 LOCATE SOURCES FOR YOUR CUSTOMERS' NAMES

No matter whether you're going to conduct a sample or a census (an issue we'll discuss shortly), you'll need a complete listing of all your company's customers. In sampling terminology, this list is referred to as the *sampling frame*. Without a complete listing of customers, any sample you draw is considered biased.

> *Biased* is the statistical term for a sample that is unfairly influenced by some systematic exclusion of particular elements—in our case, unlisted customers. A biased sample prevents accurate conclusions from being drawn since a contingent of customers is not represented.

Only with a complete listing of your customers can you be certain that any projection of results you make will be statistically accurate.

It's likely that customer lists exist (in different forms and different levels of detail) in several places within your organization. For example, your accounting department no doubt has a list of customers who owe you money, your accounts payable, otherwise your organization couldn't be collecting revenues for its products or services. Unfortunately, the "name field" in this list may quite literally read "accounts payable" or "current resident." You won't be able to conduct interviews or distribute a questionnaire to such poorly specified respondents because you would have no assurance as to exactly who was responding, and even if your respondent identified him- or herself, he or she may not be the decision maker or among the decision makers who selected your organization as a supplier in the first place.

Your sales, marketing, circulation, membership, or another department is more likely to have lists of the actual people it calls on to make sales. But sometimes these lists are missing some of the more detailed contact information of the billing database (street addresses, zip codes, etc.) You may have to find two or more such lists internally, and then merge and purge them. The action of *merging* is obvious—taking information from one list and adding it to the other. *Purging*, on the other hand, refers to eliminating information, generally because of duplication. Off-the-shelf, sophisticated database programs such as Microsoft Access offer menu options for such operations between tables (your two or more different sources of names).

 Checkpoint 2.2

1. Know exactly where you'll get a list of your organization's customers (or what new process you'll have to create to begin listing customers' identities in a systematic way).

2. If you'll be interviewing different *types* or *classes* of customers, make sure you identify each customer's type or class in the data records so that you can later sort for customer types if you want to compare their satisfaction levels.

STEP 2.3 WITH THE UNDERSTANDING THAT YOU HAVE MULTIPLE CUSTOMERS, WHICH ONES WILL YOU SURVEY?

Far too often when customer names are collected and we have more than one name for a company, we assume that the customers are of equal weight or importance. Industrial decision making is generally accomplished within what are called "decision-making units," composed of numerous individuals each with specific backgrounds, needs, and assigned tasks, and each with a somewhat different influence on the overall decision.

It is unfortunate but true that too many CSM programs take whatever customer name is made available to them and assume that the identified person has 100 percent of the decision-making authority. Given this basic problem, it is no wonder that CSM results often fail to correlate well with purchase behavior (this applies not only to the level of the individual customer but to overall results as well)!

As you establish your customerbase, you'll have the opportunity to collect information on the influence wielded by each individual you identify. Consider including this in your customerbase, as it will be very helpful in creating a single customer score if you later receive multiple responses from within any one of your customers.

All Customers Are Not Equal

Just as representatives within a customer may exert differing levels of influence on a purchase, so too are customers themselves of far different levels of importance to the future of your organization's business. The Pareto Principle, or "80/20 rule" (when applied to customers' spending), suggests that a small proportion of any organization's customers generally is responsible for a large proportion of the organization's revenues. Customers comprising the small proportion are called the organization's *high-value,* or most important, customers. It's necessary to know who they are to consider weighting your CSM results as you collect them. Don't make the mistake of simply assuming your organization knows who they are.

About 10 years ago, the author's firm was retained to conduct a concept test of a new service for a major telephone company (RBOC) in one of the country's major cities. The study design required placing a concept description in the hands of the telecommunications managers of the telephone company's hundred largest customers. (These were major companies—Exxon, Dow Jones, etc.) As we began organizing the study, we discovered a major problem. The company couldn't find a list of the names of the telecommunications managers (its primary customers) of these, its most valuable clients!

While the term *customer* sounds singular, in business it's rare that only one person makes purchasing decisions. Business decisions more often are made by decision-making units. Two or more people, each with a specific role in the unit and each with a certain degree of influence on vendor selection, populate these units:

- *Need identifiers.* The people who identify a need, who instigate the search for a product or services.

- *Information collectors.* People within the buying unit who are charged with the task of identifying appropriate alternatives and collecting information for purposes of evaluating the suitability of each alternative.

- *Gatekeepers.* Individuals who control access of persons, material, or information into the buying center.

- *Decision influencers.* The persons who influence the decision process directly and indirectly by providing information and criteria for evaluating alternative buying actions.

- *Decision makers.* The persons with authority to make the buying decision.

- *Purchasing agents.* The persons with the formal responsibility and authority for contracting with suppliers.

- *End users/consumers.* The conventional customer; those who actually use or consume the purchased product and services.

Too often a satisfaction survey is sent to the name in an organization's files (probably the purchasing department or purchasing agent). But she or he may have had little or no say in selecting the organization as the vendor of choice. To better understand who, within your customers' organizations, is actually making the purchase decision to hire your organization, you can use a process called decision mapping. *Decision mapping* seeks to identify all of a customer's staff members who may be involved in vendor selection and use, and it attempts to understand and characterize how much influence each of these individuals may have. See Worksheet 2.1 (in Appendix A) for an example of some of the questions you should ask to create a decision map for each of your customers.

As you build your customerbase, be sure to include any information you can on the importance of the customer to your organization. Total sales or revenue generated by a customer is good; profitability of each customer is even better—but generally is not easily available. This information is likely to be useful to you later on as you establish an analytical plan for the data you collect.

Identifying Customer Segments

Beyond high-value customers, there may be other customer groups whose satisfaction ratings you or your management will want to examine. Be sure to try to anticipate such requests by establishing fields in your customerbase by which to classify each customer. Remember, you won't be able to divide your data by groupings if you don't have those groups identified in your basic customerbase.

 Checkpoint 2.3

1. Though customers' names may be available to you, don't assume they're the right people to interview for satisfaction until you qualify them. You'll need to screen the names you have to confirm that they actually make decisions regarding the purchase or use of the products your organization produces. (This validation can be conducted in a separate contact or may be gathered in conjunction with your satisfaction survey in a *screening section* of your questionnaire.)

2. It may be necessary to collect more names at each of your customers' locations. Customers with multiple locations pose problems, because the decision-making responsibilities are not easily identified based on their addresses, or even titles, alone. You should probe to ascertain the decision-making participation of each of your survey participants.

3. You may wish to segment your customers according to how important they are to your organization or how much authority they exert. With such a segmentation, you will be able to more prudently allocate your interviewing efforts to those exerting the most influence on vendor selection or those generating the greatest share of your sales.

STEP 2.4 WHAT DATABASE SOFTWARE WILL YOU USE?

Where and how you keep track of the customers you identify is another issue. You should automate your contact system with a computerized database. (Even if you have fewer than a hundred customers, you will still find a computer database useful for storing, processing, organizing, and retrieving your information.) You have at least three sources for such assistance:

1. Your information technology department

2. Yourself

3. An external vendor

Whereas in previous times a customer database was a job for a mainframe computer, given the dramatic reduction in costs for computer storage media, today most PCs are easily able to accommodate customerbases, even those with millions of customers. This means your customerbase can reside directly in your department. But you still must decide not only who is going to build your database but also who is going to maintain it. Databases require a commitment; they must constantly be updated and cleaned. Having an out-of-date database is probably worse than having none at all.

Most off-the-shelf microcomputer (desktop PC) database programs will be more than adequate for your needs. Such programs include:

- Microsoft Access

- Microsoft Visual FoxPro

- Lotus Approach

- FileMaker Pro

See Table 2.1 for a full description of these and other available programs.

All these programs create what are called *relational databases.* Relational databases are superior to older computer data files called *flat* or *sequential* files. The primary difference is that the contents of relational files can easily be modified, expanded, or contracted. To import new information, one simply relates the main file or *table* to another, new table containing the additional information that is to be related. The link between the tables is established by selecting one piece of information as a *key.* The key field must appear in all the tables (files) to be linked. A unique *customer number* is a convenient field to serve as a key, though your industry no doubt has other equally unique customer-based fields. (If you adopt—as your key—a field or number that is used by other departments in your organization, you will

Table 2.1 Customerbase software programs.

Program	Vendor	Platforms supported	Special capabilities
User databases (easy to use)			
Enterprise/Piller	Hyperion	Windows/Unix	
Powerplay	Cognas	Windows/Unix	
FileMaker	FileMaker	Windows	
Approach	Lotus Development	Windows	
Programmer databases (higher functionality,more difficult to use, programming skills required)			
FoxPro	Microsoft	DOS, Windows	
MS Access	Microsoft	Windows	
Visual dBase	dBase	Windows	
Data warehouses (close to mainframe capabilities, programming knowledge required)			
MS-SQL	Microsoft	Windows NT	SQL-Structured Query Language is also supported by most of the other programs in this section
Oracle	Oracle	Windows NT/Unix	
Informix	Informix	Unix	

easily be able to incorporate information about customers in your database that is collected by other departments.)

The desktop PC programs described in Table 2.1 are all more than capable of efficiently handling millions of customers. If your firm uses a minicomputer, rather than a microcomputer network, you will find yourself using one of the following:

- Oracle

- Microsoft SQL

- Sybase

- Infomax

- DBII

The choice of particular database software shouldn't make any real difference to you, as almost all database programs follow the same basic logic and instruction sets. Their tables and file structures tend to be highly interchangeable.

Designing the Structure of Your Customerbase

You'll establish the contents for your main customerbase by identifying *fields*. Each field will contain a different piece of information and will be in a specified format (integer, decimal, text, currency, date, etc.).

Generally, the program you select to use will offer an *append function* as a convenient method with which to key in new information. Most of the database programs also support some import routines so that if your information already exists in another program's format, you can electronically import it into your new customerbase.

Security and Backups

If you're in charge of your own customerbase, make sure to establish a process by which you will routinely back up and save your information. While all routines have checkpoints to prevent unwanted erasing, no process is totally without opportunities for mistakes. A backup copy will help you avoid the problems from unintended deletions or losses.

 Checkpoint 2.4

1. You need to select the computer software, and possibly hardware, you'll use to store your customerbase and ultimately the information you collect from customers. Do you know the software package you'll use, and do you have ample storage space on the computer you intend to use?

2. You'll also need to decide where you'll store your data and whom you will use to maintain your customerbase and the information you collect. Maintenance won't be a simple task; it will require constant attention if you wish your database to stay current, and if you wish your survey results to be readily available to your colleagues in your organization.

3. Specify the backup and security procedures you envision using to protect your data.

STEP 2.5 WHAT YOU NEED TO KNOW ABOUT YOUR CUSTOMERS

To properly address your customers in your interview or questionnaire, you'll need to know a number of things about them:

- How to contact them (their name, title, mailing address, telephone number, e-mail address)

- What product(s) of yours they use

- How long their company has been a customer of your organization

- The share of your category they buy from you

Because this information is somewhat different than that which may be available in other sources within your company (such as the accounting department), you should call this database your *customerbase*. This name is appropriate because it's oriented to interacting with customers as individual decision makers. Not only will it contain information to facilitate the distribution of your survey, it will also serve as a repository for the information you collect from your customers. As such, it will become the heart of your entire survey, analysis, and reporting processes.

Create a vision or design for the fields your database will contain, but don't try to get it perfect the first time. A typical customerbase structure is shown in Figure 2.1. Most database experts will encourage you to simply establish a basic system and leave the fine-tuning for a later time. It's not necessary to anticipate *every field* or bit of information you'll ever want to maintain. With relational database structures and the supporting software that is readily available for PCs you'll be able to modify the contents of

Field name	Contents
Company name:	
Primary contact last name:	
Primary contact first name:	
Primary contact MI:	
Primary contact street 1:	
Primary contact mailing code:	
Primary contact street 2:	
Primary contact city:	
Primary contact state:	
Primary contact zip:	
Primary contact tel. no.:	
Primary contact fax no.:	
Primary contact e-mail:	
Date began business with company:	

Figure 2.1   Common fields for a primary customerbase table.

your data tables very easily. And additional information can be incorporated into your system by simply relating a new table (database) to your main table. All that's necessary is to include your relational *key* within the new information. As long as each new table includes this key, the information can be related and incorporated into any subsequent report.

 Checkpoint 2.5

1. Create a list of the minimum items you will need to know about your customers in order to begin conducting your satisfaction survey among them.

2. This information may include knowledge of how much influence they exert on the decision of whether to buy your organization's products.

3. Create your customerbase structure using Worksheet 2.2 in Appendix A.

STEP 2.6 STORE YOUR CUSTOMERS' IDENTITIES AND CONTACT INFORMATION IN THE DATABASE

As much trouble as the act of creating your all-inclusive listing of customers is, you've only just begun. Database maintenance and updating is a very time-consuming activity, but one well worth the payout. So you'll want to establish some process whereby at least three things happen:

1. New customers are identified to you, so that you may add them to your files.

2. The accuracy of all information made available to you can be checked firsthand.

3. As customers' information changes, updates are passed along to you so that you can maintain the currency of your files.

Depending on how many customers your organization has and the complexity of the information you decide to store for each customer, this requirement alone will take a considerable amount of time and effort. It is one of those hidden costs of customer satisfaction measurement that virtually nobody anticipates upfront. Make sure your management understands the importance of the issue and the costs involved.

Your organization must be willing to make several commitments:

• To support the creation of a customer list

• To commit to its maintenance over time (called *database hygiene*)

• To encourage refinement of your database's contents, over time

You'll more easily get help maintaining your customerbase if others are actively benefiting from it. That's why it is probably smart to alert other departments to the existence of your customerbase, and to try to get them to use it as well.

 Checkpoint 2.6

1. Building a customer database (customerbase) is a long-term commitment. Once you build a database, you'll need to commit to keeping it current—otherwise it will become useless, and your work in establishing it will be wasted.

2. Encourage help and participation in building your customerbase from other departments as well as your own; they'll likely find good use for the information you assemble.

STEP 2.7 DECIDE WHETHER YOU WILL INTERVIEW A SAMPLE OF YOUR CUSTOMERS OR CONDUCT A CENSUS

Traditionally when an organization considers a customer satisfaction survey, it assumes a sample of customers will be involved. There is nothing wrong with that assumption if information is the only goal of your program. This author happens to believe that customer satisfaction programs should actually fulfill two roles:

• *An informational role,* providing a source of information about customers' overall and function-specific satisfaction; and

• *A communicational role,* alerting your customers to your organization's commitment to satisfying them by understanding their needs and then monitoring how completely it satisfies those needs.

These two roles introduce the issue of how many of your customers you will include in your satisfaction survey process—a *sample* or all of your customers (a *census*). The number of your customers that you involve will be dictated by the goals you accept for your process. If all you want to do is collect information for quality control, then a sample will be perfectly adequate. But if it's important to your management to let all your customers know they are valued and their input is welcome, then a sample won't do (only those customers chosen to be part of your sample would learn that you care about their feelings and input). If you also adopt the communications goal, you'll want to conduct a census, polling *all* of your organization's customers. Most of the time the primary difference in cost (between fielding a survey as a sample or a census) will consist of the costs of interviewing customers and entering their data. A sample will always be cheaper. See Table 2.2.

 Checkpoint 2.7

1. Decide whether it's adequate for your purposes to interview only a portion of your customers, or if you'll want to interview every customer you have—that is, conduct a census.

2. If you're interviewing all your customers, you're probably attempting to not only collect information but communicate to your customers your organization's desire to dialogue with them.

Table 2.2 Comparing a census with a sample.

Census	Sample
All units in the customerbase are selected for interviews.	Only a portion of the customerbase is selected for interviews.
Expensive.	Cost efficient.
Sampling statistics (given a reasonable level of response) are theoretically unnecessary.	Must use sampling statistics to generalize to the population.
Allows a dialogue with *all* customers.	Not all customers are alerted to the organization's interest in dialoguing with them and hearing of their satisfaction.

STEP 2.8 DETERMINE THE APPROPRIATE SAMPLING METHOD (IF YOU'LL BE SAMPLING)

If you're going to sample your customers, you'll need a complete listing of them—what we've called a customerbase. Technically, the collection from which a sample (of customers) is drawn is called the *sample frame*. Your customerbase will also be your sample frame. Experts will look at your sampling frame from the following perspectives:

- *Comprehensiveness.* For a listing to be an appropriate sampling frame, it must include all customers. If your accounting department agrees to supply you with names but decides to omit poor payers, the list it provides would fail the comprehensiveness test.

- *The probability of selection.* Naively, you may assume that a list provided to you contains every customer's name only once. In this case each customer would stand an equal probability of being randomly drawn. But if the list repeats some customer's names, they would stand a greater likelihood of being selected. If the list has customers multiply listed, you need to be informed of which customers and exactly how many times each is listed. Then you'll be able to institute some controls to counterbalance for the greater frequency with which some customers' names occur.

- *Efficiency.* Is each entry a valid survey prospect, or will you have to filter out some listings? For example, what if the list provided to you contains both current and past customers, and you're drawing a sample of only current customers. You'll have to avoid selecting past customers, and drawing your sample will be a bit more complicated.

While there are many types of samples, the one you'll most likely use is called a *random probability sample.*

Technically speaking, your sample will qualify as a *random probability sample* only if each of your customers has an equal likelihood (or probability) of your selecting them. This means that every one of your customers must be represented in your sampling frame, but only *once.* If a customer isn't in the frame, it has no chance of being selected, and your sample won't be a random sample. If a customer appears more than once, it will have a disproportionately greater chance of being selected, and again, your sample won't be a random sample (unless you know of the multiple listings and control for them).

If your sample is truly a random probability sample, you'll be able to do the things you need to do with your sample's ratings, such as project your sample's satisfaction levels to your entire customerbase.

 Checkpoint 2.8

1. Can you adopt your customerbase as a representative sample frame from which to draw your sample? Ask yourself these questions:

   • Are each of your customers represented in the frame?

   • Are any of your customers represented more than once?

   • Can you determine which customers are listed multiple times, and exactly how many times they are listed?

2. Are you comfortable with the definition of a random probability sample? What about your customerbase will ensure that you have a random probability sample?

STEP 2.9 DETERMINE HOW MANY CUSTOMERS SHOULD BE IN YOUR SAMPLE

There are several methods for determining how many of your customers should be included in your sample:

• *Judgment or historical precedent.* In past surveys your company may always have interviewed about 150 of your 500 customers; this size of sample may "seem right" for your customer satisfaction project as well.

• *Analytical considerations.* You may wish to "read" your results across the four geographic regions in which you conduct business. You may know you shouldn't have fewer than 50 customers in any one analytical cell (for purposes of statistical inference), therefore your total sample will need to be at least 200 of your customers.[1]

---

[1]Theoretically, a minimum sample size of 30 to 35 is adequate from which to statistically infer results. However a sample of 50 has a greater prima facie validity.

- *Budget.* Your budget may support interviewing no more than 75 of your customers.

- *Specification of the desired level of statistical precision.* You can determine the size of your sample based on the statistical precision with which you wish to interpret your findings.

- *Prima facie considerations.* Seventy-five customers may seem like too few; 100 may look "more respectable."

To determine the necessary sample you'll need to interview there are two statistical formulas. You use one or the other depending on whether you'll be reporting percentages or average scores. They are programmed on the CD-ROM accompanying this book and are described in this chapter's Toolkit.

These procedures require you to know something about your customers and the way they're likely to answer your questions. If you've surveyed them before, chances are you have some of the information these procedures require. If you're building a CSM system from scratch, you'll have to guesstimate this information if you wish to use the procedures to help you select an appropriate sample size.

 Checkpoint 2.9

1. Specify how you will determine the number of customers to be involved in your survey process. If you'll use a census, you don't need to be concerned about *sample size;* your respondents are your population. But if you're only going to involve a portion of customers, then you need to identify how you have determined the number to involve.

2. If you use statistical methods to determine the appropriate number of your customers to sample, or use statistical methods to validate your sample size as determined by another method, what parameters have you used in your statistical calculations?

STEP 2.10 PRACTICAL METHODS FOR DRAWING YOUR SAMPLE

The actual way you draw your sample can be as pragmatic as you wish to make it. The smaller your customerbase, the less complicated a procedure you'll need.

Using the sample frame, the exhaustive listing of all your customers, you can establish an unbiased selection procedure offering each customer an equal (or known) chance (or likelihood) of being selected. Two procedures are widely used to help you select the specific customers you will interview.

The nth Customer

In this procedure, you'll divide the total number of customers in your customerbase by your required sample size. The resulting number is the "nth" interval. Now, within the first nth names in your customerbase, you need to establish which customer will be the first you'll draw. You select this customer by using a random number you can draw from a table of random numbers. (Most statistics textbooks contain random number tables.) Using such a table, without controlling your selection, place your finger or pencil on a starting point (number). Looking at the numbers subsequent to this starting point, collect as many digits as you need until you have enough to identify a number within the interval 0-to-your-nth-interval number. The customer name identified by this random starting number becomes your first selected customer. From this customer you will count (using your nth interval) to the next customer to be selected, and so on until you've selected your sample and reached the end of your customerbase by selecting each nth additional customer.

Let's assume you have 15,000 customers. You've decided to interview 1500. Dividing 15,000 by 1500 yields 10. In other words, you'll interview every 10th customer, starting at a random customer 1–10 from the beginning of the list. Looking at a table of random numbers, you might place your finger on 3. You'd then select the customer who is third on the list and every 10 customers thereafter. This means customers 3, 13, 23, 33, and so on will be selected for your sample.

Random Number Generator

Though somewhat more involved, you can repetitively use a random number table to select all your respondents. Generate as many random numbers as customers you need to interview using a computer program or computer spreadsheet. Then use those random numbers to pull from your customerbase the identities of those customers to be interviewed. For example, using the above parameters, you'd generate 1500 random numbers—all between the range of 1 to 15,000. (Numbers outside this range are simply discarded.) Once you've generated the 1500 random numbers, you use these to identify the customers you'll interview. Let's say the first three random numbers you've generated are 830, 12,341, and 92. You'd enter your customer list and select the 830th, 12,341st, and 92nd customers. You would continue this process until you have identified all 1500 customers.

Checkpoint 2.10

1. If you decide to conduct your survey among a sample of your customers rather than a census, how will you pick the specific customers you'll interview? Document your process.

STEP 2.11 ANTICIPATING AND ACCOMMODATING YOUR CUSTOMERS' RESPONSE RATE

One factor you should build into your sample size calculations is your expected *response rate*. Your customers' willingness to participate in your verbal interview or to complete your written questionnaire will vary substantially. Figure 2.2 lists many of the factors that influence response

- Your product category and industry

- The time of year in which you conduct your survey

- The positioning of your survey

- Any gratuity/incentive you offer

- The amount of work required to complete your interview or questionnaire—that is, how complicated it is

- The length (in pages, questions, or in time) of your questionnaire or interview

- The apparent value/benefit to your customer from participating in your survey

- The "appearance"/packaging of your interview or questionnaire

- The modality of your survey (mail, in person, telephone, Internet)

- The workload your identified participants are currently facing in their day-to-day responsibilities

Figure 2.2   Factors affecting response rates to interviews and questionnaires.

Table 2.3   Typical survey response rates by modality.

Modality	Typical response rate
Interviewer administered, in person	50–75%
Interviewer administered, by telephone	40–60%
Self-administered, by Internet	30–50%
Self-administered, by mail	15–30%

rates. Because you will never receive 100 percent cooperation from the customers you attempt to interview, you will always want to oversample your customers to compensate for the likely shortfall.

Response rates are fairly well known throughout the survey industry. Typical rates are shown in Table 2.3. Your results may encourage a decidedly different rate, for many of the reasons listed above.

As you determine your needed sample size, use equation 2.1 to calculate how many customer names you should draw.

$$\text{number of customers to be drawn} = \frac{\text{required sample size}}{\text{anticipated response rate}} \qquad (2.1)$$

✔ **Checkpoint 2.11**

1. What response rate do you anticipate from your customers? On what basis have you established this expectation? Previous survey results? Industry norms?

2. Identify how you have accommodated your expected response rate by oversampling.

3. What incentives, if any, are you considering to help increase the response rate?

A CLOSING OBSERVATION

It's tempting when you find yourself in a pioneering situation to strive for absolute perfection. That is why some customer database initiative projects end up with 18-month project timetables. And by the time your customer-base is finished, just about everyone has forgotten why it was needed in the first place. The best advice in creating customer databases for purposes of customer satisfaction initiatives is to start small and get a process going.

There'll always be time to add to the information later. But if your database doesn't show some immediate utility (in terms of a first wave of satisfaction interviews), chances are developmental funds will dry up fast!

In addition, consider making your customerbase available to your colleagues in other departments. The surest way to get more information from them in the future is to show that your customerbase can be of value to them. If other departments begin to rely on your information, you can be certain they'll also readily offer information to help you keep it current. Ultimately they may even help in funding the further development or maintenance of your customerbase.

Step-by-Step: The Answers for Identifying Your Customers

2.1 The term *customer* can be surprisingly ambiguous. Make sure you define the *exact* requirements for the people you will be interviewing. Make sure your management similarly agrees. See pages 29–31.

Possible criteria: A current customer is a customer who has purchased from you in the last six months (or in at least two of the last three expected purchase cycle periods).

2.2 Make sure you have access to information that both identifies and provides you contact information for those you will consider current customers. See pages 38–40.

Suggested profile:

1. Company name

2. Primary customer contact's last name

3. Primary customer contact's first name

4. Primary customer contact's street address

5. Primary customer contact's mail drop code

6. Primary customer contact's city, state, and ZIP+4

7. Primary customer contact's telephone number

8. Primary customer contact's fax number

9. Primary customer contact's e-mail address

(continued)

2.3 Establish a special database for the customer information you'll need and will collect. This will include both the contact information you assemble to distribute your survey, as well as the responses you receive back from customers. We call this database your *customerbase*. Use one of the accepted off-the-shelf database programs to create your customerbase. Don't allow someone to sell you on the necessity of creating a proprietary system. See pages 36–38.

2.4 You'll need a timetable to describe the time necessary to build your customerbase's structure and functionality, to enter the information about your customers, and then to verify the accuracy of the information.

2.5 ANSI/ISO/ASQ Q9001-2000 standards do not specify how many of your customers you should audit for satisfaction. This text has indicated that a *sample* is sufficient for improvement information. However, if your organization also wishes to communicate its commitment to each of your customers, a *census* is the only way to convey that to all of your customers. See pages 41–42.

2.6 If you'll sample your customers, a random probability sample is the only way to assure your management that findings from your sample can be generalized to all your customers.

2.7 You can determine how many of your customers you will interview based on the following: your budget, prima facie "respectability," historical efforts by your organization, or statistical means (to provide the level of statistical confidence you require in your findings). See pages 44–45.

2.8 You'll need to contact more customers than you require in your final sample because not every customer you contact will cooperate. Guesstimate what your cooperation rate will be and then over-recruit customers to compensate for the shortfall.

Chapter 2 Deliverables

In this chapter you've assembled the following components of your CSM:

1. An exact description of who you consider to be your current customer. You may have many different types of customers: current, past, potential, and so on. You're most likely to select current customers as an immediate target for your first satisfaction survey. An exact description of who you consider a current customer is critical to finding a source for names and contact information.

2. Worksheet 2.1—is a list of issues about which you should collect information in order to tell more about the purchase influence each of the contacts (whom you have identified at each of your organization's customers) exerts.

3. Worksheet 2.2—a description of the information you believe you must know about your customers (both to contact them and to place their survey responses within a meaningful context).

4. A statement of whether you'll interview a sample of your customers or your entire customerbase (at least as many as will talk with you). This should include the rationale for the procedure you have selected.

5. If you'll use a sample, a description of the process by which you plan to draw your sample and of the source you'll use as your sample frame. A statement of the criteria that will allow you to declare your sample a random probability sample.

6. The number of your customers you'll include in your sample and the derivation you've used to arrive at that number.

7. A statement of the response rate you anticipate for your survey and what plan you may implement to attempt to increase that rate.

TOOLKIT

Sample Size Calculators

If you're choosing the statistical precision method for estimating sample size, there are three constructs you'll need to familiarize yourself with:

- The *standard error of the estimate* (SE)

- The *confidence interval* you'll accept

- The *confidence level* you require

These constructs are almost totally interdependent, which makes affixing them, individually, somewhat difficult.

The Standard Error of the Estimate

Determining how many customers will constitute an "adequate" sample requires one to have knowledge of the actual population, including the population's standard deviation (commonly approximated by the sample's standard error, or SE), for the phenomenon being measured. Paradoxically, the standard error (or an estimate of it) is one of the findings you'll ultimately discover through your survey! In this way such statistical phenomena are circular; though the survey is the only way to quantify them, you require an estimate of them to determine among how many of your customers your survey ought to be conducted.

There are several ways around this apparent conundrum:

1. The question can be answered with historical data. For instance, it may be that your organization has conducted some surveys among customers in the past. If so, you can use the results of those surveys to produce estimates of the likely standard error associated with questions similar to the ones you'll be asking. Simply average over these standard errors to arrive at an average standard error for your survey. Using historical data is not inappropriate. It's been claimed that variance (the source of SE) changes more slowly over time than do means (the actual levels of outcomes). Thus, even though you're conducting a new study to see how means may have changed, it's probably safe to assume the population variance underlying your new means hasn't changed significantly.

2. Because rating scales have both an absolute beginning and an end, the mean and variance of such scales are interrelated. Assuming a 7-point scale, if a mean of 5.5 is observed, then there must necessarily be a large number of ratings of "7" and "6" creating a relatively tight distribution of scores—hence a smaller variance. If a mean is closer to the scale's midpoint, say 3.5, conceivably the spread of observed scores is much broader,

Table 2.4 Estimated standard errors based on the range of your rating scale.

Number of positions in your rating scale	Likely SE	Typical range of variance
4	0.500	.1–.5
5	0.583	.15–.65
6	0.667	.2–1.1
7	0.750	.3–1.5
10	1.167	.8–2.5
11	1.333	1.5–3.0

creating a larger variance. Using this logic, estimates have been made of variance associated with rating scales of different lengths. See Table 2.4.

3. Guesstimates can be used to create a likely SE. Recognizing that in a normally distributed mean 99.5 percent of all sample means will fall within ±3 standard deviations (6 in total), one can estimate the standard deviation ($\sqrt{\text{variance}}$) by taking an assumed range of likely answers and dividing the range by 6. For example, on a 10-point scale, if we assume that all answers (for a particular variable—say, overall satisfaction) will fall between 3 and 10, then the standard deviation would be ⅞ = 1.33, and the variance would be $(1.33)^2 = 1.77$.

The Confidence Interval (The Degree of Precision)

A confidence interval describes a range of scores about an observed sample outcome (typically a mean) that includes scores we must accept as all representing the *same* underlying population mean. If a sample's observed mean on a 10-point satisfaction scale is 7.5, the confidence interval places a numeric range (e.g., ±0.5) about that observed mean within which we would expect the majority of means from an indefinite number of additional samples to fall. The width of the confidence interval depends both on the magnitude of the observed mean and on the satisfaction professional's required degree of precision. The degree of precision describes our tolerance of an imprecise estimate (our acceptance of a *wide* confidence interval) or our desire for a highly precise estimate (our requirement for a *narrow* confidence interval).

The width of the confidence interval is entirely up to you to specify. Here's one way to assign it. Suppose your last CSM showed that overall satisfaction with your organization was 7.5 (on a 10-point scale). Your management assumes (hopes) overall satisfaction has subsequently improved. Management's goal is an average of 8.0. Your objective would be to establish a confidence interval narrow enough (about the old mean of 7.5) that a new observed mean of 8.0 could not be interpreted as a sample mean from a population whose mean was *still* 7.5, but rather represented a sample mean from a *new* population whose true mean satisfaction was now 8.0— a true significant increase. To make this statement, the confidence interval you would place around 7.5 must be smaller than ±0.5. (Notice that 0.5 is the difference between the new target level for satisfaction, 8.0, and the former measured value, 7.5.) Let's choose an interval of 7.5 ±0.45.

Assume you wish to read the results at a 95 percent level of confidence. This means that 8.0 must lie beyond the range of 7.5 plus 0.45 or 7.95. With this confidence interval, you can rest assured that 95 percent of all observed means from a population whose mean is still 7.5 will lie in the range 7.5 − 0.45 to 7.5 + 0.45 or 7.05 to 7.95. A new observed mean of 8.0 would indicate it did not come from the same distribution of satisfaction scores. One could safely conclude, in this case, that satisfaction had increased!

The Confidence Level (the Degree of Confidence)

The level of statistical confidence one may ascribe to a survey's findings is again, entirely at the discretion of the satisfaction professional. The default level in social research is 95 percent. It is ironic that most social surveys are subjected to so precise an outcome when many medical experiments (with considerably higher stakes riding on them) may lack such demanding confidence. The 95 percent confidence level is probably used too automatically in many satisfaction surveys. Many satisfaction professionals may not know they have the liberty to choose the level, or they may not understand the ramifications of changing it. In many cases, a confidence level of 90 percent, 85 percent or even 80 percent may be quite sufficient. The reason to adopt a lower confidence interval is the substantial impact the confidence level has on sample size. Decreasing the confidence level from 95 percent to 90 percent can relax the number of customers who must be interviewed, lowering the survey's cost dramatically. Lower levels of confidence may be especially defensible in *caretaker situations*, where no substantial change (either improvement or deterioration) is suspected.

Essentially, the confidence level you choose denotes your willingness to risk being wrong (i.e., to say satisfaction has increased when it has actually remained constant). At the conventional 95 percent level, you are requiring that 95 times out of 100 you wish to be correct. That is, you will tolerate only 5 errors in 100 tries. Stated this way, the reader may see why we've questioned the blind observance of a 95 percent level. For many business decisions, a 9 out of 10 record (i.e., a 90 percent confidence level) would be quite satisfactory—maybe even 8½ or 8 times out of 10!

By all means consider the severity of consequences of your actions that will be based on the CSM outcome. Also consider your likely starting

Table 2.5 Values of the standard normal deviate (Z).

Desired level of confidence	Area under the normal curve
60%	0.84
70%	1.04
75%	1.15
80%	1.28
85%	1.44
90%	1.64
95%	1.96
99.5%	2.81

point. If your overall satisfaction is likely to be low initially, as long as you see improvement at a lower level of confidence (80 percent to 85 percent) that may be sufficient. On the other hand, if you must determine which operating region is satisfying its customers best, then you'll probably want to invoke a more stringent confidence level.

The level of confidence you select influences the Z-score, or normal deviate used in the calculation of sample size. For a 95 percent level of confidence, the Z-score is 1.96 (2 is an acceptable substitution and makes calculation easier). Other values of Z may be read directly from a table of normal deviates. The most commonly used values are shown in Table 2.5.

Calculating the Appropriate Sample Size with Metric Data (Means)

Using these constructs, you can determine how many customers you should interview according to one of several formulas. If you are measuring metric data (overall satisfaction on a 10-point scale), the appropriate sample size is given by the relationship in Equation 2.2.

$$\textit{sample size (n)} = \frac{Z^2}{\left(\dfrac{\text{confidence interval}}{2}\right)^2} \; \sigma_{\bar{x}}^2, \tag{2.2}$$

where:

Z = the standard normal deviate (Z-score) appropriate for your level of precision (1.96 for a 95 percent level of confidence);

confidence interval = the range about the sample mean you're willing to accept ($\pm 0.5 = 1.0$); and

$\sigma_{\bar{x}}$ = standard error of the estimate.

Calculating the Appropriate Sample Size with Nominal Data (Proportions)

If your primary criterion variable is a proportion, then you can use Equation 2.3 to determine your appropriate sample size. Notice that in Equation 2.3 the standard error of the estimate (for a proportional answer) is approximated by the term (pro(1 − pro)).

$$\text{sample size (n)} = \frac{Z^2}{\left(\frac{\text{confidence interval}}{2}\right)^2}\ (\text{pro}(1-\text{pro}))^2, \qquad (2.3)$$

where:

Z = the standard normal deviate (Z-score) appropriate for your level of precision (1.96 for a 95 percent level of confidence);

confidence interval = the range about the sample proportion you're willing to accept (±3 percent = 6 percent); and

pro = the expected sample proportion (i.e., 80 percent saying "extremely satisfied").

Some Misconceptions about Sample Size

There are three common misconceptions about sample size:

1. *The adequacy of a sample depends on the fraction of the total population surveyed.* This is based on the naive misunderstanding of statistics that representation of some minimal proportion, say at least 5 percent, of a total population will make a sample accurate. The fact is that sampling error is completely independent of the fraction of the population included in a sample. Conversely, the size of the population has virtually no impact on how well a sample of a particular size can describe the population.

2. *Standard opinion industry sample sizes are best.* It is commonly believed that a good national sample consists of 1500 respondents. (This is a frequently cited number in public opinion polls, and so on) While this sample size may be reasonable given the particular characteristics of a national sample, each phenomenon has its own statistical properties, and samples should be decided based on the specific properties of the phenomenon being estimated.

3. *Sample sizes can be easily calculated from the level of acceptable error or the precision of the results desired.* Some warn it is unreasonable to base a sample size decision on a single variable because most surveys

contain numerous variables and estimates. It is also probably unrealistic to specify an acceptable margin of error from only sampling since error is introduced from many other sources in addition to sampling.

The appropriate way to determine sample size is first to identify an analytical plan. The key component of any analytical plan is usually not an estimate of confidence intervals but rather an identification of the analytical groups within the population for which separate estimates are required (i.e., *high-value* customers, *long-term* customers, *first-time* customers, etc.). The appropriate question is how many customers within each of these analytical groups should be interviewed; the total sample then becomes an aggregate of the minimum acceptable number to be interviewed within each of the analytical groups.

Central limit theory tells us that regardless of the distribution of the underlying population, as samples exceed 30 customers in size, the sample means will be normally distributed. We will suggest 50 customers as the minimum number of customers advisable in an analytical grouping, but 100 customers is probably a *safer* number (safer in the sense that you will receive fewer questions about statistics based on subsamples of 100 than you would with subsamples of only 50).

3

Identifying Customer Requirements

Many satisfaction surveys are actively administered today that fail to provide any real guidance to the companies sponsoring them. These surveys should be called *smile surveys* because the intent appears to be to make the sponsor happy—to give an organization's CEO a high score for his or her "balanced scorecard," rather than actually *listening* to customers with the intention of improving satisfaction. Smile surveys are usually a product of internal thinking and generally tend to measure how well an organization is doing the things it is currently doing. (The reader may recognize this as a question of *efficiency*—the tactical, operational side of things. More about this later.)

Properly formulated customer satisfaction surveys, however, will be equally concerned with determining whether there is something the organization ought to be doing that it currently is not. This is a question of *effectiveness*—the strategic side of things: "What should we be doing that we're not currently doing?" This second question is more germane to a properly run organization because it promises to steer the course of the organization back in a direction in which customers would like it headed.

In order to conduct a satisfaction process oriented to measuring effectiveness, we need to know what customers require, need, and expect. This is most commonly understood through a *requirements audit*.

FOR AN UNDERSTANDING OF CUSTOMER NEEDS, ASK CUSTOMERS

If your organization assumes it knows all the answers about your customers' views of your product and category, you're probably living an isolationist's view of the marketplace; you would be said to be approaching your market from the perspective of *inside, looking out.* This means you, your colleagues, and your management project *your view of your market and category* (however right or wrong) out to the marketplace. You assert that you know the true state of the marketplace; this is a very dangerous posture!

One of the consequences of this *internal view* as it pertains to a satisfaction measurement program you create may be that your survey, created from this perspective (because of the questions that would be included), would more likely measure your organization's *efficiency* rather than its *effectiveness.* When an organization assumes it's doing all the right things, it tends only to be concerned with *how well* it's doing them. Measuring how well your organization is doing that which it *already is doing* is a question of efficiency. Efficiency is an *internal perspective* oriented toward maximizing returns on current effort and resource allocation. It is reasonably easy to construct a questionnaire to assess efficiency.

The alternative position toward the market and your category is to attempt to see and understand it through the eyes of your customers. This view is referred to as *outside, looking in,* and it is a major part of what customer requirement assessment and satisfaction measurement is all about! Your customers' perspective is more likely to be influenced by whether or not your organization is *doing the right things.* Doing the right things is

---

The numerous dot-com businesses initiated during the late 1990s exemplify businesses that believed so much in their technology or their product that they assumed customers would flock to their enterprises. Their corporate egoism bred an arrogance resulting in their failure to test their businesses with consumers and/or involve consumers in the design or functionality of their services. Although customers were not consulted in the design of the businesses, they ultimately participated in their defeat by ignoring these businesses or by finding interaction with them to be more trouble than the perceived value of the benefits to be derived.

what *effectiveness* is all about. But effectiveness is a more difficult issue for management to confront. It requires an organization to question all its processes, to open-mindedly examine its products, maybe even the roles of entire departments. Traumatic as it may be, the customer's perspective, the external perspective, is an invaluable asset for providing insights to improve the effectiveness of organizations.

Some of the things your organization is doing are undoubtedly the right things, and for those issues questions structured to measure efficiency aren't all bad. But likewise, you're probably not doing *all* the right things. An investigation of your customers' requirements is really a question concerning what else your organization ought to be doing; in other words, your organization's *effectiveness*. This issue has also recently been represented in the "little q, Big Q" paradigm. Juran (1992, 11–13) characterizes *little q* issues as those dealing more with quality in a narrow sense—the definition of quality as conformance to internal specifications. *Big Q* issues define quality in a more global sense, addressing the satisfaction of evolving customer needs.

Step-by-Step: The Issues of Identifying Your Customers' Requirements

To most representatively identify the issues of importance to your customers, the author recommends a five-step process:

3.1 Understand how to deal constructively with the important issue of your *customers' requirements*.

3.2 Establish a procedure for investigating the requirements of your customers. Then begin by generating a "laundry list" of issues (the more possibly relevant issues that you identify in this list, the better).

3.3 Screen each possible customer requirement you've identified, classifying it into one of several major categories you'll create.

3.4 Select the specific issues you'll measure making sure you represent all the basic, evaluative dimensions you discover while still keeping your questionnaire to a manageable number of questions.

3.5 Commit to ongoing monitoring of the continuing importance of each of these issues and the possibility of new, emerging issues.

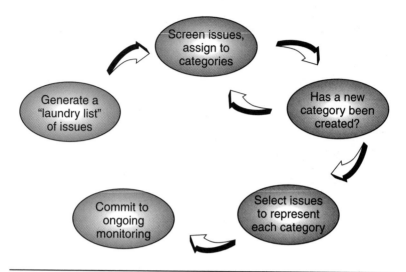

Figure 3.1   A process for identifying your customers' requirements.

The foregoing steps describe an effective process that is diagrammed in Figure 3.1. In this chapter we'll review each of these five steps.

The revised ANSI/ISO/ASQ Q9001-2000 standards recognize that an effective organization uses the requirements of its customers as inputs to its entire business process. From the standard:

7.2 Customer-related Process

7.2.1 Determination of requirements related to the product.

The organization shall determine

a) requirements specified by the customer, including the requirements for delivery and post-delivery activities,

b) requirements not stated by the customer but necessary for specified or intended use, where known,

c) statutory and regulatory requirements related to the product, and

d) any additional requirements determined by the organization.

Source: ANSI/ISO/ASQ Q9001-2000.

STEP 3.1 UNDERSTAND REQUIREMENTS

Hayes (1998, 9) defines customer requirements as "those characteristics of a product or service that represent important dimensions." Hayes encourages working those dimensions into specific examples or performance-related statements for administration in a survey.

Juran (1988, 39) is more precise. Consumer needs, Juran believes, can be represented in a hierarchical structure, a "pyramid" or chain of needs. He envisions customer requirements in a three-component hierarchy composed of primary, secondary, and tertiary needs. His model suggests that consumers might respond to questions about their desire for a product or service in one of three levels or steps as shown in Figure 3.2:

- Their *primary needs* (their "motives" prompting their purchase of the product)

- Their *secondary needs* (essentially their "requirements" of the product or category)

- Their *tertiary needs* (the measurable manifestations of the requirements or motives)

Juran's supposition sets up the following possibility. One of a consumer's primary motives for purchasing an automobile might be to achieve *status*. Probing this need, the secondary need or requirement of *being recognized* might be disclosed. Finally, at the most basic level, an impacting tertiary need (or performance measure) might be the *styling* of the motor vehicle. The only element missing from Juran's discussion is a clear understanding of what determines into which level a specific need would fall.

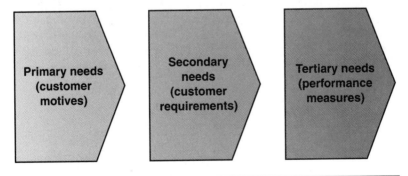

Figure 3.2   The chain of customer requirements.

The Structure of Customer Requirements

Consider the following interpretation. The highest level of customer needs, the most pervasive, should be considered *purchase motives*. These motives represent global needs or end states that dictate whether a product or service is considered at all relevant to a consumer's situation. They are the driving motivations directing a consumer in a particular need state to consider a specific product or service as likely to satisfy that need state.

The second level of needs, it is proposed, should be considered as *customer requirements*. Requirements decompose the more generic purchase motives into more pragmatic and less conceptual areas. Finally, the third level of needs can be interpreted as *performance measures or attributes*. These are the most basic (and common) means for evaluating the satisfactoriness of the product or service. They are, to borrow Juran's (1992, 109) terminology, the "language of things." (See Table 3.1) It is at this level that we generally question our customers about the performance of our product or service.

 Checkpoint 3.1

1. Establish a systematic approach for investigating your customers' requirements. This should probably include both an exploratory and a confirmatory phase. Specify the exact procedures you will employ in both of your investigation stages.

STEP 3.2 GENERATE ISSUES

To create the most all-encompassing CSM process you can, you'll need to explore every possible influencing factor. If you start too small, too constrained, your process may exclude an important issue. The best process to use is one we'll refer to as *funneling*. This is a simple way of starting by creating the broadest possible list of issues, and then gradually reducing the list until you are left with only the *core issues* you'll address in your customer satisfaction questionnaire.

You are generally advised to use a two-step process: (1) an *exploratory phase*, using qualitative techniques, and (2) a *confirmatory phase* using quantitative techniques.[1]

---

[1]We'll discuss qualitative and quantitative research techniques in chapter 4.

Table 3.1 The language of things.

Personal Banking		
Purchase motives	**Customer requirements**	**Performance measures**
Manage financial assets	Accessibility	Flexible hours ATM/credit card access Numerous branches Telephone inquiries after hours
	A variety of investment options	Savings accounts Stock accounts IRA accounts
Increase wealth	Costs/benefis	Competitive interest rates Low maintenance fees Low balance requirements
	Advice/consultation	Good research reports Makes frequent recommendations
Assure financial security	Secure transactions	Insured accounts Controlled access to account information

Exploratory phase. There are two basic ways by which to generate a list of requirements and needs: artifactual or attitudinal. Both are empirical, but one is more passive, deriving ideas by observing the current business, while the other actively solicits customers' reactions and inputs.

Confirmatory phase. Once you've generated a relatively rich and extensive list of requirements and needs through exploratory techniques, you'll need to "winnow down" your list. You may do this using confirmatory techniques. (We'll discuss these methods in Step 3.)

Exploratory—Artifactual Methods

You can turn to several sources that may already exist for information about requirements your customers may have. Consider each of the following:

- Customers' complaints and compliments

- Your help desk and customer service departments

- Warranty claims and reports

- Company mail or e-mail

A company's mailbag, e-mail log, or Internet site will most generally receive and accumulate numerous items of feedback from customers every day. It will often be the case that this information is collected and stored by another department, somewhere else in the organization. You should find out where this information is archived—it's likely to be a gold mine of insights.

Find out where your customer service function exists, and pay a visit to the head of that department, if you don't already know her or him. Ask to see how your organization's *customer service reps* record and report the information they hear about product and servicing malfunctions. You may find customers' calls are dealt with on a *case basis*, with little or no diagnostic information retained on closed cases. If this is so, you may wish to suggest to this department that it begin to retain data on closed cases to help identify recurring requests, problems, comments, and complaints. If such a historical file already exists, dig through it, looking for specific issues as well as overriding themes. You may wish to create a modest Pareto analysis of such information.

Warranty claims and repairs are another wonderful existing source of information. Perhaps you haven't previously incorporated this information into your satisfaction systems, but when you're trying to understand customer needs, listening to what they *don't like about current products or services* can tell you quite a lot about what they may feel they *need*.

Exploratory—Attitudinal Methods

Oftentimes one of the most obvious solutions is simply to ask customers what their needs are. Depending upon your industry and the sophistication of your purchasers, they may be able to tell you exactly what they desire. In more consumer-oriented industries, your customer may be able to tell you what is missing (that which he or she may have experienced before), but it is less likely that consumer-customers will be thoughtful or creative enough to voice some actual product category enhancements.

In this more *proactive* mode of gathering requirements, you need to choose the process you'll use as well as the method you'll use to collect information. Processes are any format that will put you into contact with customers. Among the more popular are the following:

- *Customer listening groups.* Invite a group of your customers to come together at a central location (a hotel meeting room; a focus group research facility) to discuss their reactions to your products, services, servicing (of their needs), and operational policies. Host the group yourself, or hire a trained moderator. You'll be amazed at the insights you can derive, once you convince them of your sincerity. (This method can be problematic if your customers are aggressively in competition with one another. If so, they may consider it inappropriate to meet with each other, especially to describe their unique needs.)

- *On-site visits.* To best understand your customer's needs and concerns, what better place to do it than his or her own factory, office, or facility? The goal is to involve your customer in a candid discussion of what he or she likes and doesn't like about you and (if the customer is willing) your competitors. You may conduct such a visit among a group of a customer's personnel.

- *One-on-one interviews.* If you meet with and interview your customers one at a time, this is referred to as a one-on-one interview. It can be conducted in person, over the telephone, even in an Internet chat room. Frequently a *discussion guide* (similar to a listening group moderator's guide) is prepared to guide the sequence of questioning and to make sure all important issues are covered.

- *Surveys of lost customers.* Customers you've lost are apparently dissatisfied. They should be able to generate a rather comprehensive list of things you should have done if you had wanted to keep them. You can survey lost customers in one of two ways: as a population, on a recurring basis (such as once or twice a year), or by establishing a continuing process that is administered to customers as they indicate they're quitting you—a so-called *exit interview.* Exit interviews may be a good tool for understanding the dimensions of dissatisfaction regarding your organization. But whatever your interviewers do, don't allow them to become defensive or begin to offer explanations for the actions customers describe as dissatisfactory. Deal with the situation as objectively as possible. Listen, record the information, and thank your past customers. (In certain cases, such an interview is an appropriate contact point to at least ask, should you solve the problem(s) they've described, whether the customer would like a sales call placed to them by your sales staff. But this should clearly be a separate endeavor from your satisfaction interview.)

Whichever of these contact processes you select, it is recommended that you employ an information collection method that will help both you and your customer create as diverse a list of requirements as possible. Here are some of the procedures you can adopt:

- Kelly's repertory grid technique

- Moments-of-truth explorations

- Explanations of reasons for switching brands

(Each of these methods is described in more detail in the Toolkit at the end of this chapter.)

 Checkpoint 3.2

1. Establish a systematic approach for investigating your customers' requirements. This should probably include both an exploratory and a confirmatory phase. Specify the exact procedures you will employ in both of these investigation stages.

2. You may have information currently available to suffice for the exploratory stage. Make a list of each area within your organization that has interaction with current customers. Contact each area asking if it maintains records of customer comments, concerns, or requests. If so, such lists can be a good source of issues.

3. Beyond already-existing information, what, if any, additional activities do you plan to use to generate further ideas concerning your customers' requirements?

STEP 3.3 CONFIRM AND CLASSIFY YOUR ISSUES

Once you have created a reasonably exhaustive listing of possible customer requirements, you enter the next phase of the funneling process, the stage of *screening and confirming*. In this stage you need to assess just how many different, discrete customer requirements you have tapped. Obviously not all of the different statements you have collected will represent separate issues. Your task is first to understand how many different, basic requirements are represented, and then to choose from among the groupings those requirements that will be most easily communicated to other customers in your satisfaction questionnaire. You want to reduce your list to minimize any redundancy that may have crept in and yet retain the most important issues. There are two basic ways of simplifying the list: *judgmental* and *statistical techniques.*

Judgmental Procedures

Judgment is probably the least satisfactory way of reducing the number of performance items you will carry forward. Because customers have been included in the discovery process to avoid internal biases, it seems self-defeating to end this process with an internal, judgment-driven reduction. Why won't the same biases that operated at the outset now cancel out customer-volunteered issues because they are devalued or disbelieved? One defense may be the very nature of learning. Managers may be so impressed with the discrepancy between their list of supposed customer priorities and the new list that they totally rethink their view of the customer. If that happens, then reduction of items through judgment may not be as biased as might have been presupposed. It is realistic to add, however, that not all managers are this open-minded. If judgment is to play a role in your reduction of issues, you should ask several different managers to review your list of issues. For each item they suggest be excluded, ask them to explain their reasons.

Judgment will, no doubt, have to be used to some extent—either as a substitute for a statistical reduction procedure or possibly to conclude such a procedure.

Statistical Procedures

Several different statistical procedures can be meaningfully used to help reduce the number of issues carried forward to your CSM. Among the techniques most frequently used are the following:

- Factor analysis
- Cluster analysis
- Correlation analysis

All these procedures require that some intermediate data are collected from customers. To apply the procedures, you'll have to take your expanded list of possible requirements to a sample of your customers and ask them to provide you some feedback (importance ratings, pile sorts, similarity-dissimilarity ratings, etc.) on them.

Checkpoint 3.3

1. Create a list of the basic, core groupings of requirements from your exploratory work. Mark each as either *expected* or *discovered* (depending on your prior knowledge of them).

2. What reduction technique will you use to reduce your listing of customer requirements: judgmental or statistical procedures? If you'll use judgment, list some of the ways you'll prevent "internal wisdom" from compromising new insights.

3. You may wish to issue a memo or report discussing your customers' requirements if a substantial number of the groupings are newly discovered groups. These groups conceivably represent an evolving need that is not yet well acknowledged or understood in your industry or organization.

STEP 3.4 SELECT YOUR CORE ISSUES

The previous sections have described several methods for empirically identifying attributes your customers and your management describe as defining quality in the product or service you sell. It is a good idea to reflect at some point on how exhaustive the attributes (and their underlying "dimensions") are in describing the category. Fortunately, some external lists exist to serve as useful "checklists" with which to compare your listings. This cross-check can provide a "reality check" to determine how many different dimensions your list taps and whether, for whatever reason, you've missed a dimension.

Checklist 3.1 Selecting Your Customers' Requirements to Be Represented in Your Satisfaction Questionnaire.

1. Compare your issues against the internal metrics you already collect on your processes. See Figure 3.3. Just as you can't manage what you don't measure, it's difficult to meaningfully react to customer perceptions without some objective measure (from inside) of your performance on an issue or process. Internal metrics give you this objective benchmark. With this additional information, you'll know better how to react to the directionality of

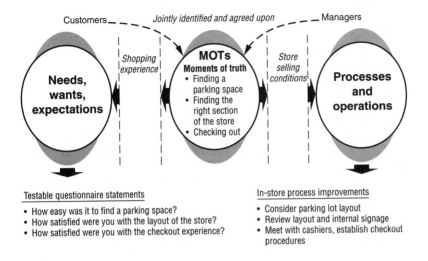

Figure 3.3 Matching customers' needs with internal practices.

your customers' evaluations (e.g., if your customers' satisfaction ratings are decreasing, is that decline [in your apparent performance] substantiated by a parallel decline in related internal metrics?).

2. Make sure all major processes or departments in your organization are represented by your selection of questions and issues. Often it's helpful both to you and to customers completing your questionnaire if you aggregate issues related to a similar process. See Figure 3.4. You may also sequence questions related to processes in the approximate order in which your customers experience the processes. Using such an organizational method, your questionnaire might provide signposts such as the following:

Section A. First, we're interested in your evaluations of our
order process . . .

Section B. Now, please give us your satisfaction with our
order-tracking capabilities . . .

Section C. Moving on to our *shipping procedures*, how do
you rate us on . . .

Hopefully, you can see how such a potential structure for your questionnaire or interview will assist you in representing all the areas or departments involved in your customer's satisfaction with your organization.

Business process	Customer need	Internal metric
	Reliability (40%)	% Repair call
Product (30%)	Easy to use (20%)	% Calls for help
	Features/functions (40%)	Function performance test
	Knowledge (30%)	Supervisor observations
Sales (30%)	Response (25%)	% Proposals made on time
	Follow-up (10%)	% Follow-up made
Installation (10%)	Delivery interval (30%)	Average order interval
	Does not break (25%)	% Repair reports
	Installed when promised (10%)	% Installed on due date
	No repeat trouble (30%)	% Repeat reports
Repair (15%)	Fixed fast (25%)	Average speed of repair
	Kept informed (10%)	% Customers informed
	Accuracy, no surprises (45%)	% Billing inquiries
Billing (15%)	Resolve on first call (35%)	% Resolved first call
	Easy to understand (10%)	% Billing inquiries

(Overall satisfaction)

Figure 3.4   Linking questionnaire constructs to internal metrics.

3. You may also draw upon the insights provided by two external frameworks to determine which issues to include in (or that may be missing from) your draft questionnaire. These frameworks can serve as objective sources for common dimensions of customer reactions to products. The two most useful frameworks are Garvin's (1988) *dimensions of product quality* and Zeithaml, Parasuraman, and Berry's SERVQUAL model (1990) identifying *dimensions of service quality*. These frameworks are shown in Figures 3.5 and 3.6.

Study the contents of the two systems carefully to gain a full appreciation of what these experts have discovered about how customers assess products and services. Hopefully the frameworks will give you ideas for items that may be missing from your current inventory of issues. But by all means, use their dimensions as a checklist against which to compare the listing of requirements you've generated by talking to your customers.

If your listing of performance attributes fails to include one or more attributes to represent each of these dimensions, you may want to rethink the comprehensiveness of your list. It should be easy to create your own attribute to represent the missing dimension(s). On the other hand, you can always go back to customers and probe the meaning and/or relevance of the dimension(s) in your category.

4. It is also fair to use the collective expertise of your organization's senior staff. Most organizations have several individuals who are exceptionally in tune with customers. You probably already know who these executives are. Consult with them, drawing on their unique insight.

Again, the new standard is quite specific about the need to understand and satisfy your customers' requirements.

Dimensions of Product and Service Quality

1. *Performance.* The satisfactoriness of the primary operating characteristics of the product.
   The acceleration of my Honda is excellent.

2. *Features.* The secondary characteristics that supplement the product's basic functioning.
   The brightness control on the monitor is very useful.

3. *Reliability.* The likelihood of the product failing or malfunctioning within a specified time period.
   The printer has performed reliably without breakdowns since I purchased it.

4. *Conformance.* How closely the product's design and operation match preestablished specifications or users' expectations.
   The sharpness of the picture is exactly as the literature described it.

5. *Durability.* The amount of use one gets from a product before it physically deteriorates or becomes obsolete.
   The printer lasted as long as I expected.

6. *Serviceability.* The speed, courtesy, competence, and ease of repair of a product.
   When needed, it was easy to have my vehicle serviced.

7. *Aesthetics.* Subjective elements of personal judgment regarding how the product looks.
   The external appearance of the monitor is very attractive.

8. *Reputation.* The general image and reputation of the company.
   Motorola has an excellent reputation for computer chips.

Figure 3.5 Dimensions of product and service quality.

Adapted from: David A. Garvin. *Managing Quality.* New York: Free Press, 1988.

Dimensions of Service Quality

1. *Reliability.* The ability to perform the service dependably and accurately.

   When CNA Insurance promises to do something by a certain date, they do it!

2. *Responsiveness.* Willingness to help customers and provide prompt servicing.

   Employees of Fleet Financial Services are never too busy to respond to my requests promptly.

3. *Assurance*

   - *Competency.* Possessing the required skills and knowledge.

     Microsoft customer service reps are always able to identify and help fix problems.

   - *Courtesy.* Politeness, respect, consideration, and friendliness of service personnel.

     Employees of United Airlines are always polite and courteous.

   - *Credibility.* Trustworthiness, believability, and honesty of the service provider.

     Allstate Insurance agents can be trusted completely.

   - *Security.* Freedom from danger, risk, and doubt.

     AARP works hard to keep my insurance coverage adequate to my needs.

4. *Empathy*

   - *Accessibility.* Approachability and ease of contacting.

     You never have to wait to get an appointment to see someone at Prudential.

   - *Communication skills.* Keeping customers informed in language they can understand and listening to their response and questions.

     AAA of New Jersey reps can explain the many issues of automobile insurance understandably.

   - *Understanding the customer.* Taking the effort to get to know customers and their particular needs.

     Employees of the Ritz-Carlton always see that I get all the special requests I've made on previous stays.

5. *Tangibles.* The condition of the "physical evidence" surrounding the delivery of the service.

   The branch offices of Prudential are very professional looking.

Figure 3.6   Dimensions of service quality.

Adapted from: Valerie A. Zeithaml, A. Parasuraman, and Leonard L. Berry. *Delivering Quality Service: Balancing Customer Perceptions and Expectations.* New York: Free Press, 1990.

5.2 Customer focus

Top management shall ensure that customer requirements are determined and are met with the aim of enhancing customer satisfaction (see 7.2.1 and 8.2.1).

Source: ANSI/ISO/ASQ Q9001-2000

 Checkpoint 3.4

1. Describe the exact process (or sequence of "filters") you envision using to pare down your exhaustive list of customers' requirements.

2. Which internal processes or metrics align with which of your survey issues? Prepare a grid showing the alignment between your survey questions and the internal metrics collected by your organization. The internal metrics will help you calibrate movement in your attitudinal measures to internal quality control issues.

STEP 3.5 COMMIT TO ONGOING MONITORING

The only thing that's certain, goes the saying, is change itself. You can be sure that your customers' requirements will change from year to year. Change occurs as the result of:

- Evolving practices in your industry

- Changes in technology

- Practices in other industries

Even if the domain of issues doesn't change, chances are what were the most important issues of today will change tomorrow. These expected changes issue a challenge to you: "Keep tabs on us!" they say. You mustn't rest a moment. You must be prepared to revisit your understanding of your customers' requirements on an ongoing basis. (See Figure 3.7.)

To this end, most CSM programs embrace a built-in process to monitor for change. But such monitoring incurs two types of costs:

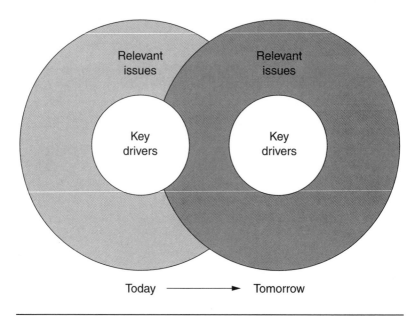

Figure 3.7   The evolution of customer requirements.

- Your surveying and processing costs

- The inconvenience your customers suffer from being interviewed twice a year. (This presumes you can't collect both types of information in a single survey. The author happens to believe that requesting too much information in a single contact will tend to denigrate the quality of all the information you collect.)

From an analytical point of view, importance can be collected or derived in several different ways. This means that you may be able to accommodate all concerns while nevertheless minding your customers' possible shifts of importance. Consider two ways of determining importance:

- Determining importance *explicitly* by collecting it directly from customers

- Inferring importance *implicitly* by calculating it from information you already have (your satisfaction data)

These two procedures—explicit and implicit determination—can be employed nicely to minimize the inconvenience visited on customers. The author happens to like:

- Measuring importance *explicitly* every second year

- Calculating importance *implicitly* on the first and consecutive other "off" years

If you adopt such a schedule, you'll be reexamining your customers' importance ratings each year, but in a slightly different manner. And you'll only be accepting one major trade-off—to eliminate the yearly, second interview with your customers. The trade-off is one of content. The implicit methods are by definition *closed systems*—constrained to the issues (questions) you're already measuring. That means you'll easily identify your customers' shifting importance weights (among those items you're currently measuring), but you won't be able to determine if new issues have come along, that are not currently included in your questionnaire, whose importance may now supersede some of the issues you're measuring.

Explicit methods are essentially *open systems*—they allow customers to volunteer new issues not included in your current inventory of issues. Consequently, explicit methods do a somewhat more thorough job of assessing importance on an absolute basis.

 Checkpoint 3.5

1. Describe the ongoing process you are considering implementing to track the continuing evolution of your customers' requirements. How frequently will you use this process? Who will conduct the data gathering?

2. How do you envision responding to each new list of customer requirements? (While customer satisfaction surveys should change and evolve, you nevertheless need a foundation of underlying, basic requirements that are continuous through several waves. Don't engage in wholesale change.)

Step-by-Step: The Answers for Identifying Your Customers' Requirements

3.1 It's important to accept a customer's view of your organization—the *external perspective* as opposed to an *internal perspective*. There is an implied hierarchy linking customers' *judgments of performance measures* or attributes to *customers' requirements* and ultimately to *customers' motives*. By understanding this hierarchy you'll be in a much better position to seek out and identify your customers' most meaningful requirements. See pages 60–64.

3.2 The best way to identify your customers' requirements is to use a two-phase approach. In the first phase, try to identify as many different requirements from as many different sources as possible. In the second phase, reduce them down to a manageable number (that can comfortably be administered in an interview), reducing internal redundancies. See pages 64–68.

3.3 You can act on your list either through intuitive methods or with statistical procedures. Either way, your goal is to reduce the issues to meaningful "buckets" or dimensions. These represent your customers' basic ways of evaluating you and your competitors.

3.4 You'll finally select the specific issues to include in your questionnaire or interview by drawing leading issues from each classification (or bucket). You'll also compare these selected issues to evaluative standards (such as Garvin's and Zeithaml's lists of dimensions) as well as the expertise that has evolved within your organization. Your goal is to create the shortest possible list of issues that still includes representative issues from all the dimensions you have identified. See pages 68–75.

3.5 Once you've identified your customers' requirements, don't be complacent about your list. Assume customers' requirements change as quickly as anything else. You'll want to establish a procedure for monitoring their evolution and change. As you detect new requirements, they should be represented in your satisfaction survey. See pages 75–77.

Chapter 3 Deliverables

As a result of your work in this chapter, you'll have completed the following:

1. ANSI/ISO/ASQ Q9001-2000 required document #1—a statement describing your customer requirements and a brief explanation of the importance of this information to your organization

2. A method by which you can gather and update the requirements of your customers

3. A refined list of those requirements that appear to be most important to include in your satisfaction questionnaire by virtue of their criticalness to your customers and their linkage to internal metrics you may be collecting

4. A cross-referencing of your requirements with critical dimensions identified in two conceptual models

5. The description of a process you'll use to update your list of critical customer requirements

TOOLKIT

Data Collection Methods

- Laddering
- Moments-of-truth workshop
- Kelly's repertory grid
- Exit interviews—why customers switch brands/suppliers

Laddering

Thomas Reynolds and Jonathan Gutman (1988) advanced a process for harnessing "means-end" chaining that possibly can be useful in elaborating on customers' requirements. Building on earlier theories characterizing personal values as either *terminal* or *instrumental*, laddering assumes customers choose between organizations by selecting that organization they perceive as most potentially instrumental in helping them achieve their desired consequences.[2] Laddering uses a series of directed, probing questions to elicit perceived linkages customers construct between attributes, consequences, and values. In the present case, it is believed that laddering could become a useful procedure for identifying the linkages between customers' *motives*, *requirements*, and *product attributes*.

Laddering, which melds qualitative interviewing with quantitative analysis, is accomplished in the following sequence:

1. Use a discovery procedure (repertory grid, preference ordering, or differences by occasions) to help customers identify performance attributes they associate with your category. (Reynolds and Gutman find the typical participant is generally capable of generating only 10 to 12 different distinctions within a product category.)

2. Select the most important attributes to carry forward (to select them you may use judgment based on previous knowledge, or it's fair to ask participants to rank-order the attributes, in which case you proceed only with the top six or so).

3. Advance the selected performance attributes into the laddering exercise. This phase presents the customer with one performance attribute at a time. For each attribute the customer is asked a series of importance probes:

   a. Why is it important to you that a product have/offer (performance attribute)?

   b. Why is that (reason from [a]) important to you?

   c. And why or in what way is that (reason from [b]) important to you?

4. Code the attributes, requirements, and motives generated in the above steps and tabulate the relationships forming common attribute-requirement-motive chains.

5. Create a final, hierarchical value grid displaying the overall linkage of performance attributes, customer requirements, and customer motives.[3]

---

[2] Milton Rokeach (1979) is generally credited with proposing a model of personal values including values that represent desired end states (*terminal values*) and behaviors and actions required to achieve these end states, the *instrumental values*.

[3] The interested reader is referred to Reynolds and Gutman, "Laddering Theory, Method, Analysis, and Interpretation" (1988), for a more complete description of this admittedly complex data collection and analytical procedure.

Moments of Truth

Borrowed from the *moment de veridad* of the Spanish bullring (the moment when the matador and bull size each other up), a customer's *moment of truth* is every bit as dramatic. It is in moments of truth, Jan Carlzon (1987) said, that organizations are either *created* (their image shored up in a customer's mind) by living up to the customer's expectations or *destroyed* by failing a customer's expectations. Inventorying moments of truth is becoming a routine tool for improving the quality of services (Vavra 1997). For example, the IBM Consulting Group in its Business Transformation Process^sm dissects customer interactions into moments of truth to help its clients better manage the delivery of quality services or quality processes.

A moment of truth analysis often starts with a *blueprint* or *brown paper* of an interaction with a customer. A blueprint or brown paper is nothing more than a diagrammatic representation of an organization's interaction with a customer. The term *brown paper* is derived from the fact that many such analyses are drawn on brown butcher shop or kraft wrapping paper (the only paper easily available in unlimited lengths). Blueprinting was first suggested for the management of service quality by Lynn Shostack (1977). The resulting diagram should show every bit of interaction: written, verbal in person, verbal on the phone, and so on. Evidence of such interactions is actually attached to the diagram (which can often cover the wall or walls of a standard conference room).

A variation of the moments-of-truth exercise is the *critical incidents method.* Patterned after psychologist John Flanagan's (1954) critical incident methodology, critical incidents have been popularized in marketing by Bitner, Booms, and Tretault (1990). Bitner, Booms, and Tretault found that so-called critical incidents can be identified through a four-question sequence, as follows:

Consider a time when you had a particularly satisfying or dissatisfying experience with (brand, product, or organization):

1. *When did the incident happen, or what comprised the experience?*

2. *What specific circumstances led up to this situation?*

3. *Exactly what did (brand or organization) or its employees say or do?*

4. *What resulted that made you feel particularly satisfied or dissatisfied?*

This questioning will result in a list of *critical incidents*—events that are so important that satisfaction or dissatisfaction with them flavors the customer's satisfaction with the *entire interaction* with your organization.

As incidents are volunteered by a sample of customers, they'll have to be processed. You can establish your own coding categories, or you can conduct a Pareto analysis on the incidents. Bitner, Booms, and Tretault found that three categories (regarding the actions of the organization) nicely accomodated the critical incidents they collected. The categories are:

- An employee initiating an encounter at his or her own volition

- An employee responding to a product or service failure

- An employee answering a customer's special request

The value of the moments-of-truth analysis follows Juran's mandate to "be the customer." Similarly, the American Indian challenged others to "walk a mile in my moccasins" to better understand a situation. In moments-of-truth excursions, the analyst essentially becomes the customer and examines the situation and the evidence (or lack of it) supplied by the organization. It's always eye-opening, usually highly productive, and can foster breakthrough insights that help organizations turn themselves around.

Kelly's Repertory Grid

In the repertory grid technique, Kelly (1955) suggested that subjects (customers) be presented with several triads of products or brands within an industry. For each (randomly assembled) triad, the customer should be asked:

1. Of these three products, which two are most similar?

2. How are these two similar? (In what ways, methods, and behaviors are they similar?)

3. How are these two different from the third product? (In what ways, methods, and behaviors are they different from the third?)

The results of these questions, as they are asked of a customer about multiple triads, will be a full listing of the needs and requirements customers face within a category.

Explanations for Switching

When customers "vote with their feet" (by switching brands or suppliers) they have apparently reached the end of their rope. Whatever they have been requiring of their current supplier or whatever inconvenience they have been suffering has simply not been offered or remedied. Interviews conducted at the time a customer switches suppliers (exit interviews) or a general survey eliciting motives for switching are excellent methods by which to discover some key requirements. Consider questions such as these:

1. When you switched suppliers, exactly what was happening with your previous supplier that caused you to search for alternatives?

2. Exactly what did your new supplier offer that solved the problems you had been experiencing?

3. Are there other benefits you have experienced since switching?

4. Is there anything you've found that you no longer receive with your new supplier?

Statistical Techniques for Reducing Lists of Requirements

Several different statistical procedures can be used to help reduce the number of issues to be carried forward to your CSM.

- Correlation analysis

- Factor analysis

- Cluster analysis

Each of these techniques requires you to collect some preliminary data from customers. In general, it's good practice to survey a sample of more customers than you have trial performance items. For example, if you have 50 items (that you want to reduce to perhaps 15 to 25), you should attempt to get evaluations of the 50 items by at least 50 of your customers. If this is not practical, you can use ratings from fewer than 50 customers, however, the resulting analysis will be less definitive. For correlation and factor analysis, you should prepare a brief questionnaire asking for either a rating of your organization's current performance on the issues (you're attempting to reduce) or customers' ratings of the issues' importance to them.

Correlation Analysis

Submit the ratings to a correlation procedure (either in a spreadsheet package like Excel or Lotus 123 or a statistical package like SPSS). Then, you'll want to review the "off diagonal" correlation coefficients. Sample these coefficients, ranking them from smallest to largest. Once you have this ranking, select a coefficient—a "critical value" (near the middle if you wish to reduce the number of issues approximately in half). Then, review all of the issue-to-issue coefficients again. Each coefficient exceeding this "critical value" will represent a pair of issues or questions which are very highly correlated and which you can consider as measuring approximately the same basic construct. You should choose one question of the pair to retain, discarding the other. In this way you'll work your way through the correlation matrix. If you need to eliminate any additional issues, simply readjust your "critical value" and reexamine the coefficients of the pairings among the remaining questions.

Reducing Issues with Factor Analysis

Factor analysis is a statistical technique which identifies correlations among lists of issues or items in a more sophisticated manner. The way it does this is by establishing "factors" or evaluative dimensions for each of the major pieces of information your customers have conveyed in their ratings of your organization on the issues or items you're seeking to reduce. Then, each individual item's correlation with the construct factor or dimension is represented by a correlation coefficient. Factor analysis goes a bit beyond simple correlation analysis by forming these groupings of questions, helping you understand the more basic underlying constructs represented by your collection of performance questions.

You'll need to use a more advanced package of statistical programs like SPSS to conduct a factor analysis using your preliminary data. Ask the package to "rotate" your results. A good rotation criterion to use is the "Equamax" rotation criterion. Although the output from a factor analysis may look somewhat confusing, it's actually fairly easy to interpret. Find the final stage of the analysis; it should be labeled "rotated loadings matrix." This matrix is akin to a table of correlation coefficients between each of your performance items and the construct variables, or "factors." You'll generally have 2 to 10 factors. When two or more of your performance items both correlate highly with ("load on") the same factor, this is evidence the performance items are both measuring essentially *the same judgmental construct*. In such a case, it is safe to eliminate one of the two items without losing any incremental information from your customers.

Reducing Issues with Cluster Analysis

Cluster analysis is a technique related to factor analysis. While some cluster analysis procedures are actually special extensions of factor analysis, there is a set of cluster analysis procedures called hierarchical procedures that approaches the similarity between your performance questions from a somewhat different perspective than correlation and factor analysis. First of all, you'll need different, "less metric" data. To reduce 50 items to a more manageable 15 to 25 items, you can use as few as 10 to 25 of your customers. Present each of these customers with a deck of cards. On each card you will have listed one of your performance questions to be judged. Each customer will have a deck with as many cards as you have items to be judged. Your instructions to these customers will simply be to "sort the 50 items into a number of piles according to issues which are 'similar,' that is they represent the same basic concerns or issues." Your customers may institute as many or as few piles as they require. You'll find customers generally adapt rather easily to this task.

To record their judgments, you'll form a type of correlation matrix (a square grid with as many columns and rows as you have issues—50 in this case). Construct this sort of grid for each customer participating in your pretest. Then, record each customer's judgments as follows. When you come to the junction of two questions in the data grid (say issue 4 and issue 10). Find those issues in the customer's piles. If issues 4 and 10 happen to have been placed in the same pile, enter a "1" in that intersection of the data grid. If issues 4 and 10 have been assigned to different piles, leave the intersection blank or assign it a "0" value.

Once you have tallied all customers' pile sorts into separate data grids, accumulate the individual grids into a new, total sample grid. Each cell in this summation grid will contain a number from 0 to the total number of customers you have involved in the task. It will look slightly like a correlation matrix, and it is, of course, similar. The larger the number in a cell, the more "correlated" the two issues represented by the intersection (because they have been placed together in the same piles by a number of your customers). This grid will be your input into a cluster analysis program.

Hierarchical clustering programs produce dendograms or "tree diagrams" which depict the relationships of your attributes. The sooner two attributes are linked in the resulting dendogram, the more similar they are. Removing one or more of the linked attributes will not substantially reduce the amount of incremental information you collect from your satisfaction survey. You should retain the one(s) with more inherent meaning or more actionability. You should avoid the temptation to combine linked issues into one question. Merging issues will confuse your customers and will make your interpretation of results more difficult.

II.

Design and Deployment

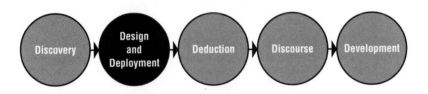

How Should You Measure Your Customer's Satisfaction?

You need to create a viable survey program that will collect the more important information you've identified yet maximize your customers' participation. To properly design your survey process you'll need to state your measurement objectives and identify key criteria and performance measures that you'll collect in the survey.

4

Deciding When, What, and How to Measure

Just as a successful journey requires a good map, a successful customer satisfaction program requires a good process. In this chapter you'll:

- Decide the class of survey you're conducting—and get your management's approval

- Select a field method and survey type with which to distribute and administer your questionnaire

- Settle on the logistics to maximize response and completion rates

- Create comprehensive interview and follow-up processes

A BASIC RESEARCH PRIMER

While the intent of this book is to offer actionable work plans rather than discussions of theory, it will be to the reader's advantage if we establish a basic understanding of social research techniques—the kind of research employed when measuring customer attitudes. Research in the social sciences is divided into two main thrusts:

Table 4.1   A comparison of research methods.

Qualitative research		Quantitative research
To generate insight; understand customers' range of perspectives.	**Purpose**	To quantify and measure *how much*.
Uses qualitative methods: observation in-depth interviews focus groups	**How conducted**	Uses quantitative methods: surveys using structured questionnaires
No—underlying hypotheses are not yet postulated.	**Directed by underlying hypotheses**	Yes—purpose is to test and quantify stated hypotheses (understandings).
Small number, typically fewer than 50	**Number of customers involved**	Larger number, always at least 35.*
A *convenience gathering*, any customers who are available, and/or cooperative.	**How participating customers are identified/recruited**	Drawn through statistically random procedures.
Costly on a CPI** basis; time consuming on a customer-by-customer basis.	**Costs/time involved**	Benefit from economies of scale; the more customers interviewed, the lower the CPI.**
In-depth interviews are sensitive to the skills of the interviewer; focus group participants frequently influence one another.	**Possibility of contamination/ interaction of results/opinions**	Fewer opportunities for biasing results, though demand and interviewer biases can still be present.
No—only in situations in which all customers can be involved, and contamination effects must still be a concern.	**Can results be projected (to those not included)**	Yes—results can be generalized to the entire customerbase (subject to statistical confidence intervals).
Not easy—summaries of learnings are generally qualitative themselves, i.e., anecdotes, descriptions of proper or improper performance or service.	**Ease/format of reporting results**	Very easy—numerical levels help to show (1) growth over time, or (2) comparison between groups.

* A minimum number of customers is always required for statistical analysis to be employed; this minimum is conventionally described as between 35 and 50. At and beyond this sample size, the properties of the normal distribution begin to apply, and parametric statistics may be employed.

** CPI is a term used to denote cost per interview. It is calculated by taking the entire project costs and dividing by the number of customers ultimately interviewed (alternatively, one may use the interviewing field costs to determine the CPI).

- *Qualitative,* or *exploratory, research,* generally subjective and experiential

- *Quantitative,* or *confirmatory, research,* which, in contrast, is objective and measurable

Both efforts can appropriately be called research, but their purpose, conduct, and results are substantially different. Table 4.1 compares these two very different initiatives.

In addition, research information is frequently classified by the purpose for which it is collected. You may find much information already existing in your organization that details some aspects of your customers' satisfaction. The author has already suggested tracking down where your organization collects and processes the communications it receives from customers (mail, e-mail, telephone calls). That information, because it already exists and because it was collected for another purpose (other than for your satisfaction measurement program), is called *secondary data.* In contrast, the information you will collect from the process you establish is called *primary data.* Primary data are data that are always collected firsthand, for the exact purpose for which they are used. There are several implied trade-offs between these two types of data, as shown in Table 4.2. In general, if you use secondary, existing information, you will be trading off *specificity* for *cost savings.*

Table 4.2 A comparison of secondary and primary data.

	Secondary data	Primary data
Is it necessary to collect it?	No—information already exists; it is "second hand" or "hand me down" information.	Yes—information must be collected "firsthand," it does not already exist.
Costs involved	Relatively few, if any.	Can be quite expensive.
Applicability of information to your satisfaction measurement process	Questionable—some "force fit" or sacrifice will need to be made, since information was originally collected for a purpose other than satisfaction measurement.	Will be directly applicable, since it is collected for the specific purpose of measuring customer satisfaction.
Typical example	Letters of complaint or compliment received by your organization's customer service department.	Results from the customer satisfaction survey you conduct.

While the ANSI/ISO/ASQ Q9001–2000 standards do not prescribe the type of research (secondary or primary, qualitative or quantitative) you should employ, it is the author's firm belief that in almost all cases, fairer, more meaningful, and certainly projectible results can be gathered only using *quantitative methods* to collect *primary data*.

Qualitative and quantitative research efforts are not at all competitive; they are, in fact, very effective partners. If time and budget allow, you will almost always wish to use qualitative techniques to better understand your customers' general status. The procedures discussed in chapter 3 were all qualitative techniques, and you learned how they could be used to build a foundation for a more quantifiable survey. The interviewing and questionnaire techniques described in chapter 5 will all be quantitative methods. In this chapter the author will assume that one or more of the following conditions prevail in your organization regarding the establishment of your customer satisfaction measurement (CSM) program:

- You have a sufficient number of customers among which to conduct a quantitative survey (always more than 35)

- You have the budget necessary to fund conducting quantitative research

- You wish the information you gather (from those customers you interview) to be projectible to all your customers through methods of statistical inference

If you have decided, for whatever reason, not to pursue a quantitative process, you do not need to read the remainder of this chapter nor chapters 5 and 6. You may skip ahead to chapters 7 and 8.

FORM AND PROCESS ARE EVERYTHING

An intentional overstatement? Yes. But from the author's perspective there's never quite enough attention focused on the content, format, and process of customer satisfaction surveys. Unlike marketing research projects in which a desired piece of information often is sought, a customer satisfaction survey is an ongoing process *entrusted to dialogue* with the most precious asset an organization has—its customers. When CSM is seen in this role, it is easier to understand why the author believes that far too many customer satisfaction processes fail to encompass all the procedures they should to deliver on their full potential.

The most important planning step you can undertake is that of fully planning out your customer satisfaction survey's many phases—beyond the simplest phase of collecting information. Figure 4.1 provides a rather thorough list of all the basic, necessary steps to conduct a customer survey. This chapter's Step-by-Step process identifies many of the more important elements. The ultimate success of your project will depend on your and your management's willingness to accept the responsibility for the full complement of CSM activities.

A Typical Survey Process Plan.

1. Identify your measurement objectives.

2. Create a list of your customers' requirements, needs, and issues.

3. Prioritize the requirements, identifying those you can handle, setting aside those you will reserve for later waves of your survey.

4. Compose your questionnaire.

5. Pretest your questionnaire.

6. Produce your questionnaire (as a printed format, in an interview format, or as an Internet survey).

7. Train your interviewing staff (if your questionnaire is to be interviewer administered).

8. Distribute your questionnaire to customers or conduct your customer interviews.

9. Receive returned (completed) questionnaires or interviews.

10. Code, edit, and clean responses.

11. Enter your data into a computer for tabulation.

12. Analyze your numerical and verbal data.

13. Create graphics of your key findings.

14. Write your report to document your process and convey your findings.

15. Present your findings.

16. Identify appropriate improvement initiatives.

17. Implement your improvement initiatives.

18. Begin measurement process again to monitor impact of improvement actions.

Figure 4.1   A typical survey process plan.

ISSUES

Step-by-Step: The Issues of Deciding When, What, and How to Measure

To create the process for ascertaining the satisfaction of your customers, follow these steps:

4.1 Specify a measurement objective, and identify the key performance criteria you'll use.

4.2 Prioritize the many issues you've identified, and select the few you can administer in your questionnaire.

4.3 Decide when you should interview your customers and how frequently.

4.4 Select a distribution method for your questionnaire (and determine how completed questionnaires will be returned to you).

4.5 Present your survey to your customers in a way that maximizes their cooperation and response rates.

4.6 Create the process you will use to report your findings to your management.

4.7 Decide whether you will institute a response process to solve problems of individual troubled customers.

4.8 Identify how (and where) you will enter your data for analysis.

4.9 Consider how you will actually conduct your survey: in house (yourself) or using an external research organization.

STEP 4.1 SPECIFY A MEASUREMENT OBJECTIVE AND IDENTIFY THE PERFORMANCE CRITERIA YOU'LL USE

Before you launch the "build" of your survey process you must be *very precise* in establishing exactly what you're measuring. You'll need to get your management's agreement before moving forward. Don't allow your program to fall victim to that old adage *Having lost sight of our objective, we redoubled our efforts!*

To simply say you're going to measure satisfaction is insufficient. You'll find you need to be far more specific. There are at least four major *classifications* of customer satisfaction surveys. The classifications are based on the informational objectives of the survey, but they are also related to when the survey is likely to be administered:

1. *Overall status surveys* generally assess *overall satisfaction* and *functional performance* in very general areas. Such surveys are generally fielded on a periodic basis, among either a sample or a census of customers. For example, most CSM programs assess overall satisfaction on an annual basis. A survey is distributed that attempts to get a general fix on both the overall satisfaction of customers as well as the organization's performance on certain key performance variables. These surveys provide a "pulse beat" measure of the overall health of your organization's commitment to customer satisfaction. They can't possibly provide all the information you need to make major changes or improvements, but they provide good directional guidance on a periodic basis.

2. *Transaction-driven surveys* focus on an organization's performance in conducting a specific transaction or interaction. You might wish to consider them *point-in-time surveys* because they attempt to measure satisfaction with a very specific interaction. Transactions that could be tracked using transaction surveys include:

- How the help desk handled a customer's call for information

- A customer's satisfaction with a consulting engineer's visit to a plant site

- Customers' opinions about the resolution of warranty claims

3. *Reliability surveys* are designed to see how well a product or service performs over time. They're usually initiated at an anniversary or other milestone of product or service use:

- One year of operating a new machine

- One year of service for a new software release

- Feelings on beginning the second year of an insurance policy

4. *Follow-up* or *diagnostic surveys* possibly are triggered by the responses of an earlier status survey questionnaire. The goal of this class of questionnaires or interviews is to learn more about the satisfaction or dissatisfaction registered on a previous survey by probing specific issues. If an organization has in mind a number of different fixes (for a specific problem), a diagnostic survey might even shed some light on customers'

preferences regarding the potential improvements. Examples of diagnostic surveys are:

- Contacting all those shoppers reporting an "unpleasant checkout experience"

- Interviewing all customers with a particular model of machinery that has received poor overall satisfaction scores in the hope of better understanding what could be done to improve the machine's performance

None of the survey classes are mutually exclusive; all probably have a role in an aggressive CSM program. Will you need or want to undertake all of them? Probably not. But you should nevertheless be aware of them and the perspective they offer. Table 4.3 summarizes their uniqueness and lists common performance criteria that you may adopt.

It's important for you to select one or more of the survey classes and then discuss the focus of the survey(s) you choose with your management. This way you can help them understand your survey's scope and what they can and can't expect to learn from it. Don't field a survey without having

Table 4.3   The four classes of CSM surveys.

	Overall status	Transaction	Reliability	Follow-up, diagnostic
When conducted?	On a periodic basis.	As close to the interaction as possible.	After a "wear-in" period, or reaching some other milestone of use/ownership.	Whenever particularly good or bad feedback has been received.
Coverage	As many customers as possible. Census?	Only those customers experiencing a particular interaction.	A sample or a census.	Among those customers offering responses that need to be probed.
Issues assessed	General issues, overall performance, satisfaction with perform-ance on key, basic issues. Very global.	Specific issues related to the conduct of the interaction. Very granular.	Issues dealing with overall reliability, durability, ease of servicing, ability to receive service, after-sales support, etc.	"Drill-downs" oriented to helping understand particularly good or bad performance in one or more specific areas.

gained *buy in* (acceptance) regarding its primary intent and coverage from those who will depend on your information.

Within the survey class you select, you'll have two types of variables:

- *Overall, criteria variables.* These will be your global, bellwether variables, such as overall satisfaction, expressed willingness to repurchase, willingness to recommend, and so on. These measures are meant to indicate the overall health of your organization—from your customers' perspective.

- *Performance variables.* These will allow your customers to provide ratings of your organization's performance on very specific issues using performance attributes, such as gas mileage, accessibility of your market team, on-time delivery, accuracy of software upgrades, and so on.

We'll defer discussing the specific questions or scales you'll use to measure overall satisfaction and performance issues until chapter 5.

 Checkpoint 4.1

1. What survey class or classes do you plan to create or are you currently administering?

2. For all the classes of survey you employ, describe your informational objectives.

3. Make a list of the specific elements of your organization's activities about which you'll be able to ask for customers' reactions.

STEP 4.2 PRIORITIZING THE MANY ISSUES YOU'VE IDENTIFIED FOR ADMINISTRATION IN YOUR QUESTIONNAIRE

In chapter 3 we discussed how to identify your customers' requirements— that is, the major elements they look to your product or service to supply or offer and the expectations and needs for which they buy your organization's products or services. To minimize the possibility of overlooking an important issue, you were encouraged to identify as many as possible. Later, in chapter 3, we advocated using a *funneling process* to help you reduce the total number of performance attributes you might administer to your customers by identifying the more important issues. At this stage, you may still have to perform further prioritizing to cut the attributes down to a truly administrable number. The worst crime you can visit on your customers is to ask them to evaluate your organization on every possible issue you and your colleagues have identified. If you field an impossibly long and complicated interview, you'll suffer the consequences:

- Your cooperation and response rates will suffer because of your questionnaire's inappropriate length.

- Among the answers you receive will probably be an unusually large number of shortened, abbreviated, or cryptic responses. (Unknowingly, you have traded off: *thorough information* for *breadth of coverage*—an arguable decision.) The customers who have labored through your questionnaire may also have adopted response practices like "gang answering" to make their task somewhat easier. Gang answering is the author's term to describe the practice of circling all of the same response boxes for a series of performance questions, rather than checking each response box individually. The practice suggests the respondent hasn't considered each question individually, but assumes the topic of all the questions is sufficiently similar to warrant the same rating. Respondents sometimes gang answer by drawing a vertical line down through all the response boxes within a series of questions. See Figure 4.2. The quality of responses marked in this way is always in doubt.

- You'll likely frustrate a number of your customers who may come to expect many more practices to change (as a result of your having covered so many issues) than your organization can hope to improve at one time.

You must act responsibly and adjudicate how many issues your survey should address. Just because you don't include all issues in one wave of your survey doesn't mean you can't rotate them into subsequent waves. This is especially useful when dealing with contemporary issues. Ask them while they're meaningful, then delete them, making room for other more recent issues.

You should probably always maintain two lists of questions:

- Your *short list*—the questions you're currently asking

- Your *long list*—questions you plan to rotate into your survey sometime in the future

	Excellent	Very Good	Good	Fair	Poor
ate the care provided to you by the Service Advisor (person who wrote up your C Truck, Inc? *(Please mark "not applicable" if it does not apply.)*					
ng your service order	☐	☑	☐	☐	☐
cific problem(s) with your vehicle	☐	☑	☐	☐	☐
vice needs	☐	☑	☐	☐	☐
ncerns with the servicing of your vehicle	☐	☑	☐	☐	☐
you	☐	☑	☐	☐	☐
ments made to you	☐	☑	☐	☐	☐

	Excellent	Very Good	Good	Fair	Poor
valuate this Mercedes-Benz Center on the following items? *(Please mark "not app*					
ance	☐	☐	☐	☐	☐
ng appointment for service or repair	☐	☐	☐	☐	☐
d promptness in greeting you	☐	☐	☐	☐	☐
handling service or repair work	☐	☐	☐	☐	☐
xpertise of service personnel	☐	☐	☐	☐	☐
all work requested	☐	☐	☐	☐	☐

Figure 4.2   An example of gang answering.

Here's a tip to help you keep track of the issues you've embedded in your current questionnaire. You'll find a feature included in most current-day word processors to be very helpful. Try building your questionnaire using your word processor's *outline mode.* This feature offers a convenient way to create areas of your questionnaire (customers' satisfaction with your ordering process, with your product's design, with your servicing provisions, etc.) and then list specific performance questions within each section. In this mode, you can track the evolving overall structure as well as the location of each individual issue. When you find yourself getting lost in the trees, back out (using the *collapse* function) and voilà, you're at forest level! If you need to be at tree level, simply use the *expand* function. The author finds outline processing to be extremely helpful. Figure 4.3 demonstrates how a questionnaire can be expanded and then contracted for ease of construction.

The outline mode is particularly useful when you need to reorder or modify your questionnaire. You may easily rearrange questions using the *promote, demote, move up,* or *move down* operations.

Section A: The Entire Questionnaire

I. About Your Rolls-Royce Motor Car

    1. In which name is your Rolls-Royce motor car registered?
      Self
      Company
      Leasing company
      Other (please specify)

    2. Did you part exchange (trade in) a car for this Rolls-Royce?
      Yes
      No

II. Your Attitude about Our Dealers

    3. How would you rate the Rolls-Royce dealership on the following?

      3A. About the Dealership
          Convenience of location
          Ease of access (parking...)
          Exterior appearance of the showroom
          Interior appearance and layout of the showroom
          Quality of sales personnel
          Availability of literature and information
          Convenience of opening hours

      3B. About Your Salesman
          Level of product knowledge/ability to answer questions
          Demonstration of the motor car, its features and contents
          Professionalism of the negotiation and sale
          Explanation of after-sale service and warranty
          Tour of service facilities

      3C. Condition of Your Rolls-Royce at Time of Delivery
          Cleanliness of interior
          Cleanliness of exterior
          Vehicle's mechanical condition
          Delivery on time

    4. Why did you select this dealer to purchase this Rolls-Royce?

    5. Would you recommend this dealer?
      Yes
      No
      Please comment

    6. Please give us your overall ratings.
      Overall Satisfaction
      With your selling dealer
      With your Rolls-Royce motor car

Figure 4.3   Using an outline processor to build your questionnaire.

III. About Yourself

    7. What is your date of birth?
Month/Date/Year

    8. Would you confirm the industry you are in and the products or services you deliver (e.g., property developer). If convenient, please attach a business card.

    9. And your position in the business.

    10. Are you self-employed?
Yes
No

    11. Who is the principal driver?
Who else may drive the motor car?

Section B: Collapsed to Question Level

I. About Your Rolls-Royce Motor Car

    1. In which name is your Rolls-Royce motor car registered?

    2. Did you part exchange (trade in) a car for this Rolls-Royce?

II. Your Attitude about Our Dealers

    3. How would you rate the Rolls-Royce dealership on the following?

    4. Why did you select this dealer to purchase this Rolls-Royce?

    5. Would you recommend this dealer?

    6. Please give us your overall ratings.

III. About Yourself

    7. What is your date of birth?

    8. Would you confirm the industry you are in and the products or services you deliver (e.g., property developer). If convenient, please attach a business card.

    9. And your position in the business?

    10. Are you self-employed?

    11. Who is the principal driver, and who else may drive the motor car?

Section C: Collapsed to Section Level

I. About Your Rolls-Royce Motor Car

II. Your Attitude about Our Dealers

III. About Yourself

Figure 4.3 *(Continued).*

Checkpoint 4.2

1. Try to set a limit (either in questions or minutes) for the length of your intended survey. Next, sketch out the approximate content (in terms of issues you're likely to include). Use this prototype as a *talking piece;* encourage your colleagues to familiarize themselves with its content.

2. Make a list of issues or items you have set aside and won't immediately address. As you prepare to get executive approval for your effort, use the list to derail any reactions as to why a particular issue might be missing from your proposed questionnaire.

STEP 4.3 WHEN AND HOW FREQUENTLY SHOULD YOU INTERVIEW YOUR CUSTOMERS?

Transaction Surveys

The question of when to interview is most easily answered for the transactional survey: as close to the transaction as information availability allows. If you are designing a transactional survey, allocate plenty of time to identify just *how* your organization knows a transaction has taken place, and exactly *how much information* is collected in the course of the transaction. (It is critical to know the name of your customer's representative or contact who directly interacted with your organization in the transaction; otherwise your measurements will be meaningless. But the customer contact's identity without contact information is just about as bad.) Because of this survey class's specificity, you'll need more detailed information with which to conduct it than for the other classes of surveys. You may need to suggest some additional information be added to records regarding the initiation or culmination of the transaction to allow you to astutely field your survey. Almost certainly, you'll need the information listed in Checklist 4.1.

Checklist 4.1 The Information You'll Need in Order to Field a Transaction Survey.

1. Name of the customer's employee or employees (representatives or contacts) who participated in the transaction. (By *participate* we mean *were involved in* the transaction—that is, the person who signed for the delivery, received the supplies, tested the new prototype, etc.)

2. Contact information (mailing address, telephone number, e-mail address) for this employee.

3. Notes on anything that happened during the transaction that might influence the customer contact's ratings or the spirit in which the contact receives your follow-up transaction survey. (If your order or machinery arrived damaged, sending a transaction survey is likely to further agitate an already unhappy customer. You will probably decide to set aside customers involved in such obviously unsatisfactory events. You may later wish to send them a different transaction survey, perhaps assessing your "disaster recovery" actions. In that survey you'd probably be asking disappointed customers how well your organization recovered from its disappointing performance.) If your performance was marginal, you may still wish to send along your standard transaction survey, but with the appropriate notation. You may wish to acknowledge the extraordinary circumstances to show the customer you track your mistakes.

Overall Status and Follow-Up/Diagnostic Surveys

For overall status and diagnostic surveys, you will have much greater latitude in your choice of when to field them. Traditionally overall status is assessed at least annually. But if you interview all your customers at the same time, once a year, you set up the situation of "customer satisfaction

Consider the subtle, yet pervasive, message conveyed both to shoppers in front of a salesclerk's desk and to sales personnel behind the desk by banners in a retail store that proudly proclaim, "Customer Appreciation Month." What does such an announcement suggest happens the remaining 11 months of the year?

week (or month)." Customer satisfaction could then be looked upon as an event, not an ongoing concern within your organization.

The author much favors continuous measurement over the course of the year, with a fraction of customers being interviewed each week, month, or quarter. This is the ideal situation both for your program and for the philosophy of satisfying customers. By operating your assessment continuously, you'll have frequent information to pass along to management on a regular basis (monthly, quarterly). With continuous measurement and reporting, customer satisfaction is more likely to become an integral part of your organization's culture.

By measuring continuously you also minimize the impact of any extraordinary events on your customers' satisfaction. Think for a minute about the possible consequences of a natural disaster occurring during your customer satisfaction measurement wave. What if a snowstorm closed down your factory for a week delaying all the orders scheduled to be shipped? What if a business problem were to occur—say your union employees strike, momentarily eliminating your on-site installation capabilities? If either of these situations were to occur during your single, annual measurement period, the data you collect would be unnecessarily influenced.

Continuous surveying or interviewing over the course of the year always offers satisfaction ratings that are more representative of how your organization generally conducts itself. The author has been involved with the satisfaction survey of guests (shoppers) of the Toys "R" Us retail chain. Toys "R" Us faces a tremendous seasonality in its business—hence its ability to offer

---

The author has received (for several years) a satisfaction questionnaire from his stockbroker's firm. The questionnaire arrives every November. In November 2000, the U.S. stock market was down overall 20 to 25 percent. What level of satisfaction can clients of this firm be expected to express as they complete the year 2000's satisfaction questionnaire? How will the firm compare evaluations from 2000 with similar ratings from 1999? How much (if any) can the likely decrease in overall satisfaction be attributed to operations of the firm as opposed to the performance of the market? Such are the possible difficulties associated with measuring satisfaction at only one point in a year.

"delightful service" is more challenging in season. Because guest satisfaction is measured continuously through the year, satisfaction ratings in November 2000 can be compared directly with satisfaction ratings from November 1999. Note, however, that continuous measurement—even on a quarterly basis—becomes difficult when the number of customers is very small (under 100—which would mean fewer than 25 customers to be interviewed per quarter).

When your customerbase is small (fewer than 100 customers), you have two options:

- Reduce the periodicity of your surveying even more (from monthly to quarterly, or quarterly to half-yearly); or

- Maintain your interviewing frequency, but reduce the number of customers you interview. When you interview fewer than 35 or so customers, you won't be able to report your findings from so small a sample. In such cases you can use rolling averages. A rolling average amasses interviews over several measurement points until a statistically meaningful number of interviews is accumulated. (Say you have 100 customers. You decide to interview eight customers a month [100 ÷ 12]. After four months you'll have 32 interviews. From that point on, you'll add your most recent eight interviews and drop those interviews that are now five months old.) Rolling averages offer a useful way of helping us accumulate meaningful numbers of interviews from which to report our findings.

Regardless of overall population sizes, never remeasure satisfaction (of an individual customer) at intervals so close together that your organization won't have had sufficient time to assert some noticeable improvements in its policies, products, or procedures. Otherwise, you'll frustrate and anger your customers who will tell themselves, "I told them what to do already, and they have failed to listen to me, or are uninterested in improving!"

Reliability Surveys

To gain a customer's accurate impressions of your product's reliability (performance over time) you'll need to establish some reasonable or logical checkpoints. Perhaps you or your industry already has certain measurement points established. In the automotive industry, one year's ownership of a new car is an accepted measurement point for assessing reliability. Perhaps you can think of logical anniversaries that make sense in your industry and given your product. Consider millionth part produced, in service for one year, and so on. Such checkpoints would be milestones at which you would field or distribute your survey to measure reliability.

Checkpoint 4.3

1. For the class of survey(s) that you specified in Checkpoint 4.1, identify exactly when you plan to interview your customers and what will trigger that interview.

2. Of which class (of the four basic satisfaction study classes discussed) is each of your surveys characteristic? Why have you chosen that class?

STEP 4.4 HOW WILL YOU DISTRIBUTE YOUR QUESTIONNAIRE (AND HOW WILL RESPONSES BE RETURNED TO YOU)?

Your options for the conduct of your satisfaction measurement program continue to expand. Several methods are available for distributing your interview or questionnaire (often called your *field method*). The field method is interrelated with the *interviewing process* you plan to use. Consider that you can either ask customers to *self-administer* your interview or you can *administer it to them* (using interviewers or machines—generally computers). The relationship between the interviewing process and field method produces a great number of options, the most common of which are shown in Figure 4.4. Each of the three interviewing processes shown is uniquely operationalized by one or more field methods. Table 4.4 compares all three interviewing processes (or *field methods*), describing their strengths and weaknesses.

 Checkpoint 4.4

1. Specify the contact method you plan to use, and describe why you've chosen it.

2. Create a process chart to describe how you will field your survey. Indicate all resources you will use for the dissemination of your interviews/questionnaires and the return process you will use.

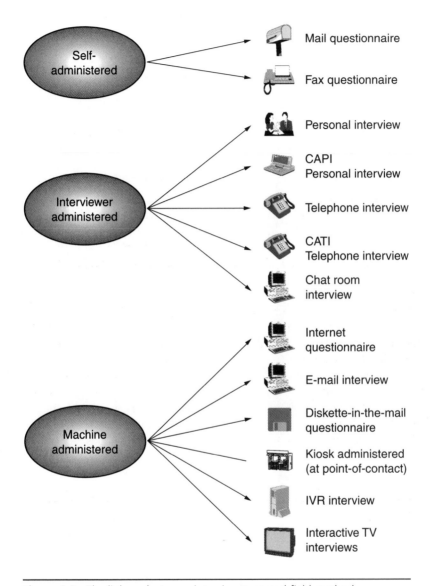

Figure 4.4 The linkage between interview type and field method.

Table 4.4 A comparison of field methods.

Characteristic	Interviewer administered	Machine administered	Self-administered
Degree of control maintained How much control is maintained over the customer's use of the questionnaire?	Substantial	Substantial	Little
Obtrusiveness/impact How much attention does the method command? How intrusive is it on the customer's activities/schedule?	Substantial	Moderate	Little
Cooperation rate How much cooperation does the method evoke?	High	Moderate to high	Low
Cost How costly is the field method?	$$$	$$	$
Time required for data collection How quickly can results from the survey be expected?	Shortest time	Moderate time	Longest time
Ability to reach a widely dispersed customer base How easily can customers who are geographically dispersed be interviewed?	Difficult	Easier	Easiest
Complexity of questions accommodated What level of question complexity does the method accommodate?	High complexity	High complexity	Low complexity
Volume of information collected How much information can generally be collected?	The greatest amount	Moderate amount	The least
Allows interruptions Can customers start and stop answering the questionnaire to attend to other obligations?	No	Yes	Yes
Allows collection of observational data Can observations about the customer be collected during the interview?	Yes	Some	No
Minimizes order effects Does the method allow for the control of order effects, or is the customer prevented from seeing the entire interview by looking ahead?	Yes	Yes	No
Allows complex skip patterns How complex can skip patterns be?	Moderate complexity	High complexity	Low complexity
Ability to embed customer's language/terms When the customer uses specific terminology in answering one question, can this be captured and used in subsequent questions to maximize the customer's understanding?	Somewhat	Yes	Not easily
Minimizes interviewer bias Does the method control interview bias?	No	Yes	Yes
Ability to present visual material Can visual material be offered to customers for their response?	Yes	Perhaps	Perhaps
Interviewer training required?	Yes	No	No

STEP 4.5 POSITION YOUR SURVEY TO MAXIMIZE COOPERATION AND RESPONSE RATES

Too many satisfaction surveys are presented to customers offering no conspicuous benefit to the customer for participating in the process. "Well, it's *obviously* beneficial to the customer," you may say. The presenter extraordinaire Dale Carnegie reportedly once said that the sweetest word in the English language is *me*. You should remember Carnegie's idea as you position your CSM questionnaires. Emphasize the benefit to your customers by introducing your questionnaire with a basic "you benefit": *Your answers to this questionnaire will help us improve the products and services we offer and deliver to you.*

In business-to-business situations, you should be mindful that your customer will probably need to complete your questionnaire at his or her office, during work hours. If the benefit to your customer's employer isn't obvious, it may be hard for your customer to justify spending his or her employer's time completing your questionnaire. In business-to-customer relationships, your interview will similarly disrupt your customer, but in his or her home—competing with household chores or leisure-time activities.

The overall "appearance" of your questionnaire (or survey process) says much about the importance your organization attaches to your survey. And make no mistake about it, sophomoric presentations will elicit a feeble response! Figure 4.5 lists some of the more important considerations you face as you try to encourage customers to pay attention to your endeavor and to invite their response.

In conducting some customer listening sessions for a client several years ago, the author recognized some considerable disinterest among the group's members toward the satisfaction questionnaire being discussed. Leaving process, the author challenged the session members: "I'm sensing a lack of interest in this questionnaire. If this is correct, can you help me understand it?" Back came the response, "Look at all of these *marketing questions* they're asking. It's *all for them*! What's in it for *us*, their customers?" Clearly, the customers felt there wasn't even a balance of benefit; the survey sponsor was the *only* beneficiary.

Factors Influencing Survey Cooperation

- *Customer benefit.* Be specific about the benefits to your customers of completing your questionnaire or interview—the more obvious and immediate the benefits, the higher your response rates.

- *Survey's sponsor.* Consider if your survey will be openly sponsored by your company—this is the traditional method for CSM studies. This is the only way to justify your knowledge of a customer's purchase behavior as evidenced in the questions you ask. Overtly sponsoring your process is also the only way you receive the goodwill benefit from being acknowledged as an organization that truly cares about its customers.

  However, some practitioners use anonymous questionnaires in an attempt to either control for bias (favorable or unfavorable) or allow asking for ratings of competitors' performance alongside ratings of their own organization.

- *Survey's appearance.* Take care with the "appearance" of your questionnaire or interview, considering the following factors:

  - The sound of your telephone interviewers—the more professional they are, the more importance customers will attribute to your process and the more cooperative they'll be.

  - The look, design, and texture of your printed questionnaire— customers use all sorts of cues to determine the significance of an initiative. If you've cut corners in printing and design, that appearance will suggest you attach a low importance to your process. Aesthetics can be very important. At the same time, you don't want to field a survey process that screams, "Extravagance!" That would be a destructive posture, especially if your company is in the process of raising its prices.

- *Time and effort required.* Your customer's perception of how much time and effort will be necessary to complete your questionnaire matters. The less effort and time apparently

Figure 4.5   Factors influencing survey cooperation.

required, the higher will be your response rates. Keep your printed questionnaires short, with easy-to-understand instructions and recording conventions. Instruct your telephone interviewers to offer potential responding customers a fair idea of the time your questionnaire or interview will require. You may position this by saying, "This interview will require only 15 minutes of your time, but its value to *your organization* will be eternal!"

- *Complexity/simplicity of your questionnaire.* Customers prefer to complete simple, straightforward questionnaires. Even though you may need to administer some rather involved tasks, it's up to you to make every aspect of your questionnaire/ interview appear easy and straightforward.

- *Relevance of the questionnaire.* Is your survey *event driven* (as in a transactional survey), or is it simply a *feel good* periodic assessment? The more contemporaneous and relevant (to the customer's current state), the higher your response rates.

- *Imposed timing.* Does your questionnaire arrive at a difficult time (inventory time, end of year, manufacturing changeovers, etc.)? Try never to conflict with industry deadlines or demands. Although you may hesitate to request a tight turnaround, experience shows that imposing a response deadline provokes higher response rates. But always be realistic. A message such as, "Please respond within seven days, to make your answers most useful" can be productive.

- *Job conflict.* Can completing your questionnaire or interview be construed as part of your customer's job? Many customers are employed in the public or governmental sectors. They face rather severe constraints in the way their time can be allocated outside the daily routine. But if your introduction makes it clear that a response will help you improve the quality of your goods or services, your responsiveness to problems, and your policies and procedures, even the strictest governmental regulation might allow compliance.

Figure 4.5 *(Continued).*

Incenting Your Customers to Respond

Be cautious and tactful when considering using gratuities or incentives. They are absolutely a polite and responsible practice, yet if improperly offered they can backfire and make your customers feel like mercenaries or peons. You want your customer in the best state of mind as he or she undertakes your interview or questionnaire, so carefully consider:

• The form of your gratuity

• Its perceived value or worth

• The timing—when you'll present it

Table 4.5 lists (in descending order of motivating power) the most typical incentives offered in current CSM projects.

There is the further issue here of *when* to *incent*. Many CSM professionals believe in *preincenting* customers. This means sending the incentive with the questionnaire or interviewer. The rationale supporting this practice places considerable faith in the guilt created by placing a reward in customers' hands. Supposedly, having the incentive will motivate them to complete the interview or questionnaire and thus deserve the incentive you've already awarded them.

The author is not one who believes in a preincentive. In the first place, it's extremely expensive. Consider that if your response rate is only 50 percent, you've essentially wasted half your incentives. The author would rather "up the ante" and not waste any incentives by rewarding only cooperating customers, in the form of a larger, *postincentive*. A postincentive is mailed or delivered to customers upon receipt of their completed interview.

A hybrid of the previous two versions is the *incomplete incentive*. In this version, one sends out only part of a tangible incentive—for example, the case for a pair of binoculars; the cap of a MontBlanc writing pen; or a

Table 4.5 Incentives for survey cooperation (ranked from most to least effective).

Business customer survey	Consumer customer survey
Promised improvement in products or services received	Money
"Sanitized" results from all survey participants	Free or discounted additional products or services
Money	Affinity merchandise
Donation to a national charity	Donation to a national charity

locked box (for which a combination will be offered). The author is both embarrassed and fascinated by the cleverness of this procedure. It's probably best used on populations *other than* your current customers, lest it create some degree of animosity among them.

 Checkpoint 4.5

1. Describe how you plan to present your interview or questionnaire to your customers. Try to make a checklist of benefits to your customer versus benefits to your organization. You should aim for as equal an allocation as possible.

2. If you plan to use an incentive, describe it and the fulfillment process you envisage.

3. Make sure to keep records to document the "lift" your survey receives from any incentive or reward program you implement. This way, when you are challenged over the added costs of the incentives, you will have compelling reasons why they are worthwhile.

STEP 4.6 CREATE YOUR REPORTING PROCESS

Just as envisioning when and how you'll interview your customers is important, so too is visualizing the nature of your corollary reporting process. When do you envision reporting your satisfaction results? How frequently? Don't make the mistake of unquestioningly accepting your management's initial request. It is likely they haven't thought through all the ramifications of their plan. Increasingly, as companies adopt a *balanced scorecard* mentality, CEO's are looking for customer satisfaction scores on a periodic basis similar to the frequency with which the scorecard's other measures are updated. ANSI/ISO/ASQ Q9001–2000 standards simply mandate the ascertainment of customers' satisfaction on an adequate periodic basis.

You may wish to diagram your contact and reporting process using a blueprint or flowchart. Figure 4.6 shows a prototypical diagram. This pictorial representation can be quite effective in describing a survey process to your management.

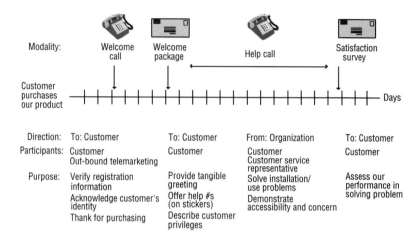

Modality:	Welcome call	Welcome package	Help call	Satisfaction survey
Direction:	To: Customer	To: Customer	From: Organization	To: Customer
Participants:	Customer Out-bound telemarketing	Customer	Customer Customer service representative	Customer
Purpose:	Verify registration information Acknowledge customer's identity Thank for purchasing	Provide tangible greeting Offer help #s (on stickers) Describe customer privileges	Solve installation/ use problems Demonstrate accessibility and concern	Assess our performance in solving problem

Figure 4.6   Blueprinting your CSM process.

 Checkpoint 4.6

1. Prepare a timeline for one year, showing your planned interviewing times and how the interviews will be combined into reports and reporting periods.

2. Create the blueprint or flowchart described above for your survey process.

STEP 4.7 DETERMINE WHETHER YOU'LL INSTITUTE A RESPONSE PROCESS TO SOLVE TROUBLED CUSTOMERS' PROBLEMS

Unfortunately the findings of most CSM initiatives are reported as (total customer) averages. But as we all know, none of us possesses an "average customer." Each of our customers is unique; each has his or her own satisfactions and dissatisfactions. Taken together, the average satisfactions may help us plan (as an organization) an improvement program, but average satisfactions do nothing to solve the problems and needs of individual customers.

When individual customers (in a customer satisfaction questionnaire) report a specific problem or issue, they no doubt expect your organization to remedy the situation for them. The problem is, most satisfaction survey processes don't include feedback or assistance to individual customers!

> A friend of mine has several times reported a
> severe problem with his automobile in the
> process of dutifully completing his manufacturer's
> customer satisfaction questionnaire. Yet despite
> his handwritten explanation and plea for
> assistance, he hasn't received a single follow-up
> from the manufacturer. His questionnaire and his low ratings
> apparently fail to set off any alarms. He's convinced it's because
> there is no warning system in place at all. His unhappy
> questionnaire is simply pigeonholed with those of other
> customers this manufacturer has failed to satisfy.

In chapter 3 we said that CSM programs can serve two objectives:

- *Collecting information from customers* for purposes of improving your quality of production and servicing

- *Communicating to customers* that your organization cares about them and is available to assist them

The revised ANSI/ISO/ASQ Q9001-2000 standard makes the second issue, communicating with your customers, an essential component of your ANSI/ISO/ASQ Q9001-2000 process. This is reaffirmation of the fact that your organization's long-term success will be further enhanced by its commitment to communicating with your customers.

To close the loop with customers who have participated in your survey, an appropriate process is to issue *red flag* or *contact-critical* reports. These reports are discussed in detail in chapter 8. You will need to establish a process and specific teams or individuals who will be available to solve the problems indicated in customers' answers, notes, and occasional attached letters.

 Checkpoint 4.7

1. Will you use a red flag report process? If so, identify the questions or conditions you view as critical enough to drive this alerting process. To whom will you circulate red flag reports? What actions do you hope recipients will take?

2. Flowchart your red flag process, indicating the time intervals between steps.

STEP 4.8 IDENTIFY HOW (AND WHERE) YOU'LL ENTER YOUR DATA FOR ANALYSIS

There are three basic ways to enter your customer responses into an electronic format:

- *Manual data entry.* Perhaps still the most common method, this requires data entry people who manually key the questionnaire responses into a database.

- *Electronic data entry.* Anytime you use a computer in your interviewing (e.g., in a telephone [CATI] interview), as the interviewer reads questions and enters customer responses, your customers' data are automatically entered into a computer file, ready for processing.

- *Self-entry of data.* Customers who complete an Internet-based self-administered questionnaire are saving you the labor of entering their information into a computer file, since that's exactly where their responses go. (Self-entry also removes another step we'll discuss momentarily: data cleaning and editing.)

Data entry is easily one of the weakest links in the survey process. Considerable amounts of time, effort, energy, and oversight are traditionally accorded to sample selection, questionnaire composition, and reporting of results. Strangely, the way the data make it into our computers for analysis is almost taken as a matter of faith. But considering the opportunity for errors, data entry deserves to be one of your focal points for quality control.

Data entry entails several steps that are generally subsumed under the label *data entry*:

1. Interpreting/editing the response to each individual question

2. Entering the response into a computer database

3. Editing ("cleaning") the response to a question to keep the response (or lack of response) logically consistent with other answers within the same customer's questionnaire.

Manual Data Entry

One of the quicker ways to get data entered, especially if you have a small number of questionnaires, is manual data entry. All you need to do is:

- Get the assistance of one or two keyboard-proficient associates

- Assign codes to the responses for each of your questions to give your associates specific values to enter

- Provide them a template, database, or spreadsheet in which to record the data

Virtually all of us who have appended a record to a database or have set up the columns on a spreadsheet designated as a database know that information can be entered into a computer relatively easily. The rub comes with how many records are to be added and how complex is the information to be entered. Excel, Microsoft's spreadsheet program, contains an excellent built-in feature called *Forms*. Forms provides a very user-friendly template for entering information into a spreadsheet—all it requires are column headings in the spreadsheet in which you'll be entering your information.

If you have a large number of customers (more than 500) or plan to regularly conduct your survey, it may pay to establish a customized data entry template. This sort of *front-end* program will be an intelligent version of the Excel Forms capability. Using Visual Basic (or another programming language) you can build (or have built) a template that not only prompts for the contents of each new "field" but also screens the information entered to see that it conforms with your expectations. Here are some examples of screening routines:

- Making sure an entered response code is legitimate—for example, a value of 0 to 10 as an answer on a 0-to-10 scale

- Checking to see if the state code entered for a customer conforms to one of the 51 USPS-approved two-letter codes

- Examining the proportions volunteered by your customer (in response to a constant sum or allocation question) to make sure they don't exceed 100 percent

- Checking to see that sales reports are input as dollars

See Figure 4.7 for an example of a smart data entry template.

Cleaning and Editing Your Data

No matter how clear the instructions in your questionnaire and no matter how well you train the interviewers who collect information for you, you are still quite likely to end up with information that has some inconsistencies: customers who conduct all their business in the United States may

Rolls-Royce Quality and Service Questionnaire

| ID –> 54235-25105 | Page: 1 |

Date Received: /   /

Overall Satisfaction

1. Please evaluate ownership
   With your car
   With your servicing dealer
   RR owner communication
   Coverage of warranty

About Your Motor Car

2. What are the strenghts?
   (E–>Edit)

<PgDn>   <PgUp>

3. What are the weaknesses?
   (E–>Edit)

4a. How important is the following?
4b. Evaluate your car.
                                    4a.   4b.
Driving enjoyment
Reliability . . . .
Quality of interior
Fuel efficiency . . . .
Driver comfort
Passenger comfort . . . .
Admired by others
Responsive to style . . . .
Cost of ownership

<Esc>

Figure 4.7   Using a smart data entry template.

answer questions about international shipping; customers who use your hardware may respond to questions about software or services. In short, you never know the quality of the information you'll get until it's in a machine-readable format. (A smart data entry template—as described above—can trap some illogical entries.) However, some satisfaction professionals run *logic checks* through the information they've collected to identify any customer records that seem amiss, and then they edit them.

Verifying Your Data

Data manually keyed in should be subjected to some degree of verification. The most common verification procedure, dating back to a verifying IBM keypunch station, requires the same data to be entered twice in succession. Thus, the data entry person enters the same data from a questionnaire two times. The second entry is used to verify the original entry. If a datum entered in the second round fails to correspond with the same datum from the first entry, the operator is alerted and he or she must reexamine his or her work to see whether the first entry was incorrect, or the second. Because the same data entry person reenters the same data, this method does not correct for entry person biases. That is, if the data entry person misinterprets a respondent's handwriting on the first entry round, it is likely he or she will similarly misread it on the second round.

The only way to minimize errors from entry person biases is to have different operators enter the same data in different rounds. That is, however, logistically difficult. It requires that the computer file containing first-round responses be maintained with the physical questionnaires containing the first-round data, so that another operator may reenter the data. Few surveys benefit from 100 percent verification by such methods. Within the survey industry, it is standard practice to verify 15 percent of the questionnaires or records. A report from such a partial verification offers an indication of the quality of the remaining work.

Provisions to Store Your Information

It's important to consider how you will store the information you collect. Failure to consider the format could render some future analyses of your information completely impossible.

While data collected in general research projects are often only identified by an arbitrary questionnaire or respondent number, it is the author's belief that *all responses* to a customer satisfaction survey ought to be attributed back to a *specific customer*. This is most easily accomplished if you've preidentified your customers on each of your questionnaires or interview scripts. Questionnaires that are personalized will easily accommodate a customer identifier. In business-to-customer automotive research, the customer designator is invariably the VIN (vehicle identification number) by which all automobile sales and claims are tracked.[1] In financial services, the designator could be the customer's account number, allowing responses to be linked to an addressable customer. If you can attach a discrete customer designator to responses to a questionnaire, you'll be able to keep track of your individual customers' feelings. (This customer identifier is likely to be the same information you've selected as your index or key for your relational database structure—described in chapter 2.)

Data from your questionnaires will need to be stored in a *record format* in computer files. You'll be able to specify the length of your data records; try to limit the total characters in a record to less than 100. The longer your data records are, the more difficult it will be to troubleshoot or review their contents. If you have as many as 230 characters of response codes, consider accommodating each respondent's data in four records of 60 to 70 characters. (You'll need to allow some characters at the start of each record for your customer's identifier and a record number, followed by the data.) See Figure 4.8.

---

[1]Though the VIN is a "natural" designator, automobile manufacturers encounter problems with how to identify owners of multiple models of their cars. Some have adopted unique customer numbers, in addition to the VIN.

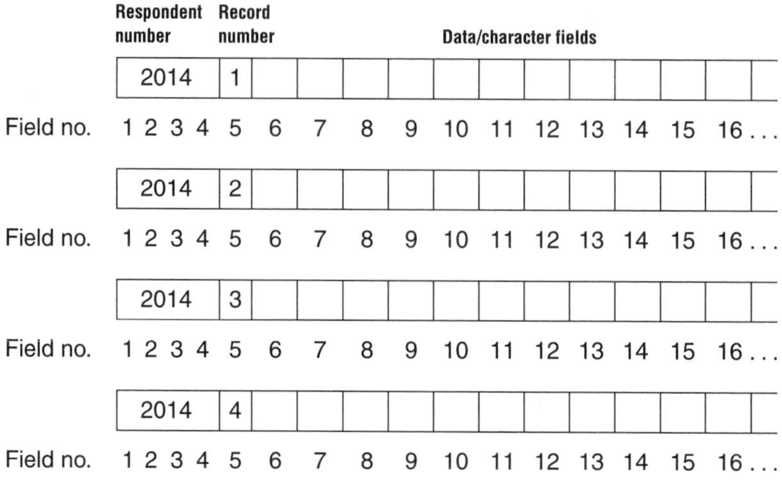

Respondent number	Record number	Data/character fields													
2014	1														

Field no.   1 2 3 4   5   6   7   8   9   10   11   12   13   14   15   16 . . .

2014	2														

Field no.   1 2 3 4   5   6   7   8   9   10   11   12   13   14   15   16 . . .

2014	3														

Field no.   1 2 3 4   5   6   7   8   9   10   11   12   13   14   15   16 . . .

2014	4														

Field no.   1 2 3 4   5   6   7   8   9   10   11   12   13   14   15   16 . . .

Figure 4.8   A record layout for data.

Though it is becoming increasingly uncommon, if your satisfaction data will be manually entered, it is advantageous to provide some entry information on your questionnaire to assist your data entry personnel. Usually such *response codes* are placed next to where your customer will enter his or her answers. The codes will be of two types: *record sequence codes* or *character fields and response codes*. Data sequence codes tell your data entry people the exact record location for each response. Should they double-up on or skip an answer, they'll quickly notice that and be able to trace back and find the replicated or missing datum. Response codes are either symbolic or numeric representations you assign to each response option. (For example, for ease of tabulating your data, you may assign a 1 to a "yes" answer and a 2 to a "no" answer. Similarly, you may assign a 0 code to a "completely dissatisfied" response and a 10 to a "completely satisfied" response. Such response codes allow you to numerically process and quantify your customers' responses.) In Figure 4.9, the 17 refers to the 17th character field (the location on the data record), while the 1, 2, 3, and so on are response codes identifying the answer your customer has given.

By convention, data entry codes and response codes are placed along the right-hand side of the questionnaire form—though they can also be placed throughout the questionnaire. In self-administered questionnaires, it is a good idea to use a smaller typeface for these codes or to screen the font used for your codes so they appear lighter in color, as shown in Figure 4.9. This will help keep respondents from getting confused by the numbers.

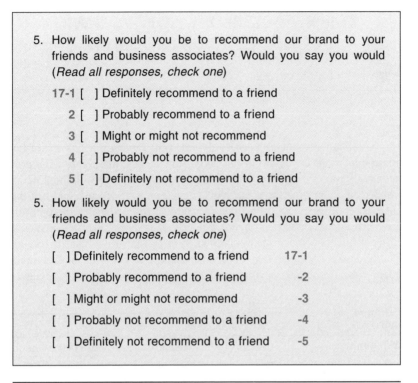

Figure 4.9   An example of how question responses can be precoded in your questionnaire.

 Checkpoint 4.8

1. Prepare a record layout for the data you will collect through your survey. Use Worksheet 4.1 (located in the Appendix) to specify this information.

2. How will your data be entered into electronic format? By interviewers using CATI? By data entry specialists? By your customers through a questionnaire Web site? Describe the data entry process you plan to use.

3. Discuss any difficulties you've encountered in assigning response codes to your prelisted responses in your questionnaire.

STEP 4.9 DETERMINE HOW YOU WILL CONDUCT YOUR PROGRAM

There are at least two ways to conduct your program:

- By yourself—in house

- Using an external, independent research company

There are advantages associated with both. Table 4.6 lists some of the more important. If you are hiring an outside agency, make sure it's a professional group to whom you can entrust your customer list without being concerned about how the agency will represent your organization. (In the discussion of interview "appearance," we touched on some of the unfortunate consequences that can befall a poorly executed project.) You should also consider how much (if any) familiarity an outside agency will need with your industry or product line. Sometimes technical categories may require a more specialized interviewing staff if your survey is to be interviewer

Table 4.6   Who will conduct your program?

Self-conduct	Use an external consultant
Less expensive, no consultant's fees.	Frees internal staff from the logistics of survey conduct and analysis, allowing more time to communicate findings to internal colleagues and serve as the agent of change.
Shows customers the organization is interested in their personal satisfaction; interviews or calls can help build a relationship.	Gives the program a more objective positioning; easier for customers to talk openly to a third party.
Knows the peculiarities of the industry; no training of an external staff in the complexities of a business.	Satisfaction is specialty; highly skilled in data collection and analysis.
Understands the internal organization, barriers to change.	Has advanced statistical capabilities, analytical know-how.
Ability to relate a customer's stated satisfaction levels with the understanding of the customer's history and relationship	Has access to external, industry benchmarks and typical satisfaction levels.
Will easily understand the possible root causes of customers' problems; greater insight into the big picture.	Works for a variety of clients, situations; transference of ideas, solutions from other engagements.
Easier entry/access to customers.	More sensitive to customers' pain; willing to listen without biasing the customer.

administered. To handle this, some organizations actually conduct a one- or two-day briefing for their research partner to assist the partner and its interviewing staff in understanding the organization's category and products.

 Checkpoint 4.9

1. Describe how you will conduct your program (fieldwork and analysis). Will you use an external vendor, or will you conduct the survey process yourself?

2. For what reasons have you made this decision?

 Step-by-Step: The Answers for Deciding When, What, and How to Measure

4.1 Considering the informational objective(s) of your satisfaction survey process, four basic types of CSM have been discussed: the annual, pulse survey; the transaction-driven survey; the reliability survey; and the follow-up or diagnostic survey. See pages 94–97.

4.2 In chapter 3 we discussed methods of reducing the questions you'll ask to a bare minimum (the fewest questions while still tapping all the important evaluative dimensions you've identified). In addition to the questions your customers want you to ask, you'll also have departments and functions within your organization hungry for information, and you need to appease as many of those needs as possible. The ultimate length of your questionnaire or interview will represent a trade-off: informational needs versus the valuable time of your customers. If you ask too many questions, your response rate (hence your projectability) will decline. See pages 97–102.

4.3 Your project's informational objective(s) (and consequently the survey type you'll use) will determine in part when and how you'll contact your customers. With each type (the annual, pulse survey; the transaction-driven survey; the reliability survey; the

(continued)

follow-up/diagnostic survey) there is a logical timing. We have posited that continuous interviewing (where possible) provides the best sample of your organization's performance, as opposed to occasional or only annual surveys. See pages 102–6.

4.4 Your basic choice of distribution method for your survey has to do with whether your survey will be administered (machine or interviewer) or self-administered. Computer-administered interviews (especially using the Internet) are far less expensive than interviewer-administered interviews. Besides your customers' time, your administration method also imposes inconvenience—especially in the return of a mail questionnaire. Consider all aspects of your survey process from your customers' perspective. See pages 106–8.

4.5 The *positioning* of your survey has a major impact on your customers' willingness to return it. Try to emphasize the benefit to your customer in responding. Also consider the appearance (the look of your printed questionnaire, the sound of your interviewer-administered questionnaire). Recognize that your interview, like any other outreach by your organization, conveys your care and concern for your customers; a sloppy process denigrates the importance of the effort and your esteem for your customers. See pages 109–13.

4.6 Carefully plan your entire reporting process. It's the internal manifestation of your program. Carefully represent the value of your information through timely and well-directed reports. Create a blueprint or process map for your reporting process. See pages 113–14.

4.7 We have posited that remedying individual customer's problems identified through questionnaire or interview returns can be of major benefit to your program. Try instituting a *red flag report* process to identify customers with specific problems to operational areas within your organization that will follow up immediately. (Ideally this follow-up should occur within 24 to 48 hours of your customer's completing your interview.) See pages 114–15.

4.8 Data entry and data storage (for retrieval) are important, often improperly anticipated aspects of a CSM program. Data entry is one of the weak links in the survey process. You'll need to create a system that is as error free as possible. It is recommended that you store your data in a file related to your customerbase so that you can review customers' ratings from prior years as you field and report on subsequent years' measurements. See pages 116–21.

4.9 You can conduct a satisfaction program internally or rely on the services of an external consultant. Often it is wise for the satisfaction professional to allocate his or her time to identifying issues and implementing change in the organization, leaving the tactical chores of survey administration and data tabulation to an external partner. See pages 122–23.

 Chapter 4 Deliverables

As a result of your work in this chapter, you will have prepared the following for your program:

1. Worksheet 4.1—contains a schedule detailing the necessary steps for the conduct of your survey and important completion dates.

2. ISO document #2—describes who will collect your customer satisfaction data and details the process to be used. Use the information from sections 4.4 and 4.9.

3. ISO document #3—requests a description of the form (modality) in which you will collect your customers' satisfaction information.

4. A statement of the informational objectives of your survey.

5

Measuring Satisfaction

Most people, it seems, imagine they can write a good questionnaire. Maybe it's their secret desire to get back at the establishment after being subjected to so many questionnaires written by others. Maybe it's their innate fascination with pondering why friends and acquaintances at times act so irrationally. Whatever the reason, few of us are wise enough to admit to not knowing all there is to know about the art of questionnaire construction.

But as simple as questionnaire construction may appear, it is the second most problematic component of customer satisfaction measurement (CSM). (The first problem, you'll remember, is identifying *whom* to interview—see chapter 2.) The fact is, far too many satisfaction questionnaires suffer from serious flaws in their construction or content. As an example of how easy it is to create confusion in a questionnaire, look at the problems even survey professionals have—witness the 2000 U.S. presidential election ballots of several Florida counties!

USING THIS CHAPTER

This chapter may admittedly seem a bit schizophrenic. We'll attempt to do two things: assist those writing their own questionnaire by laying down some basic questionnaire-writing precepts; for those readers who don't have the time to write their own, we'll offer some generic, off-the-shelf questionnaires ready for administration. Use the chapter and its contents as you need. Readers who have a desire to understand how to ask a question or how to create a questionnaire may wish to skip to the second part of the chapter for a more thorough discussion of questionnaire-writing principles. Readers who need to field a questionnaire immediately may adopt one of the questionnaires offered in the first part of the chapter.

THE BASIC QUESTIONNAIRE: CRITICAL COMPONENTS OF A CUSTOMER SATISFACTION QUESTIONNAIRE

To be effective, a customer satisfaction questionnaire (or interview) must collect at least the following items of information:

- Customer identification information

- Overall criteria ratings

- Performance ratings on more specific functional areas

Customer Identification Information

It's important to be able to trace every rating you collect back to a specific customer, for several reasons. In the first place, your customer's identity links his ratings to a specific product or group of products and a specific field staff of yours. Without knowing the identity of who is responding, you'd have to ask the very tiring questions "Which of our products or services do you use?" and "From whom do you buy our products?" Such questions are off-putting to many customers who believe it's the manufacturer's obligation to know them and what and how they're buying! (In a business-to-business situation, good salespeople or customer service people will know a lot more than just which products a customer is using. They may know how and when particular customers are using your products as well as many other characteristics about the customer.)

Second, knowing who said what allows you the opportunity to offer fixes to those customers who require them. A common misconception is that customer satisfaction surveys should be conducted anonymously. In response to that, why would one of your customers wish to take her time answering your questions if she didn't have reason to believe that your servicing of her account might improve as a result? But if you don't link her responses to her identity, she has every right to suspect that while things in general may get better, her own lot won't necessarily improve. Customer satisfaction research differs from conventional marketing or public opinion research in a number of important ways. The most important, perhaps, is that your responding customers will feel a strong sense of self-interest and involvement in your survey process. See Table 5.1 for a listing of the most important differences. The bottom line is that as a result of their participating in your survey, your customers have every right to believe that things that need improving will be improved!

Customer satisfaction surveys are undertaken among a special population—your customers. As such, they deserve to be treated to survey follow-up, to have their situation improved. (We'll complete our discussion of this process and the resulting red flag or contact-critical reports you can generate, in chapter 6.) If you are still concerned that customers may feel uncomfortable with others at your organization knowing their identities, you may offer them either a positive or negative option:

Positive option: "Please check here to give us permission to discuss your evaluations with your representative, etc."

Negative option: "Unless you check here, we'll discuss your evaluations with your representative."

The second phrasing is known as a *negative opt-out*—that is, a customer checks only if he or she doesn't want you to share his or her identity throughout your organization. You start with the assumption that it's okay to share the customer's information. The author recommends the opt-out method.

Table 5.1 The difference between marketing research and customer research.

Marketing research		Customer research
Data collection only	*Purpose*	Data collection and communication
Sample	*How many are included*	Census
Population infinite— no concern	*View of the population*	Population is precious— needs retaining
No follow-up	*Need for follow-up from the survey participation*	Requires follow-up
Fix system/product	*End result*	Fix system/product and remedy individual's problems
Aggregate data	*How information is analyzed*	Keep data disaggregated
No incentive considered necessary	*How participation is encouraged*	Offer incentive

Source: Pruden and Vavra (2000)

Overall Criteria Ratings

One of the more important evaluations you can collect is your customer's *overall satisfaction rating* with your organization's product. This global evaluation becomes the key criterion measure that you'll use in numerous ways. You make the assumption that even though your customer's satisfaction is a function of a fairly complex mental assessment, he or she can nevertheless give you the bottom line on the quality of his or her overall satisfaction with your organization's product.

It is almost always desirable to ask for this global evaluation as one of the first questions in your questionnaire; otherwise the performance questions you ask preceding it can channel or influence how your customer arrives at his or her overall evaluation of you. You want customers responding based on however they, as individuals, might make a general evaluation. If you have preceded this general evaluation with the 10 performance questions on which you require specific ratings, you run the risk of suggesting (either overtly or very subtly) that those scales define the dimensions on which customers should evaluate your products and performance. So, how a customer scores you on the performance questions may bias his or her frame of judgment as well as affect the rating he or she gives you for overall satisfaction.

True, there can still be bias with the order reversed (global first, specifics second). This type of bias is almost always present and is referred to as a *halo effect* (when a good global judgment influences subsequent, specific performance evaluations). But because each performance question directs a customer's judgment to a very specific performance element or product feature, perhaps there is a better chance for truth to prevail.

Generally you should ask seven overall criterion questions covering the following:

1. Overall satisfaction with your product

2. Likelihood of repurchasing from your organization in the future

3. Willingness to recommend your product and organization to others

4. Perception of your product as representing good value

5. Overall satisfaction with the servicing your organization has provided

The author recommends including the following two additional points because he has seen a high correlation between these variables and overall satisfaction:

6. How accessible your organization makes itself to your customers

7. How responsive your organization is to those customers who initiate contact

Although the genesis of these last two questions can be found in Zeithaml, Parasuraman, and Berry (1990) SERVQUAL inventory (for service organizations), they appear important for *any* organization to truly delight its customers.

Specific Performance Variables

To supplement your overall evaluation ratings, you'll want to collect your customers' evaluations of specific functionalities of your product. These specific issues normally relate to the requirements or needs your customers have and how well your product meets each of those needs.

Performance variables are important because they provide you some greater direction for improving customers' overall satisfaction. Without their specificity, you'd have to guess about what to do or conduct subsequent customer interviews to probe why their overall satisfaction was as it was. Borrowing dimensions from the work of Garvin (1988) and Zeithaml, Parasuraman, and Berry (1990) will help you operationalize your performance variables (category requirements) with variables that are more specific to your industry. Please refer to Figures 3.5 and 3.6 in chapter 3.

Answers to these performance variables also become an important deliverable you will offer to the various operational areas of your organization. Each of the performance variables will likely have a department or group uniquely responsible for its performance or delivery. The information you provide those departments can assist them in better understanding their current level of performance.

SAMPLE QUESTIONNAIRES

In the Appendix, you'll find three customer satisfaction questionnaires: one for a *hardware manufacturer,* one for a *software manufacturer,* and one for a *service provider.* (These are the three basic output categories recognized by ISO 9000.) Each questionnaire contains a basic number of questions derived from both the criteria and performance questions described above. The performance questions have been adapted from Garvin's and Zeithaml's frameworks (discussed previously in chapter 3) and are based on the framework shown in Figure 5.1.

	Hardware manufacturer	Software manufacturer	Services provider
1. Overall satisfaction	->	->	->
2. Explanation of satisfaction	->	->	->
3. Likelihood to repurchase	->	->	->
4. Willingness to recommend	->	->	->
5. Value for price			
6. Accessibility			
7. Responsiveness			
8.	Functional performance	Functional performance	
9.	Features	Features	
10.	Reliability	Reliability	
11.	Conformance	Conformance	
12.	Durability	Durability	
13.	Serviceability	Serviceability	
14.	Documentation	Documentation	
8.			Reliability
9.			Competence
10.			Courtesy
11.			Credibility
12.			Security
13.			Empathy
14.			Communication
15. Delivery	->	->	->
16. Installation	->	->	Alignment
17. Qualification	->	->	->
18. Servicing			
19. Any unmet needs?	->	->	->
20. Any comments, concerns?	->	->	->
21. Opt out, don't share my answers			

Figure 5.1   Framework for the output category questionnaires.

You are encouraged to customize these rather generic questionnaires before applying them in your work. However, even without further customization they should serve as sufficient templates to support a reasonable quantitative assessment of your customers' satisfaction. The more you customize them, however, the more specific you can get about your products and services.

Step-by-Step: The Issues of How to Write Effective Questionnaires

5.1 Understand the two levels at which questionnaires need to be constructed: macro and micro.

5.2 Define the structure of your questionnaire: consider the topics you'll include and how you'll order the topics.

5.3 Consider skip patterns or branches you'll need to establish in your questionnaire to accommodate different responses or customer situations.

5.4 Decide how you'll instruct your customers or interviewers to progress through the interview.

5.5 Consider the different information you'll need to collect from your customers; varying the type of information you're asking for keeps your questionnaire or interview from becoming monotonous for your customers.

5.6 Review the different types of question formats you may need to use in collecting the different types of information you seek.

5.7 Decide on the particular response scales you'll offer your customers with which to respond. This decision hinges on your use of open-ended or closed-ended questions and the type of rating scales you adopt.

5.8 Learn how to institute response codes to your questions so that you can enter your data into data records for analysis.

5.9 Learn how to pretest your questionnaire or interview before exposing it to your customerbase at large.

LEARNING MORE ABOUT ASKING QUESTIONS

In your goal of assessing customer satisfaction, you need to assure your management that you have gathered the most accurate information possible. You have already taken the following steps:

- Made sure you're contacting a totally representative sample (or total population) of your customers (chapter 2)

- Identified your customers' most important requirements or issues (chapter 3)

The next most important consideration you face is how to present and ask your questions the right way. This is the stuff of question writing and questionnaire construction. No matter whether you're conducting an interviewer-administered interview or distributing a self-administered questionnaire directly to your customers, you still need to apply all the tools we'll discuss in this section (see Figure 5.2).

Several very good reference books address the topic of writing good questions—see the Appendix for a bibliography of books you should consider reading.

STEP 5.1 THE TWO LEVELS OF QUESTIONNAIRE BUILDING

It's convenient to think of two different levels of questionnaire construction: a *macro level,* dealing with the overall structural concerns of your questionnaire, and a *micro level,* focusing on each individual question, its wording, and its response scale.

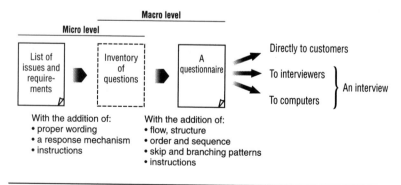

Figure 5.2   Issues, questions, questionnaires, and interviews.

We'll cover the following issues in our discussion of the macro level:

- Sequence or flow among the topics (pages 136–37)

- Routing your customer through the questionnaire—branching and skip patterns (pages 139–40)

- Instructions to assist your customers in appropriately completing your questionnaire (pages 140–43)

At the micro level we'll discuss these issues:

- Selecting a question type for each item of information you wish to collect (pages 145–47)

- Identifying a desired response mechanism (pages 147–50)

- Selecting a response scale (pages 150–53)

- Offering instructions within a question (page 154)

- Making your questions easily tabulatable (pages 155–60)

 Checkpoint 5.1

1. Check your understanding of the two levels of questionnaire construction. How would you describe the macro level to a colleague? How would you describe the micro level?

2. At which level are you concerned with the flow of your questionnaire and the sequence of your questions?

3. At which level are you concerned with questionnaire instructions?

MACRO-LEVEL ISSUES

Before setting out on a trip, you generally consult a map. In a very real way, the macro-level issues of questionnaire building deal with creating such a map for your questionnaire or interview before you actually write it!

STEP 5.2 DECIDE ON
A QUESTIONNAIRE STRUCTURE
AND ITS CONTENTS

By now it is assumed you have identified your customers' primary requirements. But as has been said several times, you still may not be able to accommodate all the issues you've identified in your first wave or year of interviewing. Oftentimes you literally won't know how many issues you can address until you actually start composing your questionnaire. You may not know with certainty until you conduct a pretest of your questionnaire to see how long (in minutes) it is.

Creating a Sequence or Flow for Your Questionnaire

Questionnaires should be thought of as having three parts:

1. The introduction

2. The main body

3. The conclusion

The *introduction* initiates your information collection task. It identifies a survey's sponsor (generally your organization), the interviewer (if interviewer administered), and the purpose of the interview.

The introduction offers a reason for your survey. It may explain how you intend to use the information you collect. It also begins the information collection process—usually with a fairly easy, nonthreatening question offering an easy-to-use response scale.

Within the *main body* of your questionnaire you should cover your topics in a logical and understandable sequence. It serves absolutely no purpose to keep your customer guessing about what topic or concern you'll address next. Your development should be very overt and logical. As was suggested in chapter 3, you may wish to adopt a chronological sequence among your topics, asking about issues in the same order in which your customer encounters them in his or her interactions with your organization. For example, your flow might progress as follows:

1. Questions about ordering your products

2. Questions about your shipping or delivery record

3. Questions about the design, features, and suitability of your products

4. Questions about your after-sale support and consulting

There is a continuing debate about whether you should openly identify your organization as sponsoring your survey. To your author, this seems an illogical question. If you truly are interested in your customers' satisfaction and wish them to be as honest with you as possible, how could you not be equally honest with them by announcing your sponsorship of the survey? (Open sponsorship is the only way to explain how you might know what products of yours they buy.)

Those supporting a blind (nonidentified) administration defend their position by suggesting that is the only way one can collect unbiased information (from one's own customers) about the performance of competitors. The response to this is that you must be conservative in how many issues you set a survey after. In this author's opinion, simply collecting information about your organization's performance is a reasonably ambitious goal, without adding further complication.

A descriptive statement can precede each section to alert the respondent to each new topic, such as, "Now we're interested in your evaluation of our parts and service operation."

This sort of topic sequence is not only logical; it also is likely to assist your customer in tracking his or her thoughts through a typical transaction with your organization. Technically, one could claim a downside to this organization. The social science purist might advise scrambling all the issues together to prevent a "topic-area response set." That is, if one aspect of your *shipping* or *delivery process* is deficient, by aggregating all your shipping/delivery issues together, there is a greater likelihood that your customer will allow his or her dissatisfactions with this issue to overflow to the other shipping/delivery items. This possible contamination is probably a small price to pay for the benefits of the more customer friendly questionnaire organization suggested above.

Finally, in the *conclusion* of your questionnaire, you will collect any additional classificatory information you need (the so-called "demographics," or perhaps more appropriately labeled, your "industographics"). Demographics, or industographics, contain descriptive information about your customers—their size, the region in which they're located, their total sales, and so on. The conclusion is also the place to again thank your customer for allowing you the time to interview him or her, or for imposing on his or her schedule to complete your questionnaire.

The "Appearance" of Your Interview

Another concern rarely thought about in the worlds of pure survey or opinion research is the "appearance" of an interview or a questionnaire. If we accept for a moment that your questionnaire or interview, distributed among your customers, becomes a kind of communication with them, then it is reasonable to assume that the way it looks (or sounds) gives your customers another bit of information about your organization. These inferences build a perception among your customers of how your organization feels about them: Does it reach out to them by way of a well-presented questionnaire, telephone interview, or Internet site? Or does it suggest, by the apparently cheap appearance of the questionnaire (or unprofessional sound of the telephone interviewer), that it doesn't really care about its customers?

Many satisfaction survey professionals never devote a single thought to this aspect of the information-gathering process. Unfortunately, expending effort to give a printed survey a special look or to hire and train a telephone staff in an organization's products and customers all require extra time and generally extra money. But in terms of payback in goodwill, such "extras" are well worth their cost!

 Checkpoint 5.2

1. Approach the structure/organization of your questionnaire or interview in a straightforward manner. Tell your customers what you'd like to know and how you'll use the information they supply. Don't play games, and don't keep them guessing. You should identify your organization as sponsor of the survey to maximize the value of the information they volunteer and to give you reason to follow up on any problems they report with corrective actions, where necessary.

2. Your questionnaire should be organized in three sections, each with a distinct purpose: the introduction, the main body, and the conclusion. Sometimes—especially with Internet-administered interviews—it's a useful idea to offer your customers a *progress meter* so responding customers can see how they are progressing through your questionnaire and how much more time it will require to complete it.

STEP 5.3 ROUTING—ESTABLISH BRANCHING AND SKIP PATTERNS

Generally it is necessary to direct customers through your questionnaire, sometimes advancing them past sections irrelevant to them or to their experience with your organization. Flow through a questionnaire is affected by branching instructions. It's a good idea to map out the questionnaire's intended sequence or flow. You can use a tree diagram (such as the one in Figure 5.3) to show branching conditions at each critical question. Several different branching patterns can be considered:

Implied branching—follow-up questions.

5A. Have you shipped by our overnight service?
[ ] no (*Skip to question* 6)
[ ] yes (*Ask question* 5B)

5B. How many times in the last 6 months? _____ (times)

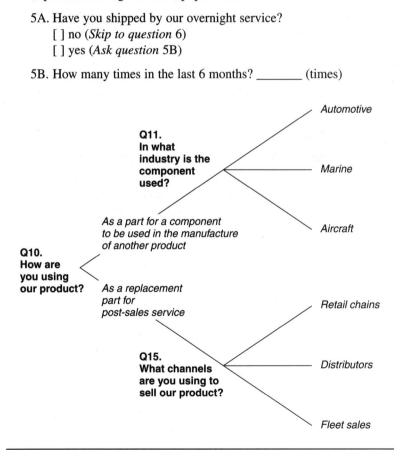

Figure 5.3 Illustration of a branching pattern.

Explicit branching—continuation and skip.

20. Have you visited our factory?
    [ ] No (*Skip to question* 30)
    [ ] Yes (*Continue with question* 21)

21. When did you last visit our factory?

    (*Skip to* Q 25)   [ ] within the last 3 months
                        [ ] 4 to 6 months

    (*Continue with* Q22)   [ ] 7 to 12 months
                            [ ] longer than 12 months ago

Branching must be effected more carefully for self-administered questionnaires than for interviewer-administered ones. Of course, computer-assisted interviews automate all branching, avoiding many of the mistakes caused by respondents or interviewers failing to correctly follow branching instructions. Still, you'll have to write out or diagram your branches so that appropriate programming code can be written.

   Checkpoint 5.3

1. Your questionnaire instructions will need to efficiently route customers through your questionnaire. If the applicability of one question depends on a response to a preceding question, you need to establish a branching or skip pattern. Try to be as thorough in your explanation of the skip pattern as possible.

2. It's very useful to diagram the sequence of your questions before actually writing out your questionnaire. That way you'll be able to see the need for skips or branches and what questions must necessarily precede each such conditional junction.

STEP 5.4 QUESTIONNAIRE INSTRUCTIONS

Any questionnaire requires instructions, whether for the interviewers who will administer it or for your customers who will attempt to answer it themselves, without the benefit of someone to clarify your information needs. Generally questionnaire writers seem reluctant to provide ample instructions.

Never assume your customers are as familiar with question types and response scales as you are. Obviously they are not. You should always provide instructions that include:

1. An introduction to the interview itself, including why you are collecting the information and how you plan to use it

2. A description of the general flow or organization of your interview

3. Intermediate instructions preceding any group of questions that are to be answered in a similar way

4. An instruction regarding each and every skip or branching pattern

5. Clear directions for how customers should return the completed questionnaire

Obviously the simpler the questionnaire structure and the clearer the instructions, the better will be the quality of the information you collect.

Conventions exist in marketing research for the appearance of interviewer instructions. These instructions are generally typed in all capital letters and placed inside parentheses. (See Figure 5.4) This is a fine practice for you to adopt for your customer satisfaction surveys. But use the convention *only if* your survey is to be interviewer administered. Otherwise, the capitalized phrases can be distracting to your customers and improperly draw their attention away from your actual questions. Try using italics or a smaller typeface for instructions in a self-administered questionnaire.

Avoid two-part instructions. When you have a grid requiring two judgments (for example, importance and performance), it'll be awkward to list the attributes twice in a self-administered survey. You can solve this possible confusion by listing the attributes only once but providing spaces for both judgments. Just make sure your instructions are divided and in sequence. (See Figure 5.5.)

 Checkpoint 5.4

1. For both self-administered and interviewer-administered questionnaires, you need to provide a clear set of instructions to guide your customers or interviewers through the questionnaire. Try to write these instructions as clearly as possible.

2. When you pretest your questionnaire, you must check your customers' or interviewers' ability to understand and follow your instructions.

Administered Format

We'd like to know how important each of several characteristics are to you in selecting a company/supplier in the (ABC Industry). For each characteristic I read, please give me a rating from 0 to 10 where 0 means "not at all important" and 10 means "extremely important." (READ ALL CHARACTERISTICS, A THROUGH K, BEGINNING AT PRE-X'D. CIRCLE IMPORTANT RATING RESPONDENT GIVES FOR EACH CHARACTERISTIC IN COLUMN A BELOW.) How important would you say (READ FIRST CHARACTERISTIC) is? (CONTINUE THROUGH ALL CHARACTERISTICS)

Now, I'll read the same characteristics again and ask you this time to rate the performance of XYZ Company on each characteristic according to how well you believe XYZ performs or delivers the characteristic. Again we'll use a scale from 0 to 10, but this time 0 will mean "poor performance" and 10 will mean excellent performance." (READ ALL CHARACTERISTICS, A THROUGH K, BEGINNING AT PRE-X'D. CIRCLE PERFORMANCE RATING RESPONDENT GIVES FOR EACH IN COLUMN B BELOW.) How would you rate XYZ Company's performance on (READ FIRST CHARACTERISTIC). (CONTINUE THROUGH ALL CHARACTERISTICS)

Self-Administered Format

Below, in the center box, we've listed a number of characteristics (a through k) you might consider in selecting a company/supplier in the (ABC Industry). We'd like to know how important each of these characteristics are to you in selecting a company/supplier. Please rate their importance by circling a number from 0 to 10 in Column A on the left side of the page. Notice that 0 represents "not at all important" and 10 represents "extremely important." Please give us an importance rating for all characteristics.

Now please reread the list of characteristics (a through k). This time please rate XYZ Company according to how well you believe XYZ performs or delivers on each characteristic by circling a number from 0 to 10 in Column B on the right side of the page. This time notice that 0 represents "poor performance" while 10 represents "excellent performance." Please make sure to rate XYZ's performance on all characteristics.

Figure 5.4   An example of questionnaire instructions.

Q6A   In **Column A** below left, please rate the importance of each of the automobile attributes a through e. Please use a scale ranging from 1 (not at all important) to 5 (extremely important).

Column A	Attribute	Column B
_____	(a) Acceleration	_____
_____	(b) Miles per gallon	_____
_____	(c) Braking	_____
_____	(d) Road-holding	_____
_____	(e) Positive steering response	_____

Q6B   Now, in **Column B** above right, please evaluate the performance of your new automobile on each attribute a through e. Please use a scale ranging from 1 (poor) to 5 (excellent).

Figure 5.5   An example of combining two tasks (importance and performance) into one question.

MICRO-LEVEL ISSUES

Micro-level questionnaire concerns are all about the details: how you'll word your questions, the response options you'll give your customers, and how you'll code their responses so that ultimately you can tabulate the responses they return to you.

STEP 5.5 WHAT KIND OF INFORMATION ARE YOU COLLECTING?

The information you collect in your questionnaire can be represented as one of the following four types:

1. *Facts.* Fact questions are generally answerable in short responses; easy for customers to answer.

    Have you taken a taxicab in the last 30 days?
    [ ] Yes [ ] No

2. *Attitudes.* Attitude questions require evaluation, the liking or disliking of a thing.

How satisfied were you with your use of a taxicab?

Not at all satisfied										Completely satisfied
0	1	2	3	4	5	6	7	8	9	10

3. *Prediction of behavior.* These questions ask about the likelihood of future behavior. (These questions seem like questions about "behaviors," but they are still really about attitudes, since no behavior has taken place.)

How likely are you to take a taxicab in the next 30 days?

[ ] I will definitely take a taxicab
[ ] I will probably take a taxicab
[ ] I might or might not take a taxicab
[ ] I will probably not take a taxicab
[ ] I will definitely not take a taxicab

4. *Demographics/industographics.* These questions elicit descriptive information about your customers' organizations, locations, sales, products/service, usage patterns, and so forth.

On average, how many times a month do you use a taxicab for travel?

_____ times

You will probably have to collect several types of information with your questionnaire. As you begin addressing an information need, ask yourself, "Is this piece of information a fact, an attitude, a prediction of behavior, or an industographic?" You'll find that collecting different types of information makes your interview more interesting for your customers. Were you to consistently ask for the same type of information repeatedly, your questionnaire or interview would quickly become monotonous for your customers to complete.

One note of caution: while the use of variety in the type of information you collect is encouraged, don't extend variety to other aspects of your questionnaire, such as the number or type of response scales you offer. In terms of their evaluations, allow your customers to learn and become comfortable with *one type* of response scale—then stay with it!

Checkpoint 5.5

1. How you structure and write questions depends on the type of information you hope to collect. There are four basic types of information: facts, attitudes, predictions of behavior, and demographics.

2. You will require several different sorts of information from your customers for a meaningful understanding of their satisfaction. Using a variety of question types in your questionnaire makes answering it less tedious and encourages a higher response rate from your customers.

STEP 5.6 SELECT A QUESTION TYPE

Distinct but not dramatically different from the information to be gathered are question types. A listing of the more common types includes the following:

- *Rating/evaluation questions.* These attitude questions are the most popular. They ask customers for their attitude on an issue. How well are they satisfied? How important is a requirement? They generally employ a rating scale, asking customers to assign a magnitude of feeling to an issue.

- *Description/explanation questions.* A close companion (in proximity, not similarity) to rating scales are explanatory, factual questions. You will use these questions (following a rating question) to ask customers to *explain* their satisfaction ratings and feelings. Description questions are almost always open-ended, requiring customers to use their own words.

A description question is most productive if you can get beyond your customer's first, "top-of-mind" response. For example, a customer (explaining the low satisfaction rating she's given your product) might respond, "Because your return policy is too complicated." This top-of-mind response would be most helpful to you if you could follow up with a response such as, "Would you please explain how it is too complicated?" Such a follow-up is called a *probe.* Unfortunately, probes cannot easily be inserted into self-administered interviews, so if you're depending on your survey to return a lot of detailed understanding, you'd better consider an interviewer-administered format. Description questions produce information that we call *diagnostic*, because the responses help us identify ways of solving customers' problems.

- *Property-assignment questions.* To assist customers in conveying their perspective of you or your policies or products, you can offer a variety of adjectives or phrases (sometimes called a *checklist*). Then all the customer has to do is select the particular adjectives or phrases (if any) that best describe his or her feelings about you or your policies or products. The obvious limitation here is that you've constrained the customer's possible responses to those adjectives that you've supplied.

- *Allocation/division—trade-off questions.* A useful measurement tool when you need to assess the relative rankings of a number of items or requirements is an *allocation task*. This is especially true when trying to explicitly assign importance to various aspects of your product. This is most commonly achieved using a *constant sum* task, in which you ask a customer to assign points among the product features (for which you're measuring importance) according to how important each feature is.

If you were asked to rate on a scale of 1 to 10 the importance of safety in your automobile, you'd undoubtedly give safety a 10. Then, if asked the importance of styling, you might again respond, 10. Again, to the question of the importance of gas mileage, another 10. Such importance ratings would hardly help Ford or Daimler-Chrysler. In such situations, a more meaningful way to collect the relative importance weights is to ask your customer to divide 100 points among safety, styling, and gas mileage. Now the customer can't assign 100 points to each attribute; you've forced him to engage in some trade-offs. Such is the beauty of allocation tasks.

Checkpoint 5.6

1. In writing questions, you will allow for four different types of responses: feelings (evaluations), descriptions/explanations, assignment tasks, and allocation or division tasks. You'll probably have the opportunity to use more than one of these methods in your questionnaire. Again, customers will appreciate a variety of response options.

2. If you need to explicitly measure the importance of your performance variables, use an allocation (or trade-off) task. Don't use an evaluation format for this type of information.

STEP 5.7 RESPONSE MECHANISMS

Once you've asked a customer a question, you must provide him or her with a way to respond. You can provide essentially three different ways for a customer to reply to one of your questions:

1. *Open-ended response.* Completely unconstrained, the customer uses his or her own words in the amount he or she wishes.

   Please describe how we could improve our after-sales servicing

   _____

   _____

2. *A response scale (numeric or verbal).* Such a scale conveys a degree of intensity (ideally suited for the measurement of satisfaction). You provide the responses; you decide how many to offer and (if numeric) how many to "label" and how they should be labeled.

   Not at all   *Completely*
   satisfied   *satisfied*
   0   1   2   3   4   5   6   7   8   9   10

3. *A question requiring your customer to supply something.* Here you make a provision for the customer to supply a description, a magnitude, or a frequency. You may or may not provide acceptable responses.

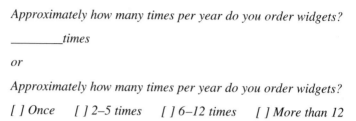

Approximately how many times per year do you order widgets?

_____*times*

or

Approximately how many times per year do you order widgets?

[ ] Once   [ ] 2–5 times   [ ] 6–12 times   [ ] More than 12

A dilemma uniting all three response mechanisms is a recurring trade-off: *summarizability* versus *completeness of response*. Generally, the more complete a customer's response, the more difficult it will be for you to condense it and assign a countable code to it. However, your needs for tabulation are really secondary to your need to understand your customers.

Numerical scales pose another conundrum. The fewer scale positions you offer, the simpler it is for your customers to make a quick response; yet from a statistical point of view it's better to have a greater number of response categories (five or more). With five or more scale positions, the responses you collect will begin to conform to a normal distribution and thereby be candidates for the more rigorous *parametric statistical tests*.

Response mechanisms serve two important roles: they assist your customers in formulating their responses to your questions, and they assist you in economically recording responses, interpreting customers' meanings, and tabulating responses.

Open-Ended Responses (Verbal Responses)

Open-ended responses allow customers to answer in their own words and to mention any issue they choose (no matter how insignificant it may seem). The issue can be objectively described, treated as an anecdote, or passed along as word of mouth. The important element is the issue of *nonconstraint*. The subject of the response, the terminology used, and the description of satisfaction are all totally up to the customer to select. In this way open-ended questions are directed at *exploration* of issues, helping surveys do the following:

- Identify salient issues (which may or may not be part of the current questionnaire)

- Sample the relevant terms used by customers to describe an issue

- Define the appropriate *evaluative spectrum* with which customers judge your product's performance

You should consider open-ended questions when you don't know enough about an issue or concept to formulate reasonably inclusive response categories (that you would need for a closed-ended format) or when the subject of a question is a sensitive issue.

Open-ended questions are also generally the most enjoyable for customers to answer because they are in complete control. It's a good idea to always ask at least two open-ended questions in a satisfaction survey. One of those should probably be used to probe, and therefore better understand, your customer's overall satisfaction rating (such as, "Why did you rate your overall satisfaction with us at this level?"). The other should probably come at the end of your survey and ask simply, "Is there anything else you would like to tell us?"

Because of their potential to help explain anticipated or especially unanticipated survey outcomes, some experts recommend distributing open-ended follow-ups throughout interviews with certain groups of customers—for example, those found to be overall less satisfied (this presumes the overall satisfaction is to be determined early in the interview).

Alternatively, open-ended questions as probes might be randomly distributed throughout *all* customers' interviews, with a fixed number (perhaps three to five) being randomly paired with the evaluative questions in each interview. This allocation method would minimize the burden or imposition on any one customer and yet collect probing follow-up information on virtually every question in your questionnaire. Such randomized follow-ups would necessarily employ generalized language:

Could you tell us a little more about what you mean?

Could you say more about what you have in mind?

I see—could you give me an example?

Despite their immense potential value, open-ended questions pose substantial challenges in analysis and reporting:

- They fail to supply a uniform response dimension; thus your customers are free to answer in any way or quantity they desire

- They produce data (results) that are difficult to compare and collapse for analysis

- They require extensive time and effort to accurately code, record, and tabulate

- They impose a more formidable response task on customers

- They may generate inappropriate reasons or irrelevant information

Response Scales

Closed-ended questions prelist the most important response options, generally in a scale or continuum. Because of the quantitative nature of this continuum, response scales easily lend themselves to *quantification*—thus, they are an efficient way to assess the popularity or priority of known or existing issues. Though you may not have anticipated (in the categories you supply) all possible responses, such an oversight will not substantially affect the major findings of your survey. (You have simply traded off all-inclusiveness for ease of tabulation.) Closed-ended questions are efficient, then, because they help control the length of the interview and therefore increase the number of customers one will be able to interview. These questions use knowledge about the customerbase to simplify information gathering. Because responses are generally prelisted or read aloud, closed-ended questions are more likely to unambiguously communicate to customers an appropriate answering frame of reference. Finally, they are very easy to report on, requiring at the very most a frequency count.

Scale Types

The motive for conducting a customer satisfaction survey is to ascribe *order* to issues and *magnitude* to levels of satisfaction. These two goals require scalar questions as opposed to open-ended questions. Responses to satisfaction questions can best be represented by a choice of position along some continuous response spectrum. A response scale is simply a verbal representation of that response spectrum. If scales are used to collect data, then results can be represented as distributions—counts of the frequency with which each scale response was chosen by customers as the response most representative of their feelings. Scales can be described as an efficient and practical means for collecting information from customers.

In general, response scales can be verbal, numeric, or pictorial. Each type has its fans and critics.

Verbal Scales

Those who favor verbal scales reason that they are the most colloquial way of assessing a respondent's state of mind. Such scales provide a continuum of verbal responses in a graduated order:

> *How satisfied are you, personally, with the acceleration of your automobile?*
>
> *[ ] Completely satisfied*
> *[ ] Somewhat satisfied*

[ ] Neither satisfied nor dissatisfied
[ ] Somewhat dissatisfied
[ ] Completely dissatisfied

Verbal response scales are patterned after sentence completion tasks allowing the customer to finish a statement:

How would you rate our shipping policies?

[ ] Excellent
[ ] Very good
[ ] Good
[ ] Fair
[ ] Poor

Some people worry about the extent to which verbal response scales share a common meaning among customers with different experiences and backgrounds. It is also difficult to find words with a uniform difference in intensity, so that it can be claimed the scale positions have *equal intervals* between them. For example, is the difference between *excellent* and *very good* the same as the difference between *very good* and *good*? Some would argue the difference between *excellent* and *very good* is greater.

There is also the worry that verbally anchored responses be entirely unidimensional—that is, that they rely on only one semantic continuum (i.e., *excellent* to *poor*). If the labels introduce more than one continuum, the scale fails to stay unidimensional. (Consider a hypothetical scale that is anchored by the two phrases *excellent* and *lacks caring*. *Excellent–poor* is certainly a unidimensional scale, as is *caring–lacks caring*. But *excellent* to *lacks caring* appears to address two different phenomena.)

Numeric Scales

Numeric scales, when anchored only at their endpoints, are more likely to escape the problem of multidimensionality. It is much easier to consider them unidimensional.

Please describe your automobile's acceleration by circling a number on the scale below:

Poor   *Excellent*
0   *1*   *2*   *3*   *4*   *5*   *6*   *7*   *8*   *9*   *10*

However, many worry about the level of abstraction customers must use to select a number between the anchored endpoints to represent their state of mind. Certainly such abstraction requires an analytically oriented customerbase and customers who are reasonably intelligent or self-assured.

The one problem with numeric scales is the possible mixed meaning of the numerical endpoints. We all strive to be "number one," suggesting 1 might be the more favorable number. Yet members of each gender look for a member of the opposite gender who's a "perfect 10." Specifying the most favorable endpoint on a numeric scale will always be difficult. The most important practice is to provide ample reminders throughout your interview of the meaning you've assigned to the 1 or to the 10 scale positions. To escape some of this ambiguity, we will advocate a numeric scale increasing in favor from 0, representing *completely dissatisfied,* to 10, representing *completely satisfied.*

Pictorial Scales

Pictorial scales are especially good for measuring the satisfaction of children and for introducing an air of informality and humanness to a questionnaire.

How do you feel about your automobile's acceleration?

But if pictorial scales appear too cutesy they may backfire. Instead of the happy face you might consider using an open pie chart, filling in slices according to the degree of your customers' satisfaction. The prevailing thought: use pictorial scales thoughtfully and parsimoniously.

Recommendation

In your questionnaire always offer your customers at least two open-ended questions: one asking them to explain their overall satisfaction rating with your organization (generally one of the first questions) and one near the end of your questionnaire, in response to which they can convey to you any additional information they haven't already mentioned. This helps ensure that they don't complete your questionnaire and still have something to tell you, which you may not have specifically asked for.

For numerical rating scales, use an 11-point numerical scale. The 11-point scale includes 0, which has relatively universal meaning as the *dissatisfied* or *totally missing* end of your rating scale. Because the 11-point scale contains an odd number of positions, it has a midpoint, a structure that some dislike. (The feeling is that customers who are traditionally fence-sitters will gravitate to such a position. By offering a scale with an even number of scales, you force them to take a position on either the positive or negative side of the perceived midpoint.)

Allowing for "No Experience"

Without a *no experience* provision in your rating questions, you run the risk of forcing customers who haven't experienced your organization's performance in certain areas to nevertheless provide a rating of satisfaction with your organization on that issue. Unfortunately, many midscale ratings (a 5 on our 11-point scale) don't really signify midlevel satisfaction. Rather, they are the expression of customers with no experience being forced to reply to all rating questions. In this situation, the customer's only alternative is to assign a midscale rating, neither *satisfied* nor *dissatisfied*, as their way of saying, "I don't know!"

It's always a good practice to accommodate such customers by providing a clearly labeled check box, away from the general rating scale, that allows them to indicate that they haven't had any (or sufficient) experience with your organization to rate you on a specific issue.

Completely *dissatisfied*										*Completely* *satisfied*	
0	*1*	*2*	*3*	*4*	*5*	*6*	*7*	*8*	*9*	*10*	*[ ] No experience*

 Checkpoint 5.7

1. You can choose from a number of formats when designing how your customers will respond to your questions. In general, customers will respond either numerically or verbally, in a closed-ended format or an open-ended format. These different formats serve different purposes.

2. Regarding your numeric response scales, we have recommended that you:

   • Offer an 11-point scale, ranging from 0 to 10

   • "Anchor" (or label) only the endpoints

   • Use the labels *completely dissatisfied* as the label for 0 and *completely satisfied* as the label for 10

   • Offer a *no experience* check box for each question, allowing customers who haven't had experience with the feature or service addressed in a question to opt out by checking it.

Instructions within Questions

Instructions for a particular question should address each of the following issues:

- What product feature or issue is being evaluated in the question

- What construct (such as satisfaction) your customer should use in his or her evaluation

- How your customer should use the response scale you've provided

- Exactly how and where to report or record responses

The importance of adequate instructions, unfortunately, is often understood only after seeing how badly customers misunderstood your intentions in their returned questionnaires. For example, consider question 3 in Figure 5.6. Because there happen to be five attributes *and* a five-point rating scale,

---

Q3   Please rate the following:

Not at all important				Extremely important
1	2	3	4	5

_____ Acceleration
_____ Miles per gallon
_____ Braking
_____ Road-holding
_____ Positive steering response

Revised Q3   How important are each of the following attributes of automobiles (*a* through *e*)? Please use a scale ranging from 1 (not at all important) to 5 (extremely important). You may use any number from 1 to 5. Please rate each attribute by placing a rating on the line to the left of each attribute.

_____ (a) Acceleration
_____ (b) Miles per gallon
_____ (c) Braking
_____ (d) Road-holding
_____ (e) Positive steering response

Figure 5.6   Importance of question instructions.

some customers might use the numbers from 1 to 5 to indicate a *ranking* rather than a *rating*. The revised question 3 attempts to better guide customers in answering.

STEP 5.8 ASSIGN RESPONSE CODES

In order to tabulate the many different responses that your customers will provide you, you'll need to assign some response codes to their answers. These response codes are the information you'll load into your computer and on which you'll perform descriptive statistics in order to summarize and report your findings.

Response codes depend on the type of question you've asked. They are relatively straightforward for closed-ended questions. Often (as in the case of numeric scales) the response your customer has selected will be the code you enter. In a 0-to-10 numeric scale, when a customer circles or checks a rating of 7, you will enter a 7 as the *code* for the *rating* of 7. In other cases, such as open-ended questions, you'll have to set up a more complex process to assign countable codes to the nuances of meaning your customers convey in their verbatim responses.

There are two procedures for assigning codes: precoding and postcoding. You can only precode closed-ended questions, because those are the only questions for which you can accurately anticipate all responses. In the case of open-ended questions, you'll have to wait until you receive enough verbatim responses from which to create a post hoc coding structure.

Precoding Your Questionnaire

Convention dictates that you'll use numbers for your codes, single digits (1–9) unless you have more than nine response options, in which case you'll need to allocate a two-digit code. You will assign the numbers to the responses as shown in Figure 5.7. In some cases, there will be a logical connection between your customer's response and the code you've assigned, as in the current example. But just as often the number code can function simply as a talliable symbol—for example, the situation in Figure 5.8. In this case the West Coast should not be considered as better (because it was accorded the number code of 4 to the East Coast's 1). As we've discussed earlier, the codes simply offer nominal, classificatory information. You will need to remember this as you enter the stage of numerical analysis. Don't perform statistical tests on response codes that are merely nominal (or classificatory) in nature. (An *average location* of 1.7 would have no meaning in this current example.)

	Completely dissatisfied		Completely satisfied	No experience
8. The basic functionality of our products	0 1 2 3 4 5 6 7 8 9 10			[ ] 11

Figure 5.7 Response codes for question scales.

Where are the majority of your customers headquartered?
(Please check one location from the list below.)

(1) _____ East coast
(2) _____ South
(3) _____ Midwest
(4) _____ West coast

Figure 5.8 Response codes for nominal data.

Without digressing into a discussion of scaling theory, we'll simply point out that the number codes can take one of four different natures:

- *Nominal.* Nominal scales are the most basic form of a response scale. The information is truly "nominal"; scale codes (1, 2, and 3) are only classificatory—like positions on a sports team (pitcher, first base, center field). As such, the only tabulation that can be performed is frequency counts. The mode is the only applicable measure of central tendency applicable to nominal scales.

- *Ordinal.* Ordinal scales convey order—from first (or *most preferred*) to last (or *least preferred*). In ordinal scales, the numeric order of the response codes conveys superiority or preference. Ordinal scales may be used to produce frequency counts; the mode and the median are appropriate measures of central tendency.

- *Interval*. Interval scales offer customers an ordered scale of preference in which the psychological distance between subsequent answers is intended to be as similar as possible (*equal-appearing interval scales*). Interval scales support the most common calculations of mean, median, and mode. Data collected with interval scales are assumed to conform to the normal distribution; this scale type produces *parametric data*.

- *Ratio*. Ratio scales are the most powerful type of response scale because they produce data with a true zero point. Many of the most common measurements in our lives are ratio scaled: length, income, speed, sales. While ratio scales support the most robust statistical analyses, they will seldom apply to the subjective concepts measured among your customers.

Your satisfaction data will be predominately nominal, ordinal, and interval with few opportunities for truly ratio-scaled data. This has some repercussions for the types of data analysis your data will support—but more on that in chapter 6.

Postcoding Open-Ended Responses

When you ask an open-ended question, you must anticipate having to code customers' responses. If your survey is a continuing survey, you'll already have a preexisting code structure. But when initiating a survey or asking an open-ended question for the first time, you'll need to establish codes for each response you wish to tally. You can use the following procedure.

Checklist 5.1 A Sequence for Creating Response Codes

1. For each question for which you've allowed an open-ended response, draw a random sample of questionnaires. Approximately 25 is a good starting point.

2. Read the first customer's response to the open-ended question. Try to encapsulate the meaning of the first thought in the response. For example: *shoddy product quality*; *attentive personal service*, etc.

3. Create a response code to represent the meaning of the response: 10 = shoddy product quality.

4. If there is another thought in the same response, review and similarly code it.

5. Advance to the next questionnaire. If the first thought is represented by a code you've already created, advance to the second or third thoughts (if present) and see if they are similarly represented by existing response codes. If not, institute new codes.

6. Proceed through your 25 questionnaires in this manner. Prior to reaching the 25th questionnaire, the need to institute additional codes should become less frequent. This will indicate you've already accounted for most of your customers' responses to your open-ended question. You are now ready to begin coding all your questionnaires. If in the process of coding, you encounter a new thought or response, you may always create a new, additional code, incorporating it into your coding structure.

Open-ended coding lists should be retained with your project, as they will be useful from one wave to the next.

Generally you'll select numeric codes (though you could use alphabetic codes). Some satisfaction professionals somewhat arbitrarily assign numeric, two-digit codes—say, ranging from 1 to 99—to the responses they identify. The author prefers to assign codes in a more systematic way. The thought is to create hierarchical codes with a meaningful structure. For example, codes under 50 might represent favorable responses, and those over 50, unfavorable. Within each run of 50 numbers, the decile value could represent the *same* performance attribute in both the favorable and unfavorable ranges. Carrying this procedure further, the hundreds location (of the code) could represent a particular aspect of the product or service. In Figure 5.9, for example, the three-digit code 253 would represent a negative comment about costs related to the hardware. Structured codes make *nets* in cross-tabulations somewhat easier to produce. For example, a net of all 1xx coded responses versus 2xx coded responses tells us quickly the frequency of *product/equipment* comments compared to *hardware* comments. Similarly, a net on all 01–49 codes versus 50–99 gives us an immediate feeling for the quantity of *favorable* versus *unfavorable* comments.

As codes are established for each open-ended question, they must be retained in a codebook, which will stay with your study from year to year. Each time you field the study, you'll use the same codes where possible. But you will also need to keep an open mind to allow for instituting new codes for new issues and points of view.

Checklist 5.2 Coding Conventions

Certain practices are advisable in establishing the numeric codes you'll use for entering your data:

1xx Product/equipment	
Positive comments	*Negative comments*
111 Quality	151 Quality
112 Reliability	152 Reliability
113 Cost	153 Cost
114 Documentation	154 Documentation
115 Size/dimensions	155 Size/dimensions
116 Delivery/issuance	156 Delivery/issuance
2xx Hardware	
Positive comments	*Negative comments*
211 Quality	251 Quality
212 Reliability	252 Reliability
213 Cost	253 Cost
214 Documentation	254 Documentation
215 Size/dimensions	255 Size/dimensions
216 Delivery/issuance	256 Delivery/issuance
3xx Software	
Positive comments	*Negative comments*
311 Quality	351 Quality
312 Reliability	352 Reliability
313 Cost	353 Cost
314 Documentation	354 Documentation
315 Size/dimensions	355 Size/dimensions
316 Delivery/issuance	356 Delivery/issuance
322 Accuracy of coding	362 Accuracy of coding

Figure 5.9 A hierarchical coding structure.

1. Use only one number or character set per data location in your records. If a question prompts multiple thoughts or responses, establish contiguous data locations for the maximum number of responses you anticipate receiving. (You'll use the same response codes—either precoded, closed-ended codes or the open-ended codes you've established—placing whichever ones apply in the response locations.)

2. For the most universal analysis of your data, use only numeric codes—not all computer programs will accept alphanumeric codes (that is, a, b, c, d). Avoid using any special characters (such as, @, *).

3. Adopt a uniform, question-to-question convention for representing response conditions such as: *no answer, don't know,* and *does not apply.* Because computer programs vary in how they read blanks, it's best to enter a character in each data location of your customer records. If you mean zero, enter a 0. If the question is not answered, enter a code for *no response.* Similarly, establish discrete codes for *does not apply.* As these codes will probably be numeric (i.e., no answer = 99, does not apply = 88), you'll have to exclude these values from any numeric computations. Many computer programs allow you to specify numeric values as codes for such missing values.

4. Be sure to make the data location fields wide enough to support all acceptable codes. If you've established three-digit codes for a particular question, be sure to provide three-character data locations in your record format for each response anticipated.

 Checkpoint 5.8

1. Response codes allow your customers to select or record an answer to each of your questions and provide a datum for your data entry people to insert into your response file. In general, you'll need response codes for every possible response to each of your questions.

2. Response codes for your closed-ended questions will often be the actual response customers have selected (an overall satisfaction rating of 8 will have an 8 as its response code). Those for your open-ended or description questions will be less intuitive; you will need to establish them.

3. Response codes will assume the *metric* of the response scales they represent. It's important to know the power or limitations of the underlying response scale. There are four response scale types: nominal (purely classificatory), ordinal (conveys preference), interval (conveys preference in increments of approximately equal intensity), and ratio (offers all of the preceding plus an absolute zero point).

STEP 5.9 PRETEST YOUR QUESTIONNAIRE

Before beginning your survey process, you are advised to pretest your questionnaire (this should include pretesting your data entry and analysis systems, though sometimes these additional opportunities are overlooked). Pretests can be conducted:

- Among a small sample of your customers—generally fewer than 25. (If you have only 25 customers, you'd want to pretest your questionnaire among 3 to 5.)

- Without the customer's knowledge that you're testing your questionnaire. (If you don't alert your customer, you can debrief him or her after the interview to determine if any questions were worded poorly or if your response categories seemed inappropriate or difficult to use, and so on)

- By alerting participating customers that they're part of your pretest. If you alert your customer, it's traditional to ask him or her for a critique of your questions and wording as you progress through the interview.

- From an interviewer's perspective, by debriefing the interviewers involved in your pretest, asking them for their observations: Did any questions seem particularly difficult for your customers? Did your customers seem frustrated or put off by any issues present or absent? What, if anything, did customers have to say about the interview?

- To help determine how long your interview is or how much time customers need to complete your questionnaire.

Based on your observations from the pretest, you should consider:

- Rewording questions or instructions that seemed to cause problems

- Changing the order of questions or issues if your customers found your order awkward or confusing

- Using different words, terms, or language in place of words that didn't seem to communicate or otherwise caused problems

- Shortening the length of your questionnaire by eliminating questions or issues

A pretest also allows you the opportunity to test your planned analytical program. Don't overlook this important opportunity—you'll have actual data, so go ahead and test the statistical runs you are planning to make and make sure the linkages between the programs make sense!

 Checkpoint 5.9

1. Don't consider using your questionnaire for a full-blown survey until you've pretested it. The pretest is important to prove that customers will understand your questions and will respond with relevant information. If you are using interviewers, the pretest will also show whether they can understand your instructions and properly administer the questionnaire.

2. Don't overlook the opportunity to check your planned data entry and analytical routines as part of your pretest.

 Step-by-Step: The Answers for Measuring Satisfaction

Research to be conducted among customers (what we've called customer research) should be conducted differently than are more general opinion surveys or marketing research. Differences should be respected in terms of respondent (customer) identities and the need for follow-up at the individual customer level.

- Traditional marketing research disavows identifying specific customers, making follow-up impossible.

- The author advocates informing customers that they may expect to be recontacted (if necessary) unless they opt out. See pages 128–29.

5.1 We have described two levels of questionnaire/interview construction: the *macro* and the *micro*. Macro-level concerns deal with the topics you'll cover in your questionnaire, the order in which you'll address those topics, how you'll route customers through the interview, and the instructions you'll offer both to customers and to interviewers. Micro-level issues deal with the structure, wording, format, and response options you'll offer for individual questions. It's important to consider both levels as you build your questionnaire. See pages 134–35.

5.2 We've identified three sections of a well-organized questionnaire: the *introduction*, the *main body*, and the *conclusion*. Each of these sections plays a vital role in making your questionnaire successful. We have also urged paying attention to the appearance of your questionnaire; the quality or shoddiness of your interview reflects on your organization. See page 136.

5.3 Routing and skip patterns are important because you want to avoid asking customers questions that are irrelevant or unnecessary. Whether your interview is to be administered or self-administered, you need to flowchart how customers will proceed through the questions. Consider the consequences of each possible response and the legitimacy of subsequent questions. See pages 139–40.

5.4 Properly thought-out and written instructions often mean the difference between an effective questionnaire and an ineffective one. Create the most helpful instructions you can. See pages 140–43.

5.5 You will find that there are essentially four types of information you can collect: *facts, attitudes, behavioral intentions*, and *demographics/industographics*. Knowing the type of information you are looking for can assist you in matching it to the best question format. See pages 143–44.

5.6 We've identified four question types that you can choose from in writing your questionnaire: *rating questions, description questions, assignment questions*, and *allocation questions*. See pages 145–47.

5.7 There are two basic response types for questions: *closed-ended* (generally rating scales or checklists) and *open-ended* (verbal) questions. The author urges you to use at least two open-ended questions, though more (in the form of drill-downs) can be very helpful. For rating/evaluation questions (satisfaction measurement), the author suggests using an

(continued)

11-point, end-anchored, numerical scale with 0 designated as *completely dissatisfied* and 10 designated as *completely satisfied*. See pages 147–53.

5.8 Be aware of the type of information your survey process will collect as it impinges on the type of statistical analysis you can conduct on your findings. Generally, responses to a customer satisfaction survey will be *interval scaled*. Response codes that you assign to your answers will be how you enter data into a computer for analysis. Because these response codes are generally numeric, people tend to forget they may not be as metric as they look. Be careful, and remember how you have instituted your numeric response codes. See pages 156–60.

5.9 Every questionnaire should be *pretested* before it is presented to customers. You may openly ask a few customers to review their reaction to and understanding of your questionnaire with you, or you may conduct a small-scale pilot study with a debriefing of participating customers after they've completed your questionnaire. See pages 161–62.

 Chapter 5 Deliverables

As a result of your work in this chapter, you will have completed the following for your program:

1. Readied customer satisfaction questionnaires for distribution or administration for hardware producers, software producers, or service providers. These questionnaires are properly organized and contain ample instructions for customers or interviewers.

2. Envisioned a pretest procedure with which to test the fieldworthiness of your draft questionnaire. You will also capitalize on this event as a way to check on your data entry and data analysis plans.

3. Checked your ability to properly tally your customers' responses to both closed-ended and open-ended questions containing both numeric and verbal data.

III.

Deduction

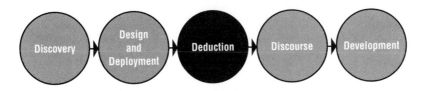

How Will You Analyze the Information You Collect?

Once you have fielded your questionnaire or interview, you'll have a wealth of information. But raw information begs for interpretation and structure. You need to mine the nuggets of insight buried in your data. Be forewarned—you'll need to organize your search and be as creative as possible as you look at your information. The more different ways you view it, the more likely you'll make a new discovery!

6

Analyzing Your Data

" "**P**aralysis of analysis!" is an epithet often thrown at programs that become stagnated at the analytical stage. Such stagnation can be the result of either a loss of direction or an almost hypnotic reaction caused by the complexity of and opportunities offered by a dataset. Your program needs to avoid such traps. You'll avoid paralysis by carefully plotting out the steps in your analytical plan before you are mesmerized by all the data you've collected and by the countless different ways of collapsing and combining your data for innumerable different analytical perspectives.

A LIKELY SEQUENCE

Most quantitative customer satisfaction analytical programs follow a fairly similar sequence. That sequence is logical and generally adheres to common analytical sequences:

1. Calculate your organization's current performance (on your overall and performance measures) using summary statistics.

2. Interpret your current performance levels by comparing them with benchmarks such as managerial goals, historical performance, or industry norms.

3. Use statistical testing to determine the significance of (1) the changes from previous measurements or (2) the difference from managerial goals or competitors' performance.

4. Explore other aspects of your data using more complex, multivariate statistical techniques such as determining which issues are key drivers of your customers' satisfaction.

This process can be undertaken for your customerbase as a whole or for specific subsamples (groups of special customers).

Step-by-Step: The Issues of Analyzing Your Data

6.1 Understand the types of quantitative analyses available for numerical data.

6.2 Select a measure to use to summarize your customers' feelings and reactions for your management.

6.3 Commit to an analytical process and impose a hierarchy on the questions in your questionnaire—some will be ideal for classifying customers' ratings, others will simply be directed responses. You need also to understand the basics of interpreting results from a sample of your customers and how and when you can generalize results to your total customerbase.

6.4 Learn how to establish customers' perceptions of your current performance—overall and through performance variables using an internal analytical perspective.

6.5 Focus on how you're perceived competitively against others in your industry—the external analytical perspective.

6.6 How can you determine when you've surpassed or failed to achieve your numeric goals? When is a numerical increase or decrease really meaningful? Testing for statistical significance is the method we use to answer these important questions.

6.7 Learn to use composite measures of satisfaction and satisfaction indices.

6.8 Understand the types of analyses available for verbal data.

STEP 6.1 TYPES OF ANALYSES FOR NUMERICAL DATA

With your numerical data, you have at least four major analytical options:

1. Use *descriptive statistics* to understand the basic parameters of your data.

2. Use *correlation analysis* to understand the relationships among your data.

3. Use *cross-tabular analysis* to provide an interpretive understanding of your data.

4. Use *advanced analysis* to better understand the structure of and dependencies within your data.

These options are listed in approximate logical order of applicability or use. You should first familiarize yourself with your data by using descriptive statistics and possibly correlation analysis; then you will be in the best position to appropriately order or meaningfully create cross-tab tables of your data. (You will ultimately revert back to your correlations for one approach to identifying the *key drivers* of your customers' satisfaction.) Advanced analysis (primarily *multivariate statistical analysis*) can be used both prior to building your basic cross-tab tables to provide a better understanding of the inherent structure of your data and later in your analytical process, to help build more advanced models from your data.

Assigning Your Variables As Classification or Response

A primary key to the success of your overall numerical analysis, which some pursue out of intuition alone, is assigning and using some of your variables as *classifications* and others as *responses*. This allocation guides how you analyze and table your results, and it makes your analyses more managerially useful.

- *Classification variables.* These are information points you have collected that can help you cluster or group your information. Typical questions that can serve as classification variables include:

  - Size/importance (dollar volume of sales) of the customer

  - Geographic region of the customer

  - Type(s)/kind(s) of your product purchased by the customer

  Classification variables can be used creatively. For example, it might be very helpful if you grouped your customers by their levels of overall satisfaction. You might divide them into three groups according to that measure. Then you could examine the ratings given your performance variables by those three groups (levels of the classification variable—*overall satisfaction*). The performance variables (your *response variables*) displaying the greatest fluctuation in ratings across the three groups could be reasoned to be the most critical in satisfying your customers.

You would also use your classification variables to identify (and name) columns in your data tables and your cross-tab *banner points*.

* *Response variables.* Your performance variables are the most obvious candidates for response variables. Response variables are elements of your performance that you expect may be rated differently by various groups of your customers (as defined by your classification variables). As you are tabling your data, always consider using the classification variables to help break down results of the response variables. (See Table 6.1 for an illustration.)

In general, the concept of classification and response variables is not leveraged nearly enough in analysis.

Types of Numerical Analysis

You can make use of three types of analyses to analyze your information:

* *Univariate analysis.* Use in situations in which one and only one variable is being analyzed and interpreted. Generally all of your descriptive statistics (your summary measures for example) will be conducted using univariate procedures.

* *Bivariate analysis.* Use in situations in which a pair of variables is being analyzed to specifically examine their apparent confluence or divergence (key driver analysis is an example).

* *Multivariate analysis.* Use in situations in which a group of variables is analyzed for purposes of investigating their:

  * Structure or relationships (using statistical techniques such as factor analysis or perceptual mapping)

  * Dependency—one variable to the group or one group to another group of variables (using multiple regression)

Univariate and bivariate analyses are more or less widely understood; not so with the multivariate techniques.

Table 6.1   Illustration of using classification and response variables.

Performance variables	Most satisfied customers (ratings of 10 or 9)	Least satisfied customers (ratings of 0 or 1)	Difference—gap
Qualification	8.9	0.7	8.3
Value for price	8.7	1.7	7.1
Product durability	8.3	2.7	5.6
Documentation	8.9	3.0	5.9
Product reliability	8.1	0.5	7.6
Installation	8.5	3.3	5.2
Conformance to specs	8.0	1.3	6.7
Features offered	8.1	2.0	6.1
Product functionality	8.7	3.7	5.0
Servicing	8.7	3.0	5.7
Product serviceability	7.6	1.7	6.0
Delivery	8.8	3.5	5.3
Sample size	*35*	*3*	*32*

We will begin by discussing primarily univariate analysis, but two of our tools (correlation analysis and cross-tabs) are bivariate methods. We will conclude with an application of multiple regression, a multivariate technique.

 Checkpoint 6.1

1. It is to your advantage to designate some of your more important variables as classification variables. This means you'll have the opportunity to view the ratings of the other, response variables by levels of your classification variables. If you use your overall satisfaction rating as one of your classification variables, you'll be able to examine all your performance ratings through the eyes of your customers in various cohort groups of satisfaction: highly satisfied customers versus very poorly satisfied customers, and so on.

(continued)

2. Analysis of a customer satisfaction survey doesn't necessarily have to include high-level statistics—though multivariate statistics can provide very useful insights. Rather,
most of your analyses will use univariate, descriptive statistics. Means or top-box satisfaction scores—your primary
summary scores—will be easily analyzed with these basic
statistical methods.

STEP 6.2 DESCRIPTIVE STATISTICS: SUMMARIZING YOUR RESULTS

No matter how complex the issue, no matter how many measures we have
quantified, we all seek the one magic number that tells the whole story . . .

"Get to the 'bottom line,' " we're told.

"Let me have it straight," we're urged.

"How're we doing?" we're asked.

If you were to attempt to answer any of these questions with an array
of frequency distributions—to do full credit to what you've learned about
your customers—you would be seen as not responding to the question.
Rather, you'd be accused of obfuscating the issue. Management today is
accustomed to receiving summary statistics that describe exactly how their
organization is doing on a variety of fronts.

Measures of Central Tendency

To satisfy the need for summary, most of us adopt measures of *central tendency* (for example, the mode, the median, the mean) to provide a convenient, easy-to-grasp, *single* number to convey the "state of the state." Each
of the three constructs mentioned is an attempt to communicate as much
as possible about the distribution of a dataset in *one single number*. The
problem is, no one number can truly describe all the nuances of a dataset.
You can easily see this in the three samples (of 100 customers' satisfaction
ratings on a 0-to-10 scale) shown in Figure 6.1. Each of the samples has an
equal summary statistic (mean) of 4.55! Despite the similarity in their
means, you would obviously want to interact with the populations underlying the three samples in very different manners if you had the luxury of
insight provided by the entire frequency distributions. The means conceal
their fundamental differences!

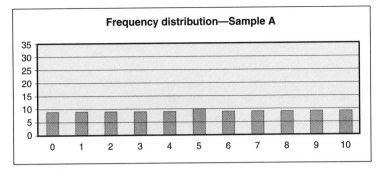

Mean = 4.55

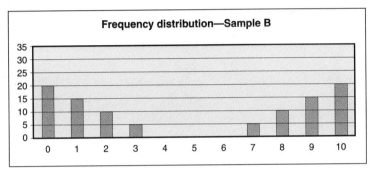

Mean = 4.55

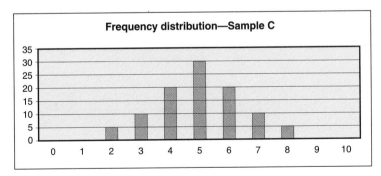

Mean = 4.55

Figure 6.1   A tale of three distributions.

The most representative picture of the responses to any satisfaction question—the foregoing discussion should show—is probably a frequency distribution of the data. But frequency distributions:

- Present a bewildering array of numbers and frequencies

- Are not easy to summarize mentally

- Cause problems when we are asked to assess the direction and magnitude of change from one measurement period to the next

Figure 6.2 displays all the possible, common summary statistics for a single dataset.

A	B	C	D
Rating	Number of customers	(B/100)	(A × B)
10	15	15%	150
9	20	20%	180
8	23	23%	184
7	15	15%	105
6	10	10%	60
5	5	5%	25
4	4	4%	16
3	3	3%	9
2	2	2%	4
1	2	2%	2
0	1	1%	0
Totals	100		735

Mean =	7.4
Mode =	8.0
Median =	8.0
Standard deviation =	2.27
Top box =	15%
Top two boxes =	35%
Bottom box =	1%
8th decile =	9.0
Percent to perfect =	73.5%

Figure 6.2 Basic summary statistics.

The author was amazed at one point in his career when he visited a distinguished professor of psychometrics, Ledyard R Tucker, for consultation on an advanced multivariate technique. He found Tucker painstakingly plotting, point by point, all the responses he'd received to a question. Expressing some amazement at seeing this apparent precomputer behavior, the author asked Professor Tucker why he was plotting the points. "Always," Tucker admonished, "look at your data *first*, before launching into a sophisticated analysis!"

Professor Tucker's advice is very wise.

The mean (or arithmetic average) is the most commonly accepted method to economically describe responses to satisfaction questions (overall as well as more specific performance questions). But, forewarned is forearmed. Don't be seduced into complacency by the compact singularity of a mean. Try, when possible, to examine the richness of your full dataset. To guard against the possibilities shown in Figure 6.1, look at the distributions underlying all of your means, when you can. They will tell you vastly more about the nature of your customers' satisfaction than a mean ever could.

Other Summary Measures

Two other measures are in use in satisfaction settings today. But unlike the mean, they are not measures of central tendency. They are just the opposite. The *top-box* or *top-two-boxes* summaries are *measures of extremeness*—a description of the proportion of your customers who are satisfied enough to award your products the very best rating (a 10) or the best and second-best ratings (a 10 and a 9). In many ways these measures are truer to many organizations' goals of moving a maximum number of their customers to complete satisfaction—delight, if you will.[1] Refer to Figure 6.2 for an example.

Another measure you could adopt would be a *percent-to-perfect* score. If you use the ratings in Figure 6.2, you'll see the highest possible score would be 1000 (100 respondents all scoring you a perfect 10). Now, in actuality, you've received the scores shown in the frequency array. Weighting

---

[1] Delight is a concept the author is fully committed to. See Keiningham and Vavra, *The Customer Delight Principle* (2001) for a discussion of the value of goaling for delight.

Table 6.2   Definitions of frequently used summary measures.

Concept	Definition
Mode	The numerical rating (6, 7, etc. from your response scale) that was assigned most frequently by your customers.
Median	If you rank-ordered all your customers' numerical ratings (to a particular question), the median would be that rating perfectly in the middle, dividing your customerbase in half, with half giving higher numerical ratings and half lower. (The median is also the fifth decile.)
Mean, average	The arithmetic average, derived by summing all your customers' ratings and dividing by the number of customers offering a rating.
Top box	The number or proportion of your customers assigning the very highest numerical rating.
Top two boxes	The number or proportion of your customers assigning the highest and second-highest numerical ratings.
Bottom box	The number or proportion of your customers assigning the very lowest numerical rating.
Eighth decile	When you rank-order your customers by numerical rating (lowest to highest), the eighth decile is that score that identifies the 20 percent of your customers who have awarded you the highest scores.
Percent to perfect	Your calculated arithmetic mean divided by the maximum or perfect score. (If your mean is 8.2 on a 1–10 scale, 8.2 ÷ 10 = 82%.)

each group of responses by the value of the rating they assigned gives a total of 735. And 735/1000 = 73.5 percent. In other words, you are 74 percent of the way to a perfect score! Table 6.2 defines each of the traditional measures as well as the summary measures we have just described.

Measures of Dispersion

Decile analysis is another method finding some acceptance in customer satisfaction measurement (CSM) recently. Decile analysis is really the general case underlying the calculation of the median. As you may remember, the median is that score (or satisfaction rating) that is directly in the center of a sorted array of all your satisfaction scores. Half your customers would have awarded a score greater than the median satisfaction score, the other half, a score lower. The median identifies the fifth decile (50 percent).

You can use decile analysis as follows:

Suppose your organization's satisfaction goal is to have at least 20 percent of your customers awarding you satisfaction scores of 9 or 10. To monitor this, you would want to calculate the eighth decile boundary. (There are only nine decile boundaries.) One can interpret a score belonging to the eighth decile as meaning, "A score of this amount is better than 80 percent of all the other scores." So as long as your data's eighth decile started at a score greater than 8, you would have met your goal. See Table 6.3.

You must decide what your primary summary statistic is going to be: means, top-box scores, or decile goals. This decision affects later analyses you will need to conduct (specifically, the tests of significance for change and comparison you will use).

 Checkpoint 6.2

1. Customer satisfaction projects require summary measures that you can use to economically report your survey findings. The most common summary statistics in use are these:

   - A measure of central tendency—the arithmetic mean (or average)

   - A measure of extremeness—the top-box score

   You will need to adopt one of these measures as an economic way to report and track your organization's performance for your management.

2. Decile analysis—a measure of dispersion—is a summary statistic that is very compatible with satisfaction improvement goals. It is an appealing alternative to a mean or a top-box score.

Table 6.3   Using decile analysis to explore overall satisfaction.

Ninth decile	10	10%
Eighth decile	9	20%
Seventh decile	9	30%
Sixth decile	8	40%
Fifth decile	8	50%
Fourth decile	7	60%
Third decile	7	70%
Second decile	6	80%
First decile	4	90%

STEP 6.3 ANALYTICAL STRATEGIES TO HELP INTERPRET YOUR RESULTS

Once you have calculated your summary measures (be they means, top-box proportions, or even deciles), you'll want to think about how to report them within your organization. Your management and your colleagues will want to know how well the organization is doing. To structure your reporting, it is useful to divide the questions you have asked in your questionnaire into two groups:

- Your *criteria variables*, that is, measures of overall performance (often selected as your classification variables—see page 169)

- Your *performance variables*, that is, measures of more specific issues and operations (likely to serve as your response variables)

Your analyses should, then, initially focus on organizing ratings *within* each of these two groupings. (While you may use most of your criteria variables as classification variables, the reverse is not likely. Not all of the variables you creatively select as classification variables need also be criteria variables.) Later, in the advanced analysis section, we'll discuss how to examine all the possible relationships between your criteria variables and your performance variables.

Some Statistical Basics

Before you report any results from your survey, you must qualify the representativeness of the ratings based on parameters of your survey. The most important point for you to realize is the following:

> The average of any of your performance measures or your average overall satisfaction as calculated from the responses of a sample of your customers is a *statistical concept*. It is your best *estimate* of how *all your customers* feel based on the limited data you have collected; yet it is subject to the whims of sampling. To confidently report the level of satisfaction of your total customerbase to your management, you must be able to extrapolate from your sample's average score (a *statistic*) to a predicted value for your total customerbase.

This process of extrapolation (statistical inference) relies on your understanding of the interaction among three elements of your survey: the size of your sample, your willingness to tolerate error, and the level of statistical significance you require or accept.

• *Sample size.* The size of your sample has a substantial impact on the confidence you can place on a *mean score* calculated from that sample. As the sample size increases (approaching the size of your entire customerbase), you can more confidently generalize your sample's average rating to the feeling of your entire customerbase, because as you infinitely increase the sample size, your sample and your population (customerbase) become one and the same. Smaller samples affect the confidence with which you can generalize findings from them to your entire customerbase. Sample size drives a concept called the *standard error of the estimated mean* (discussed below).

• *Tolerance for error.* The tolerance for error (the *confidence interval,* or spread, you accept) has to do with the range of variation you are willing to accept around any sample statistic you calculate. In the case of a single measure from a sample of your customers, say their average overall satisfaction rating of 7.5, there will necessarily be a confidence interval statistically imposed about that observed score. The confidence interval is a range about the satisfaction rating that will include a population of all means that might be sampled. The size of the confidence interval is related to the level of statistical significance you have selected and to your sample size. To determine the range of satisfaction scores in your customerbase that could support a sample statistic of 7.5, you need to declare a level of statistical significance, coupled with your sample size.

• *Level of statistical significance.* The final step is to decide on the level of significance you'll require for your analysis. Conventional practice is to use a 95 percent level of significance. That means that only five out of a hundred times will you expect to be wrong in your generalization from survey findings to your customerbase. While conventionality ordains this level, there's nothing magical about it. You could just as easily decide to use a 90 percent level of confidence. Recognize that if you stay with the 95 percent convention, you'll probably not be questioned. But buck conventionality (by adopting a different level of significance) and you'll no doubt be asked to explain your decision. (Why bother? Because potential cost savings from relaxing your level of statistical significance from 95 percent to 90 percent or even 80 percent can be substantial.)

• *Standard error of the estimated mean.* The standard error is actually the *standard deviation* of an implied sampling distribution of all sample means from a given population. The standard error describes the degree of error (departure from the population mean) to be associated with any mean calculated from a sample. The standard error

$$\sigma_x = \frac{\sigma}{\sqrt{n}}, \qquad (6.1)$$

where:

n = sample size

σ = population standard deviation. (When your customerbase's true standard deviation is unknown, you may use the standard deviation from your sample.)

When you're dealing with proportions rather than means, there is an equivalent *standard error of the proportion*, as specified in Equation 6.2.

$$\sigma_p = \sqrt{\frac{p(1-p)}{n}}, \qquad (6.2)$$

where:

p = proportion measured and
n = sample size

Because the population of all possible means from any given distribution of scores is normally distributed, the standard error can be used to construct the confidence interval about any observed mean or to test the mean for differences from other means. Means are normally distributed; therefore we can say with confidence that:

- 68 percent of all sample means will lie within ±1 standard error

- 95 percent will lie within ±2 standard errors

- 99.5 percent will lie within ±3 standard errors

These factors affect your results in a myriad of ways. Table 6.4 shows four different analytic scenarios and shows the consequences based on the size of the samples. Now we can use these factors to help determine how you should report the results of your survey. We'll examine both means and proportions.

Reporting a Mean Satisfaction Score

Let's assume, as we postulated earlier, that your survey determines an average overall satisfaction rating of 7.5. What rating or range of ratings should you report to your management? To answer this question, you'll need to use the standard error you've calculated from your data and a level of statistical significance that you choose.

Using your measured rating, the rating's standard error, and the level of statistical significance you've selected, you can now calculate the confidence interval to be applied to the calculated average rating. You would use

Table 6.4 Four scenarios.

Sampling from mean data

	Sample 1 (original)	Sample 2 (increase sample size)	Sample 3 (increase confidence level)	Sample 4 (decrease confidence level)
Sample mean (overall satisfaction)	7.5	7.5	7.5	7.5
Standard deviation	2.23	2.23	2.23	2.23
Sample size	500	1000	500	500
Confidence level	95%	95%	99.5%	68%
Standard error of the mean	0.10	0.07	0.10	0.10
Calculated confidence interval	0.20	0.14	0.28	0.08
Range	7.30–7.69	7.35–7.64	7.21–7.78	7.41–7.58

Sampling from proportional data

	Sample 5 (original)	Sample 6 (increase sample size)	Sample 7 (increase confidence level)	Sample 8 (decrease confidence level)
Sample proportion (overall sat—top box)	65%	65%	65%	65%
Sample size	500	1000	500	500
Confidence level	95%	95%	99.5%	68%
Standard error of the proportion	2.13%	1.51%	2.13%	2.13%
Calculated confidence interval	4.27%	2.96%	5.99%	1.79%
Range	60.7%–69.3%	62.0%–67.9%	59.0%–70.9%	63.2%–66.7%

Equation 6.1 and remember from the normal distribution that 68 percent, 95 percent, or 99.5 percent of all means will fall respectively within the interval of ±1, 2, or 3 standard errors of the mean.

In the example, with 7.5 as the mean satisfaction rating you've determined by interviewing 500 customers, and a derived standard error of the mean of 0.1, at the 95 percent statistical confidence level, the interval within which the true overall satisfaction (of all your customers) lies is defined by the range of 7.3 to 7.7 (about your discovered mean of 7.5). This range is the confidence interval containing the actual overall satisfaction of all your customers as surmised from a sample of your customers. In your report to management, your best message is "Our current overall satisfaction lies within the range of 7.3 to 7.7, or our organization's over-all satisfaction is 7.5 ± 0.2."

Reporting a Proportional Satisfaction Score

What if you've decided to report overall satisfaction as a proportion—that is, that 65 percent of your sampled customers rated overall satisfaction with a top-box score (extremely satisfied)? How should you report that to your management? The same procedure as above still applies, except you would now use Equation 6.2 to calculate the standard error of proportions.

With 65 percent of your 500 sampled customers awarding an *extremely satisfied* rating to your organization and a standard error of the proportion of 2.13, you'd report to management that at the 95 percent confidence level, 60.7 percent to 69.3 percent of all of your customers are extremely satisfied. Or you could report extreme satisfaction at 65 percent ± 4.3 percent.

A Simplified Reporting Process

You can adopt a reporting convention that simplifies your reporting of results. Simply average all your measured ratings, determine an average standard error, and footnote your table with the note "Averages reported here are subject to a confidence interval of ± *x*." That way you've addressed the issue of generalizability without overly complicating your reporting of each individual mean or proportion.

How to Handle Missing Data

As you collect your data, especially self-administered data, your first heart-break will be to observe that not all of your customers have answered every one of your questions! Either a customer has inadvertently skipped over a question, or he didn't easily understand the question (and left it unanswered), or she just plain refused to give you input on a particular issue. Data analysis programs that you'll use to calculate your descriptive statistics, and other results as well, will incorporate certain methods for coping with missing data. Here are the three most common:

- Deleting customers whose records contain incomplete data

- Inserting in the missing cell your *sample's average* for that question or issue

- Inserting in the missing cell the *customer's average* for all questions he or she has answered

The first method has the greatest impact. You can start with 500 returned questionnaires and yet have an in-tab sample of only 350 if every customer who has failed to answer any question is deleted from the analysis.

The author prefers the third method: filling in missing data with a customer's average response for all other questions (scored in the same manner). This at least preserves the "level" of the customer's responses. If you elect this procedure, you may have to preprocess your data yourself, because not all statistical packages support it. (If you preprocess your data, either institute a flag column for each question—to allow you to flag those responses you've filled in—or be certain to keep a pristine copy of your original data. You may ultimately wish to analyze your raw or unmanipulated data by another method.)

 Checkpoint 6.3

1. To strengthen your analysis, establish some of your questions as *overall criteria variables* and others, your more specific questions, as *performance variables*. Use your criteria variables to track your overall, global satisfaction. The performance variables will help you track changes in satisfaction to particular activities or functions within your organization.

2. As you interpret and track your customers' satisfaction, three basic statistical concepts allow you to make inferences from your results:

   - The size of your sample

   - What range of error you are willing to tolerate about your sample's results

   - The level of statistical significance you or your management requires of your findings

   These concepts help you report your results.

3. You will need to adopt a method to deal with missing data; not all of your customers will completely answer your questionnaire. The author recommends filling in missing data with the average of each particular customer's responses.

REPORTING YOUR ORGANIZATION'S PERFORMANCE

There is another use for the statistical principles described above: the need to answer questions such as "How much has the organization's performance *changed* since previous measurement periods?" That sort of question is all about comparison. And comparing two outcomes from survey research requires that you determine if the change or difference between the two scores is statistically significant. That is, could it be an anticipatable "wobble" not signifying any real change, or is it sufficiently large to indicate a real change or difference?

STEP 6.4 THE INTERNAL ANALYSIS PERSPECTIVE

With the understanding of how to most accurately report your survey results (discussed in Step 6.3), you're ready to consider your organization's comparative strengths and weaknesses. Such questions take the position of an *internal interpretation*. As such, they are *relative:* you will identify strengths and weaknesses, but only—at this stage—from an internal perspective. Your internally identified strengths could very well turn out to be weaknesses within your category or industry.

Highest, Lowest

Regarding both your criteria variables and your performance variables, consider rank-ordering them on their average (or top-box) scores from the ones customers say you're doing best on to the ones that need greatest improvement. In chapter 7 we'll illustrate some graphical ways of communicating this information, but you'll want to examine it in tabular form first. (See Table 6.5.)

Now, with your variables rank-ordered, you'll want to ask yourself the following questions:

1. Looking at the better-rated variables, how "good" are their ratings?

2. Are the performance issues we are rated best on the most important ones?

3. Which of the lower-rated performance issues should we select for immediate improvement? (In chapter 7 we'll discuss importance-performance charts, or quadrant charts as they are frequently called. These charts graphically identify those performance issues that deserve the most immediate attention.)

Table 6.5   Ranking performance variables by your current performance (ranked by mean scores).

Performance variable	Mean	Top box (%)
Product durability	7.6	36
Product functionality	7.5	31
Product reliability	7.5	33
Documentation	7.4	36
Conformance to specs	7.4	28
Features offered	7.3	39
Product serviceability	7.2	35
Delivery	7.9	41
Servicing	7.1	25
Installation	7.6	37
Value for price	7.7	40
Qualification	7.4	41

You can make your ranked listing more managerially useful by inserting a column for the importance ratings of your performance issues, but you'll have to create a way to calculate their importance weights. (See the section on advanced analysis in this chapter for a description of several possible methods for determining the importance of performance issues.)

Performance against Goals

Having established your strengths and weaknesses, one of the more obvious next steps is to examine how your organization's current performance shapes up against goals that may have been set, either by the operational areas themselves or by your overall management team. You can calculate the gap (positive or negative) between current performance and these established goals. (We'll call these gaps *goal gaps*.) Once you calculate these gaps, you should determine which are statistically meaningful and disregard the remainder. You can then rank-order your performance variables according to the size of their goal gaps from largest negative (most in need of improvement) to largest positive. In Table 6.6 the performance variables at the top of the ranking deserve the most immediate attention.

The trouble with ranking performance variables by the extent to which they satisfy goals is that a comparison with goals alone disregards the underlying importance of the variables to your customers. And, as is all too common, we very often do best on those actions that aren't that terribly important for our customers, while we tend to perform less well on the more important issues.

Table 6.6 Performance against goals (ranked by gap).

Performance variables	Mean	Goal	Difference— gap
Servicing	7.1	7.6	−0.5
Product serviceability	7.2	7.6	−0.4
Features offered	7.3	7.6	−0.3
Conformance to specs	7.4	7.6	−0.2
Qualification	7.4	7.6	−0.2
Documentation	7.4	7.6	−0.2
Product reliability	7.5	7.6	−0.1
Product functionality	7.5	7.6	−0.1
Product durability	7.6	7.6	0.0
Installation	7.6	7.6	0.0
Value for the price	7.7	7.6	0.1
Delivery	7.9	7.6	0.3

Performance against Previous Performance

Another way of assigning meaning to your current performance levels is to examine them in the context of your organization's previous performance on the very same issues. You will need to both calculate a movement, or *change score,* for each of your current performance ratings and test each to see if the observed change is statistically significant. If a change is not statistically significant you should probably not show it in a table since it is only an expected variation within the confidence interval you expect associated with your mean. Reporting such insignificant changes can't help but draw your organization's attention to them even though they are not indicative of real changes. You can ultimately add those changes (which are statistically meaningful) into your rank-ordered listing of performance variables. Then a performance variable that has been rated toward the top of your list, *and* has increased substantially from your previous measurements, can truly be counted as a current strength. On the other hand, a performance variable that is at the top of your list (ranked by current ratings) but that has slipped from a previous measurement period shows an area of needed focus. See Table 6.7.

Testing for Significance of Differences

When you need to evaluate two ratings to see if you can consider them truly different you'll use *tests of statistical significance.* Two different tests are available depending on the type of rating you're using: a mean or a proportion. For continuous variables on which it is appropriate to calculate a

Table 6.7 Performance against previous performance (ranked by gap).

Performance variables	Year 2001	Year 2000	Difference—gap
Product functionality	7.5	8.3	−0.8
Qualification	7.4	7.9	−0.4
Value for the price	7.7	7.5	0.2
Installation	7.6	8.0	−0.3
Servicing	7.1	7.2	−0.1
Delivery	7.9	7.0	0.9
Features offered	7.3	7.9	−0.6
Product durability	7.6	8.1	−0.4
Product reliability	7.5	7.2	0.3
Product serviceability	7.2	6.7	0.5
Documentation	7.4	6.5	0.9
Conformance to specs	7.4	6.4	1.0

mean, the *t-test* is the appropriate significance test to use to determine the similarity of or difference between two subsamples. For nominal or proportional data, a test of the *difference of proportions* is required. These tests can be performed almost routinely within numerous statistical analysis packages. They are programmed on the accompanying CD-ROM and are discussed further in Step 6.6 as well as in this chapter's Toolkit.

 Checkpoint 6.4

1. On your first pass through your results, you'll want to examine them from an *internal* perspective. This process will allow you to report each rating with some confidence interval attached to it and then to examine and interpret change from previous measures. Prepare a table of your results with their associated confidence intervals.

2. Internal analysis means comparing your present satisfaction results to some goal or benchmark. Two common internal goals are goals assigned by management and previous performance. What internal benchmark do you plan to use?

3. Compare the current performance of each of your criteria variables against your goals. By identifying gaps (the negative or positive difference between your performance and the goal) you'll be able to efficiently direct improvement efforts.

STEP 6.5 THE EXTERNAL ANALYSIS PERSPECTIVE

Once you have examined your results from an internal perspective, you will almost certainly be asked by your management to interpret them on an *absolute basis*. (You will be asked the proverbial question "How high is up?") Generally this means comparing your performance against outside organizations, an *external interpretation*. Your comparison can be against others in your category or industry (the best of class) or against organizations outside your industry that are acknowledged to be best in a particular activity (world-class performers).

Against Industry Benchmarks

The external benchmarks in which your management is likely to be interested first are the ratings given to others in your immediate industry, category, or ISO sector. Clearinghouses, such as www.CSM9000.com, exist to provide you with such norms. The benefit of this type of collection will be maximized if you adopt in your questionnaire as many of the clearinghouse's questions as possible. Then you will be able to compare your performance directly with other organizations' performances on exactly the same questions. Again, you should conduct this comparison by questioning whether the gaps, or differences, you observe (between your scores and the benchmarks) exceed what might statistically be expected at both the level of statistical significance and the tolerance level you have selected. If the observed gaps exceed such ranges, you may comfortably report your performance as *better* or *worse* than that of your benchmarks. You can use a format similar to that suggested for Table 6.6 to show your performance against norms.

 Checkpoint 6.5

1. Complementing internal analysis are procedures of external analysis. This means comparing your ratings to external benchmarks such as competitors' performance or industry norms.

2. Describe how you will conduct an external analysis. What benchmarks will you use?

STEP 6.6 TEST THE SIGNIFICANCE OF CHANGE SCORES, GOAL GAPS, AND COMPETITIVE GAPS

One of the harder chores of satisfaction measurement is to delineate those change scores or gaps that are truly changes (increases or decreases) from those that fail to exceed a confidence interval about the previous score or the goal or competitive performance. One of your greatest temptations will be to try to find change and differences. It's a matter of human nature. If we create a grand satisfaction measurement program, we feel more justified if we can show our program detects change or differences—even if the change or difference we identify isn't a certifiably statistically significant movement.

Your author has seen many programs tarnish their credibility by according importance to changes or gaps that are really just a matter of statistical wobble. When those same variables wobble the other way in the next measurement period, the satisfaction professional loses management's trust by apparently vacillating in findings or at worst contradicting his or her prior findings with the new results.

The best thing you can do is establish concrete rules about how much two numbers must differ before you describe the observed change or gap as a true increase or decrease, a real competitive strength or a weakness. In this section we'll discuss statistical significance testing, the way you can identify truly meaningful changes from changes that are mostly a function of statistical wobble.

Significance testing is made a bit more complex owing to the need to select a test procedure based on the type of summary statistic (mean, top box, etc.) you have adopted. There is a specific test to use if you are tracking performance using means, while your use of proportions requires you to use a related yet somewhat different test.

The Parameters of Significance Testing

We are now in a position to define two procedures for testing the statistical significance of differences. The procedures all use the concepts of sample size, confidence level, and tolerance for error we've previously reviewed (see chapter 2's Toolkit and Step 6.3 in this chapter). They differ only by the summary statistic being tested: a mean (an average satisfaction rating) or a proportion (a top-box score). You can find statistical packages that perform both tests for you. In addition, the CD-ROM accompanying this book contains an Excel spreadsheet version of each.

Significance Testing for Means

When your response scale is interval or ratio scaled, you have the right to calculate means as your measures of response. Let's say you've asked your customers to rate their overall satisfaction on a 0-to-10 scale. Now you wish to determine whether the satisfaction ratings from two subsamples (for example, customers of Factory A and customers of Factory B) are statistically different. In this case you'd use a *t-test*. Most statistical software offers a routine to calculate t-tests. It may be in a stand-alone t-test program, or you may be referred to a *one-way analysis of variance (ANOVA)*. To submit your data, you'll need a marker in your customers' data records to indicate to which group each of your customers belongs. Some software is very choosy about what characters you can use as group markers, so make sure you consult your software manual before taking the time to mark your customers' records. (Consult any basic statistics book for the formula for hand calculating a t-test.)

To determine the significance of a t-value you've calculated, you'll need to consult a table of t-values. Enter the table at the row representing the degrees of freedom in your analysis and the column representing the level of statistical significance you wish to use.[2] If your calculated t-score exceeds the value in the table, your groups are significantly different. (See the chapter Toolkit.) While it may be useful to know how to calculate a t-score, most software programs will not only calculate t-scores but will also interpret the statistical significance of the t-score for you.

The t-test is intended for pairs of means. When you have more than two subsamples whose differences you wish to test, a more effective test is the one-way ANOVA (analysis of variance). The ANOVA will first test if any pair (of all your pairs) of subsamples is significantly different. This will be indicated by a significant *F-test*. Then you may individually compare each pair of means using a t-test procedure to determine which pairs of means contributed to the significant F.[3]

Significance Testing for Proportions

Let's say your data show that your customers serviced by Factory A gave you a top-box score of 42 percent, while those customers serviced by

---

[2] "Degrees of freedom" are a representation of the complexity of your data. In the present case, your degrees of freedom may be calculated by adding the two sample sizes and subtracting 2: $(n_{Factory\ a} + n_{Factory\ B}) - 2$.

[3] The reader is referred to basic descriptive statistics books for this procedure. For example, see Bruning and Kintz, *Computational Handbook of Statistics*, Fourth ed. (1996) for the procedure.

Factory B gave you a top-box score of only 36 percent. Your need is to determine whether the proportions (42 percent and 36 percent) are significantly different or are differences you might expect to result simply from variations in sampling. The test for the significance of the difference of proportions will help you answer this question.

To test for the difference between two proportions requires that the difference be converted into a *Z-score*. Again, you will find statistical packages with a significance of the difference between proportions test. (A spreadsheet version is included on the accompanying CD-ROM.) The resulting Z-score is interpreted according to your need for statistical significance. If you've selected the 95 percent level of confidence, then you'll require a Z-score of 2 (actually 1.96) or higher to indicate that these proportions are truly different. A table of the *normal deviate* provides probability estimates for other Z-scores. This table can be found in any basic statistics text.

 Checkpoint 6.6

1. As you conduct your internal and external analyses, comparing your results to benchmarks, you will need to test the significance of the differences (either positive or negative) of your performance against the benchmarks. In this section we have described methods for testing the difference of means and the differences of proportions.

2. Create a process for checking the significance (trueness) of any differences you find between your results and the benchmarks you have chosen.

STEP 6.7 COMPOSITE SATISFACTION SCORES

It has become common in satisfaction measurement to build overarching scores that are either *composite satisfaction ratings* or *indices*. You'll want to consider the value such summary scores may offer you in your reporting process. You may find utility in adopting a composite satisfaction score to help report your findings. On the other hand, when a layperson hears "customer satisfaction," he or she almost invariably hears it in the context of a CSI report or rating. CSI, a *customer satisfaction index*, is another summary score you can use to report the overall level of your customers' satisfaction.

A Composite Satisfaction Score

Although you have probably asked your customers to rate your organization in terms of their overall satisfaction, you may still wish to calculate a composite satisfaction score. To calculate a composite score, simply average all the performance question averages you have calculated. The resulting number (the average of all averages) is your composite satisfaction score. Composite scores can be calculated at the total sample level or at the level of individual customers. At the customer level, the measure can be added as a new datum to each customer's data record. You'll have to create a storage place for the measure in your data record once you calculate it.

Some may suggest such a simple average would not do justice to all that you might know about your performance variables. Table 6.8 shows how an index of satisfaction might be calculated in several different ways. Column A is a simple average (composite satisfaction score) of the scores over 10 performance questions. But what if you've identified your customers' importance weights for each of your performance questions? You might wish to incorporate this importance information either at the level of

Table 6.8 Calculating different indices of satisfaction.

Questionnaire's performance questions	A	B	C	D	E
	Total sample			Customer 1	
	Ratings	Standardized weights	Index 2	Importance weights	Index 3
Product functionality	7.52	0.08	0.60	0.17	1.28
Features offered	7.34	0.08	0.59	0.03	0.22
Product reliability	7.48	0.08	0.61	0.13	0.97
Conformance to specs	7.39	0.08	0.59	0.06	0.44
Product durability	7.63	0.09	0.68	0.18	1.37
Product serviceability	7.24	0.07	0.52	0.02	0.14
Qualification	7.42	0.11	0.82	0.06	0.45
Value for price	7.72	0.09	0.72	0.16	1.24
Documentation	7.43	0.09	0.65	0.03	0.22
Servicing	7.07	0.07	0.52	0.01	0.07
Delivery	7.86	0.07	0.57	0.10	0.79
Installation	7.64	0.08	0.62	0.05	0.38

Satisfaction composite (unweighted) 7.4

Satisfaction index 2 (weighted—total sample weights) 7.5

Satisfaction index 3 (weighted— individual customer's weights) 7.6

your individual customers or on a total sample basis. Column C shows the composite score weighted by the population's importance weights, while column E shows the composite score weighted to each customer's importance weights (illustrated for customer 1).

Many practitioners point out that a composite measure will be more statistically reliable than any single measure. Hence, in trending, the composite measure may be a better choice.

Satisfaction Indices

The simplest approach to a customer satisfaction index is to add all the performance question ratings (on either a total sample or individual customer basis) and then divide (index to the base of) the total points possible in your questionnaire. Your customer satisfaction index will always take a value from 0 to 1.00 (or 0 to 100 percent). Often, especially in the automobile industry, the percent is reported simply as an integer number (95 percent becomes 95).

Other practitioners, such as the former Digital Equipment Corporation (now a part of Compaq), devised special weightings of their satisfaction distribution and referred to these weighted averages as a customer satisfaction index (Dandrade 1994). In particular, a formula was advocated that assigned different weights to the five response levels (very satisfied, satisfied, neither satisfied nor dissatisfied, dissatisfied, and very dissatisfied) on Digital's corporatewide satisfaction measure:

1. Add all of the percentages of responses reflecting satisfactory (very satisfied, satisfied, neither) ratings.

2. Subtract five times the *very dissatisfied* score.

3. Subtract two times the *dissatisfied* score.

This produces an index that can range from 100 to –500. The formula consciously overweighs dissatisfaction to focus business units on improvement.

Other organizations, such as Mercedes-Benz USA, have assigned weights to each of their performance questions with which to calculate an index as a *weighted average*. The weights in such an index may be analytically derived (to reflect the relative importance of each question) or may be assigned based on judgment or intuition (to focus improvement efforts on specific attributes).

A more ambitious customer satisfaction index is the multiple measure described by Kessler (1996). Touting the simplicity of one number as a score of overall business performance, Kessler suggests combining several diverse measures including customer satisfaction, supplier satisfaction, internal performance metrics, and market indicators (price advantage/ disadvantage, market share) into one weighted index or number. She shows the advantage of this in cross-competitor comparisons. This could be a valuable exercise, assuming you can gather all the competitive data necessary.

Trending the Index against Overall Satisfaction

Besides simply reporting and trending it, there are at least two analytical ways to use the composite satisfaction score or the customer satisfaction index, if you calculate one. The most common use is to longitudinally plot the scores or indices against your customers' overall satisfaction scores. The assumption is that the composite score describes how well your organization is doing, based on your *internal* definition of performance (represented by the battery of performance questions you've assembled in your questionnaire).

On the other hand, the explicit measure of overall satisfaction describes how *globally acceptable* your organization is considered by your customers. In Figure 6.3 the composite satisfaction trend line is climbing, indicating the organization is doing a good job on those things being specifically measured. Yet in the same time frame, the overall, explicit satisfaction measure is decreasing, showing customers' weakening satisfaction in a global sense. The paradox depicted in Figure 6.3 suggests several possible explanations. It may be the performance questions currently being measured:

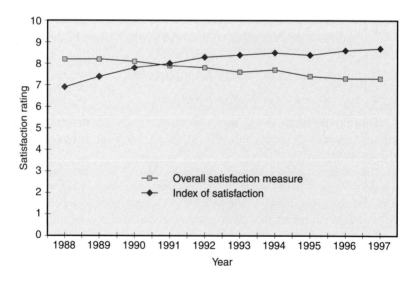

Figure 6.3 Trending overall and composite satisfaction.

- Include issues no longer relevant to the customerbase and therefore not totally correlated with customers' overall satisfaction

- Fail to include *new issues* that have recently become relevant to customers

- Identify issues that customers may be less willing to rate completely satisfactory for fear that high ratings might result in subsequent neglect

- Invite easier criticism for their specificity than the broader concept of overall satisfaction. There is often a bias toward offering more positive scores on broad, affective concepts such as overall satisfaction than on specific issues of conduct.

Consider another way of utilizing the information in these two measures. If you were to plot each customer's joint scores on a graph, you'd have a picture of how well the two measures agreed across all of the customers in your customerbase, as well as a valuable way of segmenting your customers. Look at Figure 6.4. Here 20 customers have been plotted according to both their overall satisfaction measure and their composite satisfaction score. A plurality of points lie on a regression line from lower left to upper right. For these customers, the two scores

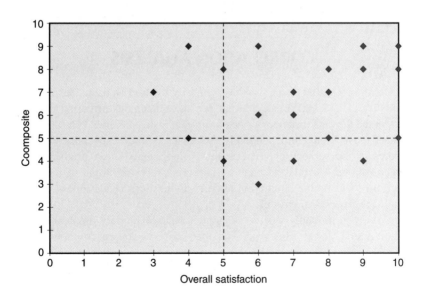

Figure 6.4 Plotting individual customer's scores.

are pretty much in sync. But now consider the customers whose scores don't agree. The customers in the upper left have higher composite scores than overall satisfaction scores. Those customers may be the first to recognize there are additional performance issues besides the ones you are currently measuring. They would be good customers for you to interview to attempt to understand what additional performance measures you should audit.

Customers in the lower right have higher overall satisfaction scores than their composite scores. Those customers may represent a loyal following (perhaps *advocates*) who despite their loyalty to your organization (and hence high overall satisfaction) are objective enough to recognize some opportunities for needed improvement on a performance issue by performance issue basis.

 Checkpoint 6.7

1. Composite satisfaction and satisfaction indices are concise ways of reporting results from your performance attributes. They are useful constructs you can use to learn more about your organization's satisfaction. Compare and trend these measures against your overall satisfaction question to help determine the ongoing comprehensiveness of your current performance questions.

CORRELATION ANALYSIS

Up to this point, the discussion has primarily focused on basic, descriptive statistics. However, consider what we have been investigating. We've examined the performance of one question or issue at a time. But rarely do issues move totally independently from one another, especially when it comes to the subjectivity of customers' judgments about products and organizations. Correlation analysis and cross-tabs (the topic of the next section) focus on the interaction of pairs of questions or variables—hence the label *bivariate* measures.

You will probably wish to calculate a Pearson product-moment correlation matrix[4] for all your data. This matrix shows you exactly how much

---

[4]As you may know, Pearson product-moment correlation coefficients take values from 0.0 to 1.0 (positive or negative). The larger the coefficient, the greater the association existing between the two variables.

each question you've asked is correlated with your other questions. The ideal though seldom attained result is:

- Little or no correlation existing among your performance variables—showing you have succeeded in measuring decidedly different aspects of your performance

- Considerable correlation between each of your performance questions and your overall, global measures (overall satisfaction, etc.). (The correlation between your global measures and your performance variables can be one way to identify which performance variables are your *key drivers*. We'll discuss this use of correlation coefficients shortly.)

Table 6.9 shows a correlation matrix rather typical of the type virtually all statistical packages (including many spreadsheet programs) will create. Because a correlation matrix is symmetric, you need only examine one-half of it. The diagonal (top left to bottom right) is populated by 1s, indicating the perfect correlation of each of your performance variables with themselves. Look at the half-matrix below this diagonal. Each row gives you the correlations of that row's performance variable with the variable defining each column of the correlation matrix. In Table 6.9, the 0.587 in the first column indicates a moderate correlation of the performance variable *functionality* with the criterion variable *overall satisfaction*.

INTRODUCTION TO CROSS-TABS

Cross-tabulation is the name given to two-way table analysis, when several two-way tables are combined in a single display table. Cross-tabs form the basis for rudimentary analysis in virtually all marketing research programs. In the ordering of cross-tabulations, we may be said to be using bivariate analysis, because we are examining the relationship existing between two variables at a time: the variable defining a group of column headings and the variable whose results are displayed in the rows of the table.

If you elect to use the support of a professional partner to help you conduct your survey, most likely their participation will include preparing cross-tab tables for you. If you conduct your own project, you'll need to know more about producing cross-tabs. Either way, you have some important decisions to make in order to have the most meaningful data display tables for your use. This chapter's Toolkit describes more completely the mechanics of cross-tabs. Table 6.10 shows a typical cross-tab table reporting some of our test data.

Table 6.9   A correlation matrix.*

	OSAT	VALUEPR	FUNCTION	FEATURES	RELIABL	CONFORM	DURABL	SERVICBL	DOCUMT	DELIVER	INSTALL	QUAL	OSERVE
OSAT	1												
VALUEPR	0.685	1											
FUNCTION	0.587	0.336	1										
FEATURES	0.587	0.597	0.363	1									
RELIABL	0.600	0.452	0.304	0.399	1								
CONFORM	0.589	0.399	0.249	0.393	0.495	1							
DURABL	0.651	0.486	0.386	0.356	0.548	0.405	1						
SERVICBL	0.533	0.510	0.373	0.398	0.489	0.423	0.398	1					
DOCUMT	0.646	0.435	0.418	0.513	0.391	0.388	0.434	0.319	1				
DELIVER	0.530	0.299	0.297	0.384	0.237	0.446	0.341	0.158	0.420	1			
INSTALL	0.594	0.416	0.435	0.558	0.339	0.366	0.358	0.418	0.498	0.377	1		
QUAL	0.815	0.624	0.463	0.578	0.629	0.602	0.613	0.551	0.529	0.514	0.497	1	
OSERVE	0.539	0.293	0.430	0.311	0.268	0.373	0.266	0.273	0.347	0.287	0.433	0.395	1

Table 6.10 A sample cross-tab table.

Hardware manufacturers study

Question 8: Please rate your satisfaction with the functionality of our products.

	Overall Satisfaction			Region			Sales level	
	TOTAL SAMPLE	Top-two boxes	Bottom-five boxes	East	South	West	Top 20%	Remaining 80%
	(A)	(B)	(C)	(D)	(E)	(F)	(G)	(H)
Total	100	35	12	35	27	38	20	80
sample	100.0	100.0	100.0	100.0	100.0	100.0	100.0	100.0
	100.0	35.0	12.0	35.0	27.0	38.0	20.0	80.0
No	3	1	1	3	–	–	1	2
experience	3.0%	2.9%	8.3%	8.6%			5.0%	2.5%
	100.0%	33.3%	33.3%	100.0%			33.3%	66.7%
Responding	97	34	11	32	27	38	19	78
sample	100.0%	100.0%	100.0%	100.0%	100.0%	100.0%	100.0%	100.0%
	100.0%	35.1%	11.3%	33.0%	27.8%	39.2%	19.6%	80.4%
10—completely	23	14	–	9	6	8	5	18
satisfied	23.7%	41.2%		28.1%	22.2%	21.1%	26.3%	23.1%
	100.0%	60.9%		39.1%	26.1%	34.8%	21.7%	78.3%
9	18	11	–	3	6	9	3	15
	18.6%	32.4%		9.4%	22.2%	23.7%	15.8%	19.2%
	100.0%	61.1%		16.7%	33.3%	50.0%	16.7%	83.3%
Net top-two	41	25	–	12	12	17	8	33
box (9, 10)	42.3%	73.5%		37.5%	44.4%	44.7%	42.1%	42.3%
	100.0%	61.0%		29.3%	29.3%	41.5%	19.5%	80.5%
8	18	–	1	5	6	7	4	14
	18.6%		9.1%	15.6%	22.2%	18.4%	21.1%	17.9%
	100.0%		5.6%	27.8%	33.3%	38.9%	22.2%	77.8%
7	7	3	–	3	2	2	1	6
	7.2%	8.8%		9.4%	7.4%	5.3%	5.3%	7.7%
	100.0%	42.9%		42.9%	28.6%	28.6%	14.3%	85.7%
6	11	5	1	5	2	4	2	9
	11.3%	14.7%	9.1%	15.6%	7.4%	10.5%	10.5%	11.5%
	100.0%	45.5%	9.1%	45.5%	18.2%	36.4%	18.2%	81.8%
5	6	1	3	3	–	3	–	6
	6.2%	2.9%	27.3%	9.4%		7.9%		7.7%
	100.0%	16.7%	50.0%	50.0%		50.0%		100.0%
4	9	–	4	2	2	5	2	7
	9.3%		36.4%	6.2%	7.4%	13.2%	10.5%	9.0%
	100.0%		44.4%	22.2%	22.2%	55.6%	22.2%	77.8%
3	3	–	1	1	2	–	1	2
	3.1%		9.1%	3.1%	7.4%		5.3%	2.6%
	100.0%		33.3%	33.3%	66.7%		33.3%	66.7%
2	1	–	1	1	–	–	–	1
	1.0%		9.1%	3.1%				1.3%
	100.0%		100.0%	100.0%				100.0%
1	1	–	–	–	1	–	1	–
	1.0				3.7%		5.3%	
	100.0%				100.0%		100.0%	
0—completely dissatisfied	–	–	–	–	–	–	–	–
MEAN	7.52	8.68 C	4.55	7.38	7.52	7.63	7.37	7.55

ADVANCED NUMERICAL DATA ANALYSIS

Univariate and bivariate analytical procedures (the tools described up to now) are absolutely fine for studying performance in a very simplistic, straightforward manner. And these are the predominant tools used in most customer satisfaction measurement processes. But satisfaction data are actually much more complex, and there are statistical tools that offer a full understanding of the relationships embedded in your customers' data.

Multivariate analysis is thus named because techniques subsumed under that classification are capable of handling more than two variables at a time. While such techniques are largely beyond the scope of this book, you are invited to review several of the sources listed in Appendix C, including the author's advanced book.[5] Multivariate techniques can provide answers to some important questions. A few are outlined here.

- What is the true structure of your data? *Factor analysis* can help you understand exactly how your customers look at your product or service. It will define the evaluative dimensions your customers use as they react to your organization's products and performance.

- Not all of your performance questions are equally important. By finding how they affect your customers' overall satisfaction with your organization, you'll be able to weight your perform-ance questions according to how they affect your overall performance. With multiple issues to be improved, knowing the relative importance of each helps you prioritize your organiza-tion's improvement efforts. You'll necessarily want to focus on the more important issues first. The more important variables are, by convention, called key drivers, critical performance indicators (CPIs), drivers of delight, and so on. Multivariate techniques are one approach to determining the importance weights for your performance questions.

- *Structural equation modeling* is another multivariate technique that promises help in creating a model of how your customers evaluate you and then carry through with their evaluations (possibly in terms of purchases).

---

[5]Vavra, *Improving Your Measurement of Customer Satisfaction* (1997).

STEP 6.8 TYPES OF ANALYSES FOR VERBAL DATA

While many overlook the notion of analyzing verbal data, a relatively rich array of techniques allow you to mine information from your customers' verbatim responses. Those techniques include the following:

- *Coding open-ended responses* to quantify what customers are telling you in their verbatim responses (covered in chapter 5, Step 5.8).

- *Sorting open-ended responses* according to a classification variable (*extremely satisfied customers* versus *extremely dissatisfied customers*, etc.).

- Searching your customers' responses *for the occurrence of particular words* or phrases representing particular issues (on-time delivery, meeting conformance specs, etc.). By convention we call such search phrases *keywords*, and occasionally we'll see the acronym *KWIC*, which stands for <u>k</u>ey<u>w</u>ord <u>i</u>n <u>c</u>ontext. This implies that a count of the occurrence of keywords is good, but seeing the keyword in the context in which your customer used it is even better.

Coding is almost always performed to help quantify the nature of information conveyed through open-ended responses. Less used, though no less valuable, are the actions of sorting responses and searching for keywords.

Sorting Open-Ended Responses

Reading through a list of customers' open-ended responses can be very enlightening, but it will generally raise additional questions, such as "I wonder which kind of our customers said that!" or "I wish I knew which of our products she was talking about!" When we use a secondary piece of information to allow us to sort the open-ended responses to a question, considerable value is added to the listing. So you can use one of your classification variables to organize the open-ended responses of your customers. In this way, answers to the question "What did you like most about our product?" can be displayed by the type of product your customers purchase, by your customers' level of overall satisfaction, or by your factory or sales office servicing them. While you and your colleagues will still need to mentally summarize the many different perspectives of your customers, you'll have wonderful lists of issues important to the groups you've surveyed by which to sort your verbatims.

Keyword Searching

Keywords are hot buttons that either mean something special to you or have been volunteered in an unusually frequent way. To conduct a KWIC search you will need to identify those words you consider key. Do that in one of two ways:

- Use your existing insight or intuition

- Examine customers' open-ended responses, looking for words, terms, or phrases that appear an unusually frequent number of times

Once you identify those words you wish to designate as key, you can use a computer routine to find them for you. It's most helpful if your routine lists the sentence or entire response containing your key word. See Table 6.11 for an example.

Table 6.11   A sample keyword in context search.

Search for keyword = "dealership"

VIN Owner ID	Motor car/comments	Dealer number
SCBZF27C6WCH12345 ID: 6632	**1998 Bentley Brooklands R Mulliner** Friendliness and approachability. I am pleased to say the new ownership of the **dealership** quite understands Rolls-Royce/Bentley owners and their requirements.	Dealer: 0305
SCDZE12F8RDW12345 ID: 3345	**1996 Bentley Brooklands** I am glad to complete this survey, as it is possible that this **dealership** saved me from great inconvenience. Yours and their programme of checking customers' vehicles discovered a worn tyre, of which I wasn't aware. They are very, very good!	Dealer: 1111
SCBZQ15C4VCJ12345 ID: 10987	**1997 Bentley Turbo R LWB** They are only five minutes from my home, therefore very convenient. I also have other cars from the **dealership** and they have generated a very good customer-client relationship.	Dealer: 2233
SCCZE13C9TCH12345 ID: 9776	**1999 Bentley Arnage** Excellent car company and **dealership**. Please let me know when the new models have been announced.	Dealer: 3355
SCDZB23C2WGH62345 ID: 12995	**1998 Bentley Continental R** I am pleased to know you now have a **dealership** in West of Scotland. I would like to know what the future is for Rolls-Royce/Bentley.	Dealer: 8888

Checkpoint 6.8

1. The verbatim (open-ended) responses you collect from your customers contain some of the richest information you can interpret. But in its raw form it's not nearly as valuable as when you process it. Using the tools described in this step, describe the open-ended processing plan you intend to use.

2. How will you establish response codes for your open-ended questions?

3. Do you envision sorting your open-ends by any classification variables? If so, outline your plans here.

Step-by-Step: The Answers for Analyzing Your Data

6.1 Add value to your analysis by marking some of your more important questions (likely your criteria questions) as *classification questions* for use in organizing and structuring some of your analyses. Then, the remainder of your questions become *response questions*. You will gain insight by examining the results of your response questions by the groupings established by your classification questions. In general, your report tables will use your classification questions to define their columns. See pages 169–72.

6.2 To succinctly report your satisfaction results, you need to select a *summary measure* to use as your main reporting statistic. This summary measure can be a measure of central tendency such as the mean or a measure of dispersion such as a top-box score. Whichever you select, you must introduce this measure to your management and train them to expect to see all your results reported in this way. See pages 172–77.

6.3 Remember that any rating from your sample is a *sample statistic*. It is subject to the whims of statistical variability; ask a different 100 customers and you could receive a different answer! You'll need to

(continued)

establish some statistical parameters of your data to help you accurately report your results. These include the *size of your sample*, your *tolerance for error* (willingness to accept a wide or narrow range of possible outcomes about your sample's answer), and the *level of statistical significance* at which you want to report your findings. These three parameters, along with your estimate of your data's *standard error*, become key to interpreting and reporting your summary statistics (be they means or top-box scores). You may wish to institute a process of reporting your results with the notation "Averages reported here are subject to a confidence interval of ±.xx." The confidence interval is particularly important when you compare numbers looking for change or difference. See pages 189–91.

6.4 In reporting your organization's performance, you'll want to examine results from an internal perspective and an external perspective. Internally, you'll compare your present survey results with any results from the past, and with any satisfaction goals your management may have established (either formally or informally). Externally, you'll want to compare your performance with competitors' satisfaction levels or with norms for your industry. See pages 184–87.

6.5 An external analysis is concerned with your customers' satisfactions compared with the similar performance of your competitors. While your internal analysis gives you a relative perspective within your own organization, external ratings are more of an absolute, showing you just how high (or low) ratings can go. See page 188.

6.6 In any comparisons you make, be certain the differences you report are validated by statistical significance. Avoid the temptation of discussing directional changes (increases or decreases) that fall short of the magnitude needed to statistically qualify them as changes. If you don't, you may find yourself discussing a decrease in satisfaction from one wave of your survey and an increase from the next—in the absence of any real change in operating practices. In such a situation, you'll lose credibility for your program very quickly. See pages 189–91.

6.7 Satisfaction indices are frequently spoken about. We've identified several methods for composing indices, either without or with question-by-question weights. The weights may be judgmentally or analytically determined. See pages 191–96.

6.8 To economically report the information conveyed by your customers in their answers to any open-ended questions you may ask, you'll need to assign tallyable response codes. Finally, don't overlook the value of more creatively processing your customers' open-ended responses. We've discussed sorting open-ended responses by industographics or categories of your classification variables (such as *extremely satisfied* and *extremely dissatisfied*). You can also search open-ended responses for the occurrence of keywords you specify (KWIC). See pages 201–3.

 Chapter 6 Deliverables

As a result of your work in this chapter, you'll have completed the following:

1. ISO document #4—a description of who will analyze your data. This description also needs to contain an analytical plan. A summary of your checkpoint responses for this chapter should suffice.

2. Your performance questions listed according to how well your organization is currently performing, from best to worst.

3. Comparisons of your customers' evaluations of your performance with your previous performance as well as your industry's norms.

4. The importance of each of your performance questions in creating delight—their so-called key driver scores.

(continued)

5. A correlation matrix examining how closely your performance questions are related to your criteria measures
   (overall satisfaction, etc.) and among themselves.

6. If you desire, cross-tabulation tables showing responses to
   each of the questions in your survey displayed by some of
   your questions you've selected as *classification questions*.

7. Tables displaying selected responses to your open-ended
   questions organized either by some industographic characteristic of your customers, by ratings on one or more of
   your independent questions, or containing words or terms
   you've selected as keywords.

TOOLKIT: CREATING A
CROSS-TABULATION OF YOUR RESULTS

The Method

Cross-tabulations (cross-tabs) are one of the basic tools of conventional
marketing research. While they may at first glance appear perplexing
(refer back to Table 6.10), they are really a rather common-sense cross-
categorization of data. They are not an analytical technique per se—they
merely display the data. Some users would claim they can test various
hypotheses based on the way they structure and produce cross-tabs, looking
for larger cell frequencies where issues or questions intersect. In this sense,
cross-tabs provide a very useful overview of one's survey results.

The portion of a cross-tab shown in Figure 6.5b simply depicts
responses to one question—overall satisfaction—by responses to the classificatory question of location (West Coast and East Coast). The cross-tab
table is merely a series of two-way data display tables linked by the column
questions and headings (referred to as the *banner*) tabulating the results of
the same row-wise question—in this case overall satisfaction. (The row
labels are generally referred to as *stubs*.)

Traditional statistical software packages (SPSS, SAS, SYSTAT) have
not produced banner cross-tab tables, further mystifying the technique.
While each of these packages has a tables or cross-tab routine, generally
that allows producing only two-way tables (two variables cross-related) or
three-way tables (two variables cross-related, for every value of a third
variable). The beauty of the *marketing research cross-tab* is that answers

to one survey question may be examined by many different other variables—all on the same table! Because the statistical packages lack such routines, you'll have to buy a special cross-tab program or use a computer tab house that can produce (among other analyses) cross-tab displays of your survey data.

Once a cross-tab table is recognized for exactly what it is, it can be parsed into a series of row-column intersections, or *cells*. These cells comprise the entire table. Generally, the column variables are instituted to represent characteristics of your customerbase: *West Coast customers* versus *East Coast customers*, or *High-value customers* versus *Low value customers*, and so on. As such, the columns represent classification variables, while the row variables represent response variables or outcomes. Of course the variables chosen for columns may have only one value or they may have multiple subvalues. Gender as a column variable would have only two values (*male, female*), while SIC codes could have an indefinite number of subvalues. The only limitation to the banner points is the number of columns that can be calculated and displayed on one page.

Most cross-tab programs limit the total number of columns in a banner to 21 or 22. Recognizing that at least one column must be reserved for *Total sample*, the satisfaction professional has approximately 20 columns across which to allocate classificatory variables. Of course, numerous cross-tabs can be run, but the reader is urged to limit himself or herself in the number of cross-tab banners ordered. The analyst's burden of comprehending the results increases geometrically with additional cross-tab banners. There simply becomes too much data to humanly digest or synthesize!

The Format

A universal standard applies to how data are displayed in the cells of a cross-tab table. A cell can contain up to four numbers, but frequently only the first three (from top down) are shown. The order and identity of these cell entries are depicted in Figure 6.5a. The topmost number in the cell should always be a whole number. This number represents the *frequency count* of those customers who fall into the cell demarcated by the banner column and the stub row. Referring to the outlined cell in Figure 6.5b, it can be seen that 15 of the 120 customers interviewed were from the West Coast and gave a satisfaction score of 9 on an 11-point scale.

The second number in the cell, usually containing a decimal value, is the *column percent* number. It is the proportion of those customers represented by the column ("West Coast") who have responded (or can be identified) with the stub row value. Think of this percentage as an *incidence*,

	Total customers	Customer's location	
		West Coast	East Coast
Total sample	140	80	60
No response	20	10	10
Total answering	120	70	50
Completely satisfied (10)	**45**	**30**	**15**
	37.50%	*42.90%*	*30.00%*
	100.00%	*66.60%*	*33.30%*
		25.00%	*12.50%*
(9)	**35**	**15**	**20**
	29.20%	*21.40%*	*40.00%*
	100.00%	*42.90%*	*33.30%*
		12.50%	*16.60%*
(8)	**25**	**10**	**15**
	20.80%	*14.90%*	*30.00%*
	100.00%	*40.00%*	*60.00%*
		8.30%	*12.50%*
(7)	**15**	**5**	**10**
	12.50%	*7.10%*	*20.00%*
	100.00%	*33.30%*	*66.60%*
		4.20%	*8.30%*

Frequency count
Column percent
Row percent
Table percent

Figure 6.5a
Cell identity.

Figure 6.5b   Sample cross-tabulation table.

that is, the proportion of the column's customers who are represented by the row stub response. In Figure 6.5b, 21.4 percent of the West Coast customers gave a satisfaction rating of 9. The third number, also a decimal value, is the *row percent* number. This number can be thought of as representing *composition*—that is, for all customers offering the row answer (a rating of 9), what proportion are represented by the column characteristic? In Figure 6.5b, the row percentage is 42.9 percent in the outlined cell. That means of all customers replying that a rating of 9 represented their satisfaction with the organization, 42.9 percent came from the West Coast. (Note if 70 of 120 reporting customers were from the West Coast, we'd expect $^{70}/_{120}$ of all 9-rating customers to be from the West Coast. How does the 42.9 percent compare with that expectation? Are there more or less "somewhat satisfied" customers from the West Coast than you'd expected?)

If there is a fourth cell entry, that will be the *table percent* number. It displays the proportion of the total sample who are both stub and banner *qualified*. The table percent number can frequently help you make a point about the incidence or penetration of a particular set of conditions (the stub and banner characteristics). In Figure 6.5b, in the outlined cell the table percent is 12.5 percent. That means of all reporting customers, 12.5 percent were from the West Coast *and* gave the organization a satisfaction rating of 9.

Ordering a Cross-Tab

To produce a cross-tab report, you'll need to go through five steps:

1. Identify the questions to be used in the banner (column headings) and the appropriate way to divide responses to any continuous variable to be so used.

2. Run frequency counts on all questions with continuous responses to identify appropriate categories for the stubs (row titles).

3. Determine how to deal with missing data—overall and for specific questions/tables.

4. Specify which individual tables in the cross-tabs would benefit from filtering. (Most tables will be reported for the total sample. But for some tables reporting questions that are conditional, you may wish to filter the customers being tabulated to only those customers who qualify on the condition, that is, "have multiple insurance policies," "eat out 2+ times per week," etc.).

5. Specify the overall appearance desired for each cross-tabulation page.

Which Variables to Select for the Banner?

We've identified the banner variables as classificatory or criteria variables. They need not be restricted to demographics. Often the greatest utility comes from cross-tabs where the banner variables are analytical. For example, one of the overriding questions of any satisfaction survey is "What distinguishes the satisfied from the dissatisfied customers?" So why not institute two columns in your banner for exactly that: *Satisfied customers* versus *Dissatisfied customers* using your overall satisfaction as a *classification variable*. Notice that these two categories needn't be all-inclusive of responses to your overall satisfaction question. For example, the *Satisfied customers* banner column could be defined as "top-box" customers (those giving an overall satisfaction rating of 10, 9, or 8) while the *Dissatisfied customers* could be represented by those giving a particularly low satisfaction rating or bottom box (say an overall satisfaction rating of 4 or less). The banner points described in this way will ignore customers who awarded your product a satisfaction rating between 7 and 5, but that's okay. The banner subpoints have been chosen to tease out the most information from the stubs by choosing extreme categories—*very satisfied* and *very dissatisfied*.

Dividing Continuous Variables

Not all of your variables (for your banner or your stubs) will yield discrete categories such as *East Coast* versus *West Coast*. The above example of dividing overall satisfaction ratings into two groups—satisfied and dissatisfied—shows how you will need to specify categories for those variables with continuous responses. For example, customers arrayed by their *Total purchases* or *Production volume* would both require categorization to make reporting them useful. The satisfaction professional will arrive at appropriate categories by ordering a frequency count run and then examining the results to identify meaningful points of division for the continuous variable.

Handling Missing Data

No matter how hard your interviewers try to get answers from every customer or how committed your customers are to providing you with complete information in a self-administered survey, you will still have questions with missing data from some respondents. Missing data on cross-tabs is best handled by instituting a row showing the frequency of *no answer* for each question. Then the remainder of the table can be based on those who responded. This is appropriate for most cases except where a no answer is actually meaningful. For example, the number of customers who cannot specify the percent of their category requirements they allocate to you may be a useful response and should be included in the distribution of answers. On the other hand, those customers for whom you lack an SIC code may not be relevant, since that is simply missing information with no informational value of its own.

Filtering

There are certain cross-tab tables whose value may be enhanced by examining them for levels of a third variable. (Remember, a cross-tab table essentially shows the association between two variables: the column variable and the row variable.) What if your column headings include High-value customers/Low-value customers and East Coast customers/West Coast customers, but you'd like to examine the results of a particular question by High-value customers in the East Coast. An economical way of doing this (without using a "nested" banner of value within location) would be to filter one or more tables by *West Coast* versus *East Coast*. For the tables you filter in this way, you'll have a distribution of stub answers by value within location.

Appearance of Your Cross-Tab Tables

Generally, far less attention is spent considering how the cross-tab tables will look than is warranted. This is probably because satisfaction professionals focus on selecting the banner variables but then delegate the format to the cross-tab house or computer programmer. This is generally a bad decision. The order of variables along the banner is very important, determining how easy it will be to use them. In addition, the information contained on each page can help or hinder the page's utility. It's best to draw how you'd like the banner to look, as well as to specify all the information you'd like included in the table.

Statistical Tests

Many cross-tab programs provide significance testing of means within their list of options. You'll need to decide for which pairing of column means significance tests are useful. When you specify those columns, the program will compute a t-test for the column means and interpret the t-score's significance for you. In Figure 6.10, the sets of columns headed "overall satisfaction" and "sales level" have been subjected to t-tests. The "C" below the mean of 8.68 in the top-two box column indicates that this rating mean is significantly greater than the accompanying mean of 4.55 for bottom-five box customers at the 95 percent level of confidence.

Pivot Tables

Even without the special software necessary to create marketing research, multi-column cross-tabs, you can create portions of a cross-tab table using the *Pivot Table* function in Excel. Refer to Table 6.10 in the CD-ROM for a demonstration.

IV.

Discourse

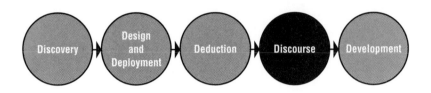

How Will You Report
Your Findings?

Conducting your survey is only part of the customer satisfaction measurement (CSM) process. No improvement will be forthcoming unless the many layers of your organization (executive, managerial, factory or platform, sales and service) hear about the knowledge you've gathered with your process. ANSI/ISO/ASQ Q9001-2000 makes action and communication an integral component of the monitoring process.

7

Reporting Your Results

The story of four blind men examining an elephant makes clear how easily reporting results can be incomplete or misleading and biased by personal perspective. Your challenge as you tabulate, interpret, and then prepare your results for dissemination is to communicate as accurate and as compelling a picture as possible. That isn't easy. We all bring our preconceived notions to any interpretation. Leaving your biases behind, your job is to ferret out the "stories" in your data and then create the most compelling graphics possible to communicate those findings. You will need every bit of graphical help you can get, because those to whom you'll be presenting your findings won't have nearly the same level of understanding as you. Your graphs will need to be both extremely inviting and also very easy to understand. With the insight you've gained about your organization's strengths and weaknesses, you must become an evangelist with the charge of making believers of all those to whom you present your information!

This chapter focuses on how to economically yet effectively discuss your survey results in a report. In chapter 6 we discussed how to appropriately analyze your data. But the tables and statistics you produced in that chapter, while essential for *your* understanding of the information, are hardly compelling calls to action. Your task now is to create a compelling description of your findings. That is the vehicle you can distribute to explain your gained insights and to stimulate improvement initiatives. This chapter also identifies the three most important satisfaction charts you can use to explain your findings.

Step-by-Step: The Issues of Reporting Your Results

7.1 Understand the basic principles of composing and writing effective reports.

7.2 Understand the basic principles of creating and presenting effective visuals.

7.3 Because not all of your performance questions are equally important, it's critical that you know how to derive their importance weights from your data. This is called implicit derivation of key drivers. Knowing the importance of your performance questions allows you to produce more meaningful graphs.

7.4 When you're not content deriving the importance of your questions statistically, you can go to your customers. This is called explicit determination of your key drivers.

7.5 Understand the unique role of each of five types of graphics for communicating a specific satisfaction outcome.

7.6 Learn the more important graphs for displaying your internal analyses.

7.7 Learn the more important graphs for displaying your external analyses.

7.8 Learn a graphics procedure to help promote and prioritize improving customer satisfaction.

STEP 7.1 BASICS OF WRITTEN REPORTS

The skill of writing a readable and usable satisfaction report is indeed precious. Most of us are not very comfortable with our skills as writers. As a result, we dread the thought of reaching the reporting stage. But lucid, effective writing is not an impossible goal. It is relatively easy to improve your writing skills, if not also your pleasure in writing. Here are five principles to consider as you prepare your written reports to make them more effective:

- *Completeness.* Your report will be complete when it provides all the information your readers need in a language they can understand.

- *Accuracy.* The need for accurate data input and analysis is absolute; fail in accuracy only once, and your future credibility may be lost forever. You'll want to carefully check all of your analyses.

- *Clarity.* Clarity is the result of clear and logical thinking and precision in the way you express yourself. By all means, avoid using jargon.

- *Conciseness.* While your report needs to be complete, avoid the temptation of excess; be selective. Tell your audience only that which is necessary for their understanding and action.

- *Organization.* Offer your readers plenty of signposts to help them follow your flow of thought and idea. Frequent headings, section summaries, and lists of implications—all of these writing conventions help ensure that a maximum amount of communication will occur.

Written communications are the final stage in most satisfaction projects. As such, they serve two purposes: to document your project's objectives and processes and to convey your key findings.

Written satisfaction reports can be subsumed under one of three different formats:

- A full-report format

- A memo-style report (an abbreviated version)

- A presentation deck

Each of these formats has its proponents, and one may be the preferred method of communication in your organization. Here is a brief discussion of each.

Full-Report Format

Full-report-format documents are very thorough discussions of your process, your findings, how you have analyzed your results, the significance of your findings, and a discussion of the implications as you see them. Typically, a full-report-format report will contain the following sections:

1. *Title page.*

2. *Executive summary/implications for satisfaction improvement.* This section, your implications section (prior to your discussion), should be the call to action to your organization. An executive reading this section should leave with a clear understanding of exactly what your organization needs to do to improve customer satisfaction. Ideally each plan or initiative should be allocated to a specific operating area or department. This section should also whet readers' appetites for consuming more of your report—this is your opportunity to hook your report's potential readers.

3. *Table of contents.* Organize your contents as logically and as simply as possible; make issues easy to find.

4. *Statement of objectives.* We've been very specific about stating what you intend to accomplish in your survey. Share those goals with readers of your report. In addition, help readers understand the limitations you accepted prior to fielding and analyzing your information.

5. *Key trends.* Your management will be keen on reviewing certain measures on a continuous basis. Obviously, overall satisfaction is one of those measures. But there will be others, idiosyncratic to each organization and industry. Make sure such measures are clearly displayed as trends with an appropriate narrative, discussing the ramifications of each depicted trend.

6. *Discussion of the findings.* Some readers of your report will wish to examine how you have arrived at your conclusions. For those readers, the detailed discussion section should provide a complete explanation of your analyses.

7. *Review of your methodology.* Don't fail to describe exactly which customers you've interviewed, how you selected them, when you interviewed them, and how you collected data from them. The more open your process, the more readily it will elicit trust. The better understood your process, the more likely you will be to receive constructive suggestions for improving it from one measurement wave to another.

8. *Specifics of your sample and fieldwork.* If only for your successors who may need to continue your work, provide a workmanlike description of what you did and how you did it.

9. *Appendix.* The appendix is a good place to locate all those things that might be questioned at some time or another but that would only encumber the more actionable sections of your report with superfluous detail.

Your full-report formatted report will likely have many tables displaying your summary data and will indicate where you have conducted tests of significance. You probably will include several visual exhibits: graphs or charts to illustrate key points. All in all, a full-report format provides complete documentation for your process and findings.

Memo-Style Report

A *memo-style report* is an attempt to make the full-report format a bit more palatable and perhaps more inviting to the time-starved managers in your organization. While you may devote a short paragraph to many of the sections included in the longer full-report format, your memo-style report will be the epitome of conciseness. Efficiency is your goal in this document. Tell your audience only that which is essential for them to know. Eliminate all the "frosting." These reports are often dubbed *top-line reports* because of their focus on only the most important issues. (*Top-line* can also imply that an additional, full-report communication will follow, so be careful in adopting this term.)

For this style report, you'll probably only have the following three sections:

1. Executive summary/implications for improvement

2. Key trends

3. Objectives/fieldwork summary

Presentation-Style Reports

More and more, corporate America is gravitating to visual presentations. These are usually created in a computer graphics program such as Freelance, PowerPoint, or Corel Draw. They consist more of "bullet-point statements" than full sentences. Visuals, graphs, charts, and flow diagrams are used to emphasize the key information. See Figure 7.1 for an example of how information can be consolidated into one slide.

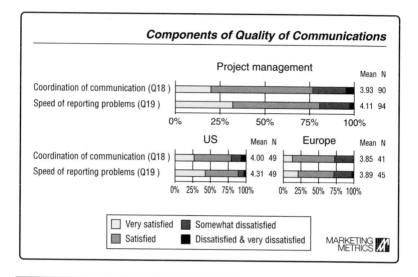

Figure 7.1 A sample presentation slide.

 Checkpoint 7.1

1. All satisfaction programs benefit from a written summary. Choose the report format you'll use from the three described in this chapter. What are your motives for this selection?

2. Your audience will benefit most if you place your findings up front in your report to highlight the discoveries of your program. Don't hide them behind tedious descriptions of your methodology and sample design.

3. What specific sections do you envision for your report?

STEP 7.2 BASICS OF VISUAL REPORTS

As you consider how you will visually display your survey's findings, keep in mind that several principles underlie the creation of effective satisfaction graphics. In general, you'll want to:

- Have a clear goal in mind for each visual

- Select the most appropriate graph for each visual goal

- Configure each graph in the most compelling way possible

We'll review these basics here, before going on.

Basic Chart Types

It's critical that you identify specifically *what* you want to communicate before you select a chart type. That's because certain charts are very effective for certain purposes, but no one chart is appropriate for all needs. Figure 7.2 establishes the four basic roles of a satisfaction visual: to show magnitude, growth or trends, composition, and order or flow. One or, at the most, two graph types best achieve each of these roles. It's critical to have a well-established communications goal for each visual before selecting a particular graph type; don't decide that pie charts look good and then force-fit all your data into the pie chart format.

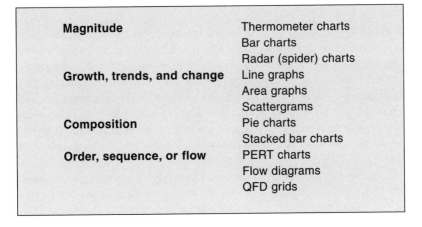

Magnitude	Thermometer charts
	Bar charts
	Radar (spider) charts
Growth, trends, and change	Line graphs
	Area graphs
	Scattergrams
Composition	Pie charts
	Stacked bar charts
Order, sequence, or flow	PERT charts
	Flow diagrams
	QFD grids

Figure 7.2   Goals for satisfaction visuals and the graph types associated with them.

Use of Color

Once you select a graph type, you face some additional decisions to help make your visual as understandable as possible. *Color* is one of the more important enhancements you can add, but it's most effective when used sparingly. If overused it can confuse or even blind a viewer to a graph's main point. A good rule of graphing is to use color sparingly and with total purpose in mind. Never use color simply because it's available!

The Inherent Communication Value of Colors

Color in a satisfaction graphic not only makes a chart more aesthetically attractive but also should uniquely convey some basic meaning. If one sees a bar chart containing both red and green bars, an immediate assumption would be that the green-colored bars represent some basically good outcomes while the red-colored bars convey bad outcomes or trouble areas. If there are more green bars than red, the viewer would most probably perceive an overall "positive situation"; if red bars outnumber the green, the same viewer would be alerted to a deteriorating situation. And all of this communication would occur simply on the basis of the astute use of two colors!

> Because of their inherent, almost universal meanings, watch your use of red and green and their partner color, orange. It is probably a good idea to not use these three colors to represent any particular customer group or performance question. Instead, reserve them to convey direction and severity of outcomes.

Linking Colors to Outcomes

If you assign a color or hue to a certain customer type or set of performance attributes in one chart, don't change your color assignments in later charts. Instead, maintain the same color representation throughout all your graphics. You'll find your management picks up on your color assignment convention quite easily and is then aided throughout the remainder of your report. (Amazingly, many reports are compiled with color graph after color graph in which colors seem to have been randomly assigned on a graph-by-graph basis with no rationale or established color key. In such cases, the chartist has failed to recognize the value of a uniform color key.)

Because many color graphs will ultimately be photocopied in black and white, it's very helpful if you assign a unique texture or shading pattern to each color as well. Then, as your color charts are black-and-white photocopied, the texture or shading pattern will retain the meanings the colors had originally represented.

Using Symbols

All your graphs and charts can be made more personal and more interesting by including symbols. One of the more compelling modifications you can make is to replace the innocuous bar in your bar charts with a symbol (or stack or row of symbols) that are more relevant to your organization. For example, you can overlay a bar with a line of cars, a stack of money, or a piece of pipe. Even without taking the time to fill the entire bar, a symbol can be placed at the end of each bar to add to the visual impact of your graphic. (See Figure 7.3.)

The Order of Your Performance Questions

Every aspect of a satisfaction visual should convey information. Why then do we often see bar charts in which the order (top to bottom or left to right) of the questions graphed has no meaning other than (perhaps) the order in which the questions were asked in the questionnaire? When the order in which questions are listed has no meaning, the chartist has missed a very important opportunity. Always establish the order in which you will display your performance questions in your visuals. It is suggested that their order should represent their importance to your customers; thus the most important questions will be at the top of the graph, the least important issues at the bottom.

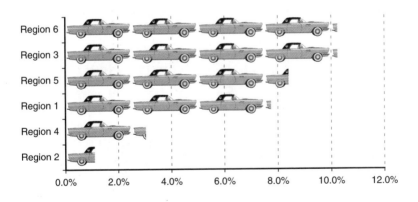

Figure 7.3 Using symbols in charts.

 Checkpoint 7.2

1. Try to learn the graph type that best accomplishes each of the four basic roles of a satisfaction graphic (magnitude, trends, composition, and sequence).

2. What colors do you plan to use in your graphs? Create a key to identify the role of each color. (It is strongly recommended that you reserve green, yellow, and red as the traditional indicators of *good*, *changing*, and *bad* outcomes.)

3. Always have a reason for the order in which you list or display information, in particular your performance questions. Do you know the relative importance of each of them? Importance is one of the most valuable orders in which to list performance issues. If you establish such a practice, keep it consistent throughout all your visuals.

DETERMINING IMPORTANCE

In chapter 6 we mentioned the value of determining the *key drivers of satisfaction* in your survey. There are two methods for calculating key drivers:

- *Implicit methods.* Methods that attempt to infer priority weights from existing information using statistical analysis

- *Explicit methods.* Methods that ask customers more directly for their judgments of the importance of issues

STEP 7.3 IMPLICIT METHODS OF KEY DRIVER DETERMINATION

Implicit methods for determining your customers' key drivers of satisfaction use information you've already collected. The analysis is based on the classification of some of your measures as criteria measures and the remainder as performance measures. If your performance measures incorporate most of the experience your customers have with your organization, then their performance ratings ought to vary with their rating of overall satisfaction in such a way that you can use that relationship to derive the weights or relationships between your performance measures and overall satisfaction. There are two ways you can accomplish this:

- Using Pearson product-moment correlation coefficients of each of your performance variables with your overall satisfaction question

- Using multiple regression to regress your overall satisfaction question on your performance questions

Arguably, multiple regression is the more accurate manner of identifying the unique contribution of each performance question, given the influence of the questions together and upon each other. It unfortunately is also the most fallible method. It suffers from a condition called *multicollinearity*, which occurs when your performance questions are not completely independent but are intercorrelated among themselves.

Pearson Product-Moment Correlations

You can easily calculate the Pearson product-moment coefficients by using any correlation routine. With your data in an Excel or Lotus 1-2-3 spreadsheet, simply identify your input data and then select *correlation*. A square matrix of as many rows and columns as you have performance variables will be produced. The column containing the correlations of each performance question with your measure of overall satisfaction will contain the coefficients you want. Refer back to the first column in Table 6.9 in chapter six. You will use these coefficients to represent the respective importance weights of each of your performance variables in driving your organization's overall satisfaction. They are the quantities you will plot on your importance graph. Their relative values also represent the order in which you should list and display your performance questions throughout your report.[1] See Table 7.1.

Multiple Regression

Using multiple regression you can also calculate multiple regression coefficients. These coefficients will be decimals between -1.00 and $+1.00$. You can access a multiple regression routine in virtually any statistical analysis package, including some spreadsheet programs (Excel and Lotus 1-2-3, for example). Simply identify overall satisfaction as your dependent variable (the concept dependent on other things) and your performance questions as the independent variables (the things possibly causing or related to your customers' overall satisfaction). You will need to answer only two other questions to receive your key driver weights. You may be asked if you want

---

[1]Rust and Donthu (1999) have advocated a procedure by which the pairwise correlation coefficients are normalized. The formula for normalizing is simply $\beta i = \sqrt{\dfrac{\rho i^2}{\Sigma \rho^2}}$.

Table 7.1   Using Pearson product-moment correlation coefficients for key driver weights.

	Raw Pearson product-moment correlation coefficients	Normalized Pearson product-moment correlation coeficients	Multiple regression correlation coefficients
Qualification	0.815	0.381	0.249
Value for price	0.685	0.320	0.193
Product durability	0.651	0.304	0.097
Documentation	0.646	0.302	0.137
Product reliability	0.600	0.280	0.050
Installation	0.594	0.278	0.076
Conformance to specs	0.589	0.275	0.071
Features offered	0.587	0.274	−0.017
Product functionality	0.587	0.274	0.138
Servicing	0.539	0.252	0.117
Product serviceability	0.533	0.249	−0.006
Delivery	0.530	0.248	0.087

standardized coefficients. Since all your performance variables will be measured on the same attitudinal scale (perhaps 0 to 10), standardization should not be necessary. You will also probably be asked whether you wish a constant (or a y-intercept of 0). Again, you should probably decline and accept a constant (y-intercept value). (A y-intercept suggests you accept the existence of some minimal overall satisfaction, even if all the performance variables you measured conceivably had a value of 0.)

With these questions answered, the package (or spreadsheet) will produce a column of regression coefficients (your potential key driver weights). The multiple regression analysis will also calculate a value of R^2, called the *squared multiple correlation coefficient*. This number, ranging from 0 to 1.00 (interpretable as a percentage), represents the total amount of variation in your overall satisfaction score that your set of performance questions is capable of "explaining" (anticipating, if you will). As such, this number gives you an idea of *how good your model (your assemblage of performance questions) really is in explaining overall satisfaction*. Don't shoot for 100 percent. It won't happen (unless your data is flawed—highly multicollinear). Remember, however, that the use of multiple regression may be compromised by the correlation existing among your performance questions.

See Figure 7.4 for an example of using multiple regression to determine key driver (or performance question importance) weights. (This is how the regression weights in Table 7.1 were derived.)

SUMMARY OUTPUT

Regression statistics

Multiple R	0.916
R square	0.840
Adjusted R square	0.818
Standard error	0.969
Observations	100

ANOVA

	df	SS	MS	F	Significance F
Regression	12	428.991	35.749	38.041	1.88718E-29
Residual	87	81.759	0.940		
Total	99	510.750			

	Coefficients	Standard error	t Stat	P-value	Lower 95%	Upper 95%	Lower 95.0%	Upper 95.0%
Intercept	-1.586	0.511	-3.105	0.003	-2.601	-0.571	-2.601	-0.571
Value for the price	0.193	0.057	3.370	0.001	0.079	0.307	0.079	0.307
Product functionality	0.138	0.055	2.505	0.014	0.028	0.247	0.028	0.247
Features offered	-0.017	0.053	-0.326	0.745	-0.123	0.088	-0.123	0.088
Product reliability	0.050	0.061	0.812	0.419	-0.072	0.172	-0.072	0.172
Conformance to specs	0.071	0.058	1.232	0.221	-0.044	0.186	-0.044	0.186
Product durability	0.097	0.059	1.656	0.101	-0.020	0.214	-0.020	0.214
Product serviceability	-0.006	0.052	-0.117	0.907	-0.110	0.097	-0.110	0.097
Documentation	0.137	0.054	2.546	0.013	0.030	0.244	0.030	0.244
Delivery	0.087	0.058	1.503	0.136	-0.028	0.203	-0.028	0.203
Installation	0.076	0.060	1.255	0.213	-0.044	0.195	-0.044	0.195
Qualification	0.249	0.070	3.581	0.001	0.111	0.387	0.111	0.387
Servicing	0.117	0.047	2.511	0.014	0.024	0.210	0.024	0.210

Figure 7.4 Sample regression output.

Checkpoint 7.3

1. Learning the relative importance of your performance questions helps you identify your key drivers of satisfaction. This is easily accomplished by statistically analyzing your dataset—a process we've called *implicitly deriving* key drivers.

2. There are two statistical procedures that can be used to identify key drivers. Which technique (correlation coefficients or multiple regression coefficients) do you plan to use, and why?

3. If you use multiple regression as a method by which to calculate the importance weights (key driver weights) for your performance variables, are you certain there is only a minimum amount of correlation among your performance questions?

STEP 7.4 EXPLICIT METHODS OF KEY DRIVER DETERMINATION

Explicit methods of determining your customers' key drivers of satisfaction require a whole additional dataset. As such they are both costly and intrusive (on your customers). Their added value is that explicit methods are *open systems*. They allow your customers to volunteer totally new questions and issues. In this way they are more likely to help you radically update the issues covered in your survey. (The implicit methods discussed previously can be considered *closed systems*—they operate only within the issues that currently make up your survey.)

Several different techniques exist by which to conduct an explicit determination of key drivers. But the overriding requirement among all of them is that they require customers to make *trade-offs* in their evaluative judgments. A simple importance rating scale (0 to 10, *not at all important* to *extremely important*) will be unsatisfactory in helping to identify key drivers. Using such a scale, customers would be free to rate many, if not all, performance attributes as extremely important. Yet your organization has limited resources with which to improve its product/service offerings. It must know exactly which attributes are the *most* important.

Judgment tasks that require customers to trade-off one attribute for another are the best way to collect importance data that will support this critical notion of prioritization. Several different tasks for collecting trade-off judgments have been used and advocated. We'll review a number of them.

Constant Sum Tasks

To assess importance using a *constant sum technique*, you would present a list of performance questions or attributes to a sample of your customers and ask them to distribute a fixed number of points across the questions or attributes in accordance with the importance to them of each item. Customers may assign as few or as many points to each question or issue as they like. The more points they assign, the more important that performance issue. The only constraint is that the total of all assigned points must equal the fixed number of points with which they started out. Figure 7.5 shows a typical constant sum question.

We need to know how important each of the following components are to you in evaluating a financial services provider. *Please allocate 100 points across the nine components below (a thru i) according to their importance to you. You may allocate any amount of points (from 0 to 100) per item, so long as your total does not exceed 100. The more important an item, the more points you should allocate to it.*

a. A broad range of products and services _____

b. Investment performance _____

c. Financial stability _____

d. Overall image and reputation _____

e. Efficient recordkeeping _____

f. Service from your relationship manager _____

g. The value of service, advice, and performance relative to fees and commissions paid _____

h. The combination of investment services and traditional private banking _____

i. Quality of securities research information offered _____

Total Points   **100**

Figure 7.5   A typical constant sum question format.

Constant sum tasks are best used when the number of attributes to be evaluated is reasonably small, usually 10 or less. (This is a condition most key driver studies will not be able to meet, as there are inevitably 20 to 30 issues being considered.) Constant sum tasks also seem to work best in situations where the customer can see the allocation task (in personal or self-administered surveys); they generally don't work well in telephone surveys. A constant sum task is best implemented with computer administration wherein the computer can keep a running tally of points assigned—customers are notoriously bad at addition. Without this sort of check, you'll have to rebase many customers' point assignments because they'll either fall short of or exceed your point total.

Constant sum results are tabulated by simply averaging the points assigned to each attribute and then ordering the attributes from the one with the most points to the one with the fewest (or no) points.

Rank-Ordering Tasks

Customers may be presented with a list of performance questions and asked to rank them from the most important to the least important question. Though this is a straightforward request, the process becomes difficult for customers as the number of performance issues exceeds 15 items. (When you have a large number of items, you can adopt a sequential pile sort task. See Vavra [1997] for a full description of that procedure.)

A secondary disadvantage is that the quality of data produced by this task is really only ordinal. Though an attribute may be considered more important than another, the distance or amount of that superiority will not be captured, nor will it be identifiable. Analysis of rank-ordered data typically involves calculating the *average rank* (treating rank positions as scores and calculating the average). Unfortunately, the metric of the rankings does not support such a calculation, though it is frequently done in practice.

Pair-Preference Tasks

Pair-preference tasks are an eloquently simple way to collect trade-off judgments. All customers know they can't have everything. So when presented with a pair of performance questions and asked to identify which issue is more important, most customers will readily comply. The judgments presented to customers, as pairs, are very easy to comprehend and respond to.

The primary difficulty with pair-preference judgments is how the number of pairs geometrically expands as the number of performance questions you have to be judged expands. If you have only 10 questions, you'll have 45 pairs, but if your number of questions doubles to 20, the number of pairs you'll have quadruples to 190! There are ways of working around this difficulty, but none are perfect. The most common solution is to *split-sample* the pairs. This means that in the case of 45 pairs, no customer is presented with all 45, but each individual customer might be randomly presented with one-third, or 15 pairs. The data from all participating customers are aggregated and averaged and are generally quite robust. It bothers some people that individual customers might be exposed to only a subset of your questions and likely will not see all performance attributes. Generally, in split-sample applications, each customer will see fewer than half of all performance questions you're reviewing.

The presentation of questions within each pair should always be controlled (for example, no attribute should always be listed first). And pairs should obviously be randomized in presentation. This type of task works particularly well in computer-administered projects.

Once you've collected the preference judgments, the data are typically analyzed by a statistical routine called Thurstone's Case V. This procedure is a very simple, yet eloquent method for metricizing the ordinal (preference) data.[2]

 Checkpoint 7.4

1. Why might you wish to conduct an explicit assessment of key drivers rather than settle for the simpler implicit assessment.

2. In what ways is a trade-off task superior to a ratings task for discovering your key drivers.

3. How do you plan to implement your explicit key driver measurement process—in conjunction with your satisfaction measurement or as a separate study? How frequently do you envision an explicit assessment?

4. Which method do you plan to use to explicitly identify your key drivers? Have you chosen that method by balancing effort from your customers against the quality of the data you'll collect?

---

[2] The Thurstone Case V method is available in SPSS and in a package of psychometric tools called PCMDS. See Smith (1996).

STEP 7.5 TECHNIQUES FOR GRAPHING YOUR RESULTS

Any summary listing of this sort is an easy target for argument; but even considering that risk, your author believes the following five chart types are all you'll really need to make a visually impressive display of your satisfaction findings.

1. *Thermometer charts*—to report relative importance of your performance questions

2. *Bar charts*—to display performance against benchmarks (goals or competition)

3. *Trend line charts*—to display longitudinal performance

4. *Quadrant charts*—to help prioritize improvement actions

5. *Quality function deployment (QFD) grids*—to rally involvement of the diverse departments within your organization that all affect your customers' satisfaction

---

 Checkpoint 7.5

1. Make sure that you are acquainted with the five basic graph types just described, and know for which of your communication goals each type is most effective.

STEP 7.6 GRAPH YOUR INTERNAL ANALYSES

To best demonstrate the relative importance of your performance questions, a *thermometer chart* is superb (see Figure 7.6). One may also use a *bar chart*, but your author much prefers the thermometer format (see Figure 7.7). The advantage is in the relatively easy way groupings of questions can be identified (based on their levels of ratings). For example, in Figure 7.6, a triage process may be easily performed on ratings. The one question that is most important is vividly obvious, as are the three questions conveying much less importance. The remaining questions show moderate importance.

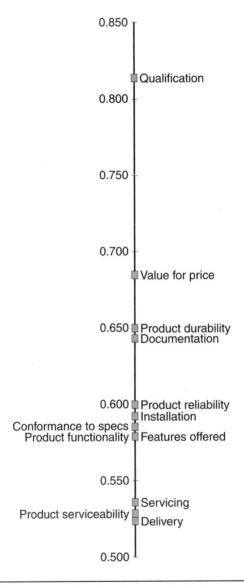

Figure 7.6   A thermometer chart for showing relative importance of performance variables.

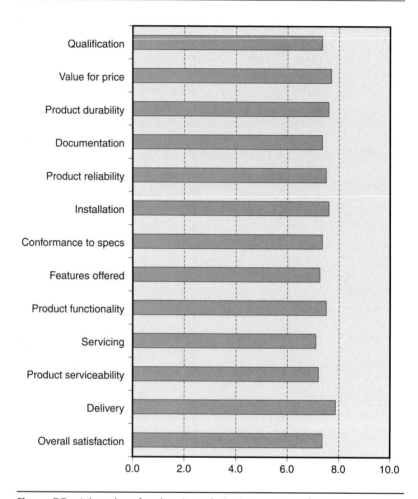

Figure 7.7   A bar chart for showing relative importance of performance variables.

When it comes to displaying ratings against corporate goals or previous history, bar charts become more attractive. Consider using only horizontal bar charts; they more easily accommodate labels identifying performance questions. In the case of performance against a corporate goal, show the goal as a vertical line as in Figure 7.8.

Alternatively, if you wish to compare the performance of various locations or the ratings of various customer groups, a *clustered bar chart* is

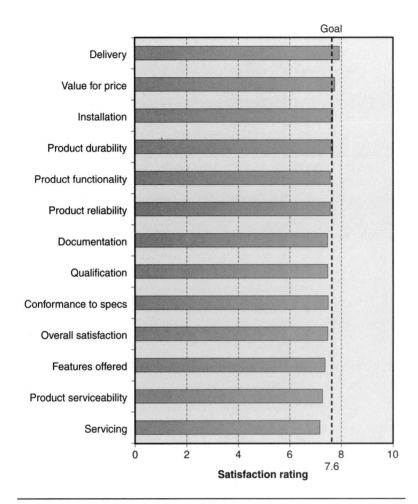

Figure 7.8 A bar chart showing performance against a corporate goal (ranked by attainment of goal).

recommended (see Figure 7.9). In this format you create a bar for each location's or department's scores for each of your performance questions.

If you want to show a trend of your overall satisfaction scores, a *line chart* is your best choice (see Figure 7.10).

To show how your performance questions have changed from another measurement period, the simplest approach is to use one of the following:

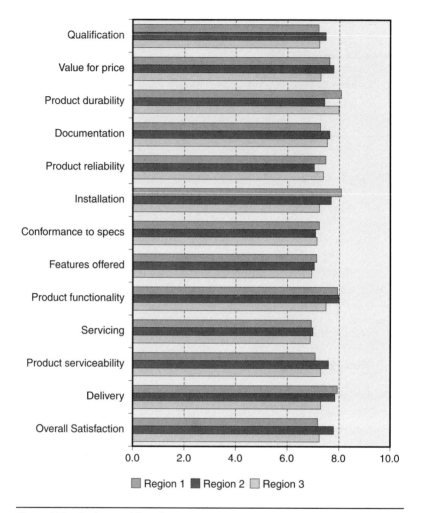

Figure 7.9 A clustered bar chart.

- A *horizontal bar chart* with change numbers placed at the end of each bar (see Figure 7.11)

- A *deviation horizontal bar chart* displaying minus or plus differences from the previous measurement (shown on p. 240 as Figure 7.13)

You will always be asked, and must also ask yourself, which of the changes you have observed (if any) are great enough to qualify as true changes if you tested them for statistical significance. The familiar *box and*

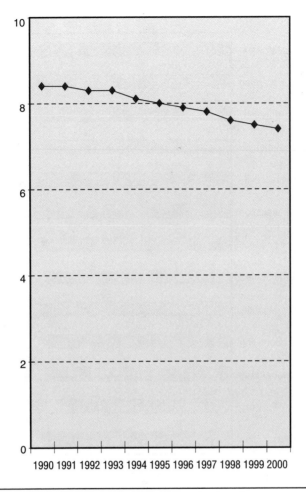

Figure 7.10   Using a line chart to show longitudinal performance.

whisker chart from stock market analysis provides a useful template to address this question. If you allow the confidence interval about the previous score to define the box, then the current score is plotted as the whisker. If the current score lies outside the box, it does—by definition—exceed the confidence interval and may therefore be considered as exceeding the range of variation defined by statistical phenomena. Hence, the new score would be considered a true change since it exceeded any variation expected based on statistics alone (see Figure 7.12).

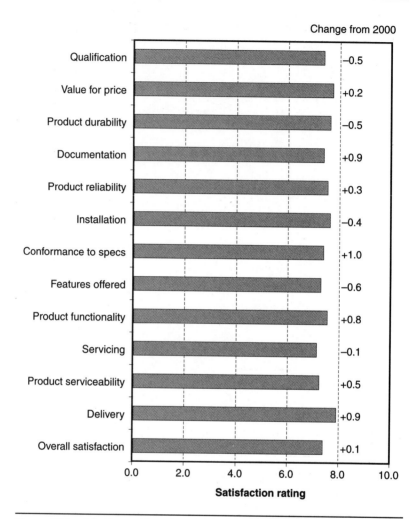

Figure 7.11 A horizontal bar chart with change numbers.

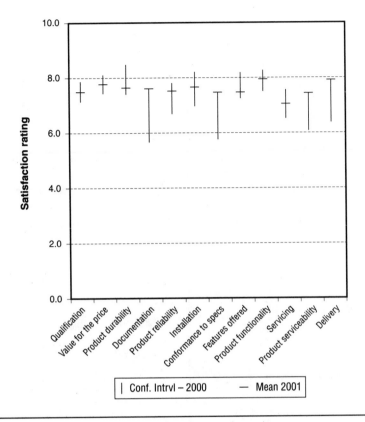

Figure 7.12 box and whisker chart with Satisfaction rating (0.0 to 10.0) on the y-axis and categories on the x-axis: Qualification, Value for the price, Product durability, Documentation, Product reliability, Installation, Conformance to specs, Features offered, Product functionality, Servicing, Product serviceability, Delivery

| Conf. Intrvl – 2000   — Mean 2001

Figure 7.12 Using a box and whisker chart to show change.

 Checkpoint 7.6

1. To graph importance weights (of your performance questions), use a thermometer chart or a horizontal bar chart.

2. To show how your performance questions are rated against an internal goal, use a horizontal bar chart showing the performance goal.

3. To show change from a historical score, you may either append change scores to the end of each bar or use a *deviation*, or *change*, graph in which changes are illustrated by a left-facing (decrease) or right-facing (increase) bar from a central axis (unchanged).

STEP 7.7 GRAPH YOUR EXTERNAL ANALYSES

External analyses are also concerned with comparison, but comparison with external operations. In particular, that means comparison with an industry norm or standard, or with a particular competitor whose performance you may have been able to assess (perhaps by interviewing some of his or her customers).

A horizontal bar chart, against the external benchmark, is again a favored graphic. A variant on this format places the benchmark's performance in the center of the chart. Then your organization's performance is shown as a deviation (a bar extended to the left of center is a weaknesses, a bar to the right of center is a strength). See Figure 7.13 for an example.

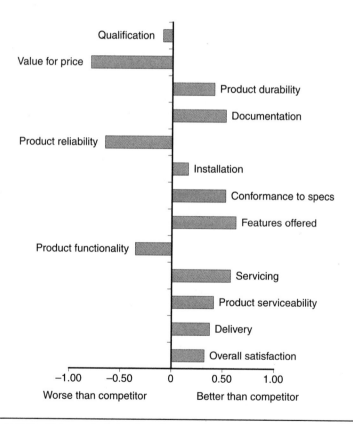

Figure 7.13 Using a deviation bar chart to show performance vis-à-vis a competitor (attributes listed in order of importance).

Checkpoint 7.7

1. By establishing an industry norm as a benchmark, you can express your own organization's performance as differences (deviations) from that goal. The horizontal deviation bar chart serves this purpose most dramatically.

STEP 7.8 A HELP TO PRIORITIZE IMPROVEMENT: THE QUADRANT CHART

There is no better vehicle, and none more widely accepted to help engineer positive change as a result of your satisfaction survey, than the so-called *quadrant chart*. A less generic, more descriptive name is an *importance-performance* (or *I-P*) *chart*. This eloquently simple chart, first suggested by Martilla and James (1977), has been universally employed as an excellent action builder following a satisfaction survey. Virtually all audiences seem to understand its composition and the dramatic message it sends.

You make a quadrant chart by creating a grid represented by importance ratings on the vertical axis and performance ratings on the horizontal axis. You'll need to subdivide each axis. On the horizontal axis (performance) draw a vertical line at your average performance rating; on your vertical axis draw a horizontal line to represent the average importance rating of all of your performance questions. With these two lines, you've formed four sectors, or quadrants.

Now you can plot each of your performance questions on this grid according to their importance and rated performance. To interpret the grid, use the following logic. If your organization is truly listening to its customers, then your performance issues ought to be delivered in proportion to their importance. That is, your performance questions plotted on your grid ought to form a *regression line* running from the lower left to the upper right of your grid. Performance issues lying on (or near) this imaginary line would verify that your customers perceived them as delivered (performed) roughly proportional to their importance. This happy condition describes an intelligent and responsive organization.

In actuality, while *some* performance issues may lie on such an imaginary regression line, a great many performance questions' importance and performance ratings will cause them to be located somewhere else in your two-by-two grid. By convention, each of the quadrants is described and carries a normative action strategy. Those descriptions and their appropriate strategies are shown in Figure 7.14.

Focus—opportunity	Keep up the good work
(Weak performance on important attributes—mandate to improve performance)	(Strong performance on important attributes—maintain and leverage)
Low importance Low priority (Performance in proportion to importance—maintain current status)	**Possible oversupply** (Strong performance on unimportant attributes—may represent oversupply, opportunity to reassign resources)

Figure 7.14   The regions of the quadrant chart.

Performance issues lying in the lower left or upper right quadrants are in *good* job locations. In these quadrants, your organization's performance is roughly proportional to the importance of the questions. Your requisite action for performance questions in these two quadrants is to maintain their current levels of delivery. They are perceived to be supplied in proportion to their importance.

The two remaining quadrants offer opportunities for change. The lower right quadrant is labeled *oversupply* because performance issues located in this quadrant are being delivered to a much greater extent than their judged importance warrants. If possible, your organization should relax its performance on these issues. This is an area where, quite possibly, you are spending more in time, money, or resources than is warranted by customers' expressions of issue importance. If possible, your organization should redirect resources from these issues to other, more important performance issues.

Finally, there is the upper left quadrant. Here, very important attributes are perceived as being underdelivered. Attributes in this quadrant signal an opportunity for improvement. But you must be careful to determine *what type* of improvement is required. Your customers' perception of underdelivery may be a "factually correct" perception.[3] If you can verify that your organization is failing to offer as much of the performance issue as is desired (for example, you may be supplying less than your competitors

---

[3] We are respecting the recognition that whatever customers perceive is by definition the reality with which your organization must deal. However, sometimes customers' perception(s) will be consistent with fact and other times inconsistent with fact. The extent to which customers' perceptions are consistent or inconsistent with fact determines *how* your organization must deal with them, not whether or not your organization accepts them.

are), then your mandate is to increase your organization's performance on these attributes. Such a problem is clearly a *product/service* problem. But what if you are reasonably certain you're supplying as much as (or possibly more than) your competitors are? If this is the case, you have a *communication* problem. That is, your customers have apparently not been made aware of your delivery of these issues to the point that they credit you fairly for your performance. In such cases your organization must increase customer awareness of its delivery through the "management of evidence" (Vavra 1995).

Managers and quality improvement teams readily embrace quadrant charts because they logically identify priorities for improvement based on each of the performance attributes measured with which to seemingly increase overall satisfaction. In Figure 7.15 the 17 performance attributes are plotted according to their importance and performance scores.

Some Analytical Considerations

Early in the discussion of quadrant charts, we alluded to how the quadrants were identified. It was suggested that the vertical line be drawn at the average performance rating (over all performance questions) and the horizontal

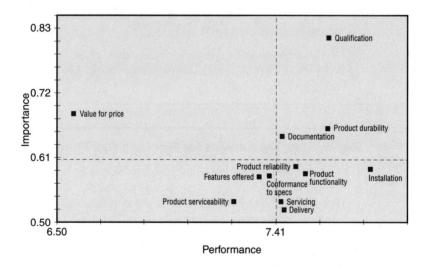

Figure 7.15   The performance attributes performance-importance quadrant chart.

line drawn at the average importance rating (of all performance questions). Your author strongly believes in making the boundaries for the quadrants relative to the current dataset, though some have argued for other procedures for identifying the boundaries. Originally, Martilla and James suggested simply dividing at the arithmetic midpoints of the horizontal and vertical scales. You may have other ideas. In fact, you may wish to be a bit more creative in how you plot your performance questions. For example, the horizontal scale could be the range of your customers' top-box ratings for all your performance questions. (Your range would then equal 0 to the highest top-box score over all performance questions.) Being even more creative, you could scale your horizontal axis by your organization's rating differences against your competitors' or your industry's best-of-class ratings. (In that case your scale would range from −10 through 0 to +10, or would constitute some other similar range).

 Checkpoint 7.8

1. Explain why, in an ideal situation, all your performance questions—when plotted in a performance-importance (quadrant) chart—would lie on the diagonal from lower left to upper right.

2. What labels do you plan to give the four quadrants in your adoption of this chart type?

3. Plot your performance questions on a quadrant chart. What proportion of your performance issues are in the opportunity quadrant?

 Step-by-Step: The Answers for Reporting Your Process

7.1 Three formats have been discussed for a written report of your survey process and your findings: a *full-report style,* a *memo style,* and a *presentation deck.* Regardless of the format you use, lead with your findings and priorities for improvement; provide the methodological information only secondarily for those also interested in your process. See pages 216–20.

7.2 Make sure you have a communications objective in mind before you select a graph type for each of your satisfaction graphics. Too often people favor a particular graph type without fully recognizing the goals for which it is most appropriate. We have reviewed the four basic roles of satisfaction graphs: to display *magnitude, trends, composition,* or *order.* For each role, one graph type is superior.

- Color is one of the more important enhancements that can be given to a graph, but it is best used sparingly and strategically. We have recommended reserving use of the stoplight colors (green, yellow, and red) because they already denote meaning. Further, it is recommended that color assignment be maintained throughout a report to assist readers in easily understanding the points being communicated.

- Every aspect of a satisfaction graphic should convey information. That's why your performance questions should always be listed (top to bottom; left to right) in their order of importance to your customers. Correlation with your overall satisfaction measure is one way to imply those importance weights.

7.3 Knowing the importance your customers place in your performance questions allows you to appropriately champion improvement and brings meaningful order to your graphs. The process by which importance weights are developed is called key driver analysis. If you focus your analysis internally at the data you have already collected, you are implicitly deriving your key driver weights. Correlation coefficients are the most satisfactory process for implicit derivation. See pages 224–28.

7.4 It's a good idea to occasionally look outside the data you already have to review your key driver weights. Implicit derivation is a closed-system process. In contrast, going back to your customers for an

(continued)

explicit determination of key drivers is an open system. Several survey procedures were discussed. Be sure to employ a questioning technique that requires your customers to *trade off* your performance variables one against another. Avoid using a rating question to collect these importance weights. Constant sum, rank-order, and pair-preference are three question types you can use. See pages 228–31.

7.5 We have described five graph types that satisfy all the basic reporting needs you'll have for your satisfaction reporting process. They are:

- *Thermometer charts*—to graph the importance weights of your performance variables

- *Horizontal bar charts*—to display your performance and to show performance against a norm or target

- *Trend line charts*—for longitudinally tracking the growth of your overall satisfaction score or the trending of your performance ratings

- *Quadrant charts*—to depict your performance questions by your customers' ratings and the importance of each question

- *Quality function deployment grids*—to help rally improvement efforts by identifying the controlling area or department for each of your performance variables

See page 232.

7.6 For the graphing of your internal analyses, horizontal bar charts allow you to plot your ratings on your performance questions in a very understandable and relative way. You can simply plot the ratings you've received; you can use separate, clustered bars to show the ratings of each of several locations or departments on the same performance questions; or you can show how your performance questions' ratings measure up against an organizational goal (shown as a vertical line). A line chart will very nicely plot your overall criteria ratings (satisfaction, recommendation, repurchase, etc.). See pages 232–39.

7.7 For external analyses, horizontal bar charts plotting the ratings on your performance questions as deviations against your industry norm or a competitor's performance ratings will produce a very dramatic picture. See pages 240–41.

7.8 The quadrant chart is a useful graph to help your organization prioritize its improvement initiatives. The judged importance and performance ratings of your performance questions are plotted in a four-quadrant grid. Important performance questions that score low on current performance deserve your immediate attention. See pages 241–44.

 Chapter 7 Deliverables

As a result of your work in this chapter, you will have produced the following materials:

1. Graphs for your internal analyses, including:

   - A horizontal bar chart showing your customers' ratings of your organization on performance questions

   - Line charts trending your criteria questions (overall satisfaction, willingness to recommend, likelihood of repurchasing, etc.)

2. Graphs for your external analyses, including a horizontal bar chart showing your customers' ratings of your organization, with your industry's norm or average displayed as a vertical line.

3. A quadrant chart showing the position of all your performance variables. From this chart you should be able to write a sequence of improvement activities, addressing those performance issues that are most important and that are currently performed least well by your organization.

V.

Development

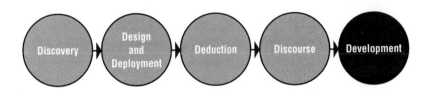

How Will You Stimulate Continual Improvement?

*Once your findings are widely dissemi-
nated, you have the further opportunity to
challenge your organization to take action
to make the improvements your customers
request. Measurement must not be considered the primary focus of a customer
satisfaction program; without a focus on
improvement, the measurement is wasted
effort and resources. Your program should
include tools for championing and mentor-
ing change. Continuous improvement is one
of the new goals of the ISO standards.*

8

Closing the Loop: Communicating Your Results

I once asked an executive vice president of a Fortune 500 organization if his firm measured customer satisfaction. "We sure do," he replied. "Those are the reports from our last five years' worth of studies," he said, proudly gesturing to some pristine-looking binders on a not too convenient shelf. Too many customer satisfaction initiatives end up similarly— their reports sitting like gargoyles on the bookcases of corporate managers who commissioned the work without knowing what they'd do with the information once they received it or how they'd act on their customers' stated opinions and recommendations.

If the existence of this information (and its potential benefit) is not widely known or understood, that's probably why such studies are allowed to remain untouched on managers' shelves. Nothing will come from your project and neither will improvements be made unless you adequately communicate your findings and act as a zealous facilitator to stimulate improvement.

It has been suggested that one "can't manage what isn't measured." That perspective buttresses measurement as an invaluable action. But measurement by itself isn't sufficient. It is, then, similarly true that "measurement alone doesn't *ensure* improvement"!

Step-by-Step: The Issues of Communicating Your Results

8.1 Clarify with your supervisor or management that asked you to undertake a customer satisfaction program who in your organization will take "ownership" of the information you'll collect and exactly how they envision it being disseminated. Agree also on a process by which you'll report your findings.

8.2 It may be useful to build proof of the value of your attitudinal customer service measurement (CSM) information. You'll do this either within your attitudinal data (showing that lower performance ratings are related to lesser likelihood to repurchase and recommend) or by linking your attitudinal data with customers' actual purchasing behavior.

8.3 You'll report your findings to management, of course. But equally important is conveying an understanding of customers' problems and needs to your organization's employees—the people who staff the processes and produce your current products. If they're to embrace the changes that need to occur, they'll do so most readily if they understand the reasons for the changes. Reporting some of or all your findings to employees will be critical to your improvement initiative.

8.4 A frequently unanticipated need is providing feedback to your customers subsequent to fielding your satisfaction survey. This important feedback has been specified in ANSI/ISO/ASQ Q9001-2000. Feedback can either be a simple "Thank you for participating" or a more strategic response and action plan based on specific actions the customer suggested or requested.

8.5 To really use your information, you'll need to establish a task force or team charged with carrying your findings back to operational departments and areas. Without such a team, the value of your information will end with your written report. You may have sufficient authority yourself, or you may need to rely on your management's authority.

8.6 Recognize that customers will identify two types of problems: (1) *actual problems* and (2) *perceived problems* created apparently because of your organization's poor or nonexistent ability to adequately inform customers of your activities and progress. Don't assume every problem is an actual one.

8.7 With an improvement task force in place, you'll need a process to associate customers' perceptions of problems to the department or areas within your organization that have the most impact on those problems. One such process is called the *quality deployment function* (QDF).

STEP 8.1 OWN AND DISSEMINATE YOUR INFORMATION

The revised ANSI/ISO/ASQ Q9001-2000 standard specifies that the review of information for improvement purposes is a necessary process. From Section 5.6:

5.6 Management Review

5.6.1 General

Top management shall review the organization's quality management system, at planned intervals, to ensure its continuing suitability, adequacy and effectiveness. This review shall include assessing opportunities for improvement and the need for changes to the quality management system, including the quality policy and quality objectives.

Records from management review shall be maintained (see 4.2.4).

(continued)

5.6.2 Review Input

The input to management review shall include information on

a) results of audits,

b) customer feedback,

c) process performance and product conformity,

d) status of preventive and corrective actions,

e) follow-up actions from previous management reviews,

f) changes that could affect the quality management system, and

g) recommendations for improvement.

Source: ANSI/ISO/ASQ Q9001-2000

Hopefully you have a "champion" to take ownership of your process. Try to involve him or her in a discussion of the vision he or she has for distributing, explaining, and acting on the information your project collects. While you are somewhat at the mercy of this person's preconceptions about (or past experiences with) satisfaction surveys, you nevertheless can affect his or her thinking and guide him or her in a constructive direction. Section 5.6 gives you considerable ammunition to help forge a useful dissemination process.

There are two, possibly three, groups that deserve to hear your results:

- Your management
- Your employees
- Your customers

And you have your choice of several different ways to communicate with them, including the following:

- Written reports or memoranda
- Presentations (oral discussions of your findings)
- Visuals: graphs and charts

While you may choose to use any or all of these methods, your organization will probably have its own favorite method of internal dissemination and communication.

While written documents will provide those interested with a thorough description of your process and findings, there's nothing better than a graph or two to stimulate action. The adage *one picture is worth a thousand words* sounds trite, yet it is absolutely correct in terms of disseminating satisfaction information and creating grassroots interest in improving it. In several satisfaction initiatives in which the author is personally involved, graphed results are regularly communicated with visual reports posted in open view for everyone to see.

- At the Rolls-Royce and Bentley Motor Car factory in Crewe, England, keyword verbatims (related to each of several departments) are posted monthly to relay the "voice of the customer" to department members, members of neighboring departments, even distinguished visitors to the factory! These reports not only serve to identify possible problem areas and areas of excellence but also help to remind the employees that their ultimate product is not a motor car but a delighted owner!

- Outside the employee cafeteria at the Motorola GTSS facility in Arlington Heights, Illinois, is a bulletin board with the title Customer Satisfaction Process Survey. The posted charts are longitudinal and are updated each month. Because this division of Motorola has employees around the world, an Intranet Web page has been designed giving those with appropriate security clearance the ability to browse through aggregated results and individual questionnaires on a real-time basis.

- When he was president of Roche Diagnostics, Carlo Medici challenged his executives to make customer satisfaction results their number one concern to help turn around that once ailing division of the pharmaceutical giant. In an extraordinary case study, Medici and his colleagues were able to improve their division's standing almost instantly simply by listening to and responding to their customers' complaints and suggestions (Keiningham et al. 1999).

Communicating your survey results requires first that you fully comprehend the results, that you have reasonable explanations for why your organization is rated as it was, and that you can relay this understanding and insight to others in your organization. This is admittedly no small order. Beyond simply communicating the information, you will of course want to inspire improvement and change (where necessary).

Checkpoint 8.1

1. Information is power; improvement requires that this power be as widely disseminated as possible. With wide dissemination, more people will understand the importance of the changes that need to be made, and those persons having to make the changes may make them with greater enthusiasm and involvement.

2. To whom will you distribute findings from your survey?

STEP 8.2 BUILD RESPECT AND TRUST FOR CSM INFORMATION

We noted earlier that customer satisfaction data, attitudinal as it is, may not be as compelling to your colleagues as other, more tangible information (for example, sales levels, return rates, warranty claims, etc.). You may find it desirable to establish the impact of your satisfaction information as quickly as you can. The most compelling way to establish credibility for your program's output is to validate your attitudinal satisfaction data by showing how it correlates with actual customer behaviors.

Correlating Satisfaction with Repurchase or Recommendation Intent

In the early stages of your program, you may have to be content with simply showing your colleagues how the *attitudes* of satisfaction are correlated with *attitudes* of repurchase or recommendation. That is because you won't have a sufficient number of measurement points to associate with various levels of behavioral data. The attitudinal data available for you to correlate with your satisfaction scores should probably be called *intentional data*. These measures can include your customers' expressed likelihood to continue to buy your organization's products or your customers' likelihood of increasing their share of category requirements purchased from your organization.

Such a correlation is typically demonstrated in the aggregate, as Figure 8.1 shows. In this figure, the impact of overall satisfaction on future purchase intentions (for an automobile manufacturer) is clearly evident. Of those customers completely satisfied (delighted), there is an 86 percent likelihood of purchasing another of the manufacturer's automobiles. Of those customers completely dissatisfied, there is only a 10 percent likelihood they'll repurchase.

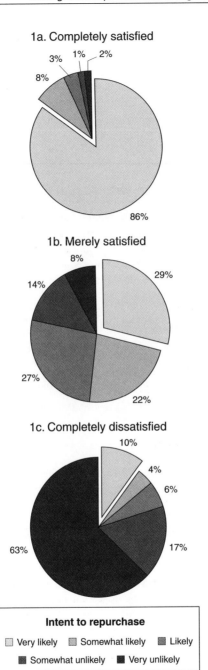

1a. Completely satisfied

3% 1% 2%

8%

86%

1b. Merely satisfied

8%

14%

29%

27%

22%

1c. Completely dissatisfied

10%

4%

6%

63%

17%

Intent to repurchase

▨ Very likely   ▨ Somewhat likely   ▨ Likely

▨ Somewhat unlikely   ■ Very unlikely

Figure 8.1   Correlating overall satisfaction with intentions to repurchase.

So, satisfaction has a very real consequence for customers' future (intended) purchase behaviors. However, as we've already established, the relationship between satisfaction and future purchasing behavior is complex; high satisfaction is no guarantee the *individual* customer will necessarily repurchase.

Admittedly, correlating satisfaction scores with intentions is not as dramatic as actually showing differences in sales levels, but sales analysis requires substantially more data.

Correlating Satisfaction with Actual Purchase Data

Empirical methods utilize known spending patterns, demonstrated longevity, or some other objective measure of customer or account value. Because this investigation deals with causality, correlation or regression analysis is a likely tool for this type of validation. Two procedures can be envisaged for analytically investigating the correlation of satisfaction with profits.

- *Longitudinal.* These methods look at the movement of *aggregate* customer satisfaction and *aggregate* profitability over time.

- *Cross-sectional.* This is a look at the pairings of profitability and satisfaction from many different customers at any one point in time.

In both these perspectives, the major problem is to identify a suitable variable to represent profitability.

Longitudinal Methods

Longitudinal methods attempt to demonstrate a relationship over successive measurement periods between aggregate, organizationwide performance and observed levels of satisfaction. These methods will be most attractive to organizations that have recently employed customer satisfaction and have witnessed increases in their satisfaction ratings. Figure 8.2 plots six measurements of satisfaction and fiscal performance, showing their correlation with a regression line to establish the relationship. With the regression line as plotted, each increase of one point in satisfaction suggests a likely increase in profitability of $165,000. Of course, we must not assume a completely linear relationship. It is likely that financial performance will relate to increases in satisfaction following a diminishing-returns model. Stated another way, the higher the starting level of satisfaction, the less the incremental financial performance is likely to respond to additional improvements in satisfaction.

The viability of this form of linkage analysis will depend on your ability to find a suitable measure of aggregate-level profitability for the vertical axis. Here are some possibilities:

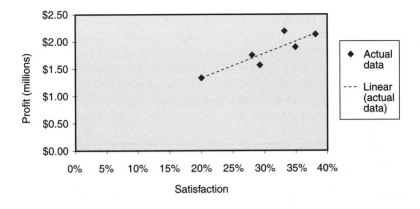

Figure 8.2   A trend line showing satisfaction and profitability.

- Organizationwide profits
- Sales levels
- Account growth (incremental sales)
- Market share
- Aggregate estimate of your share of each customer's category requirements

Cross-Sectional Methods

The cross-sectional approach assumes your organization's customers' satisfactions will be distributed over a range wide enough to allow comparison with each customer's purchases, profitability, share of requirements, or some other measure of business success at the customer level. This analysis takes place at one point in time, as opposed to the longitudinal analysis that requires measurement points over several different points in time.

Because satisfaction measures are maintained at the individual level, any linking procedure necessarily will require performance data at the individual or account level as well. It is surprising how few organizations can derive a measure of profitability for individual customers or accounts. Any company depending on direct marketing is likely to have appropriate metrics, as are not-for-profits and charities. These businesses have all learned over the years to reinvest only in those customers who create profits; therefore, they have developed workable measures of profitability.

With your customer-by-customer performance information collected, compare the satisfaction scores for each of your customers with the performance information. In Table 8.1 we've adopted *change in sales* as our performance measure. This performance measure is then correlated with the concomitant change in satisfaction score from the same period. Table 8.1 shows that for every unit change in satisfaction scores, sales may be expected to change by 19.8 units! This type of analysis should be compelling proof to even the most hardened skeptic of the importance of improving customer satisfaction.

 Checkpoint 8.2

1. Establishing belief in your survey will be important as you attempt to rally support for the changes your findings identify as desirable. The easiest way to show that performance ratings influence behavior is to cross-tabulate different rating levels with stated intentions to rebuy or recommend your services. You should see a pronounced lower likelihood among those who are less satisfied with your performance.

2. A true acid test and the most compelling of validations is to compare the actual sales or spending patterns of your highly satisfied customers with your less highly satisfied customers. What sales data do you have available that you can use to compare customers aggregated into groups with different satisfaction levels?

3. You can use sales or spending data in an instantaneous (cross-sectional) or longitudinal way. How can you best demonstrate to your organization the importance of maximizing customer satisfaction?

YOUR THREE AUDIENCES

Previously at least three possible audiences were identified as deserving of some report of your survey findings:

- Your management
- Your employees
- Your customers

Table 8.1   A longitudinal correlation—satisfaction with sales.

Customer	Satisfaction scores			Sales		
	1995	1996	Change	1995	1996	Change
135	7.1	7.1	0	80	82	2
141	6.7	6.2	−0.5	60	50	−10
165	8	8.5	0.5	110	130	20
173	8.8	9.1	0.3	25	55	30
210	7.2	7.8	0.6	10	15	5
215	7.9	8	0.1	63	73	10
252	7	6.9	−0.1	61	46	−15
307	7.8	7.3	−0.5	33	33	0
388	7.6	8.1	0.5	26	32	6
420	7.9	7.9	0	60	67	7

Regression output:

Constant		3.7149028
Standard error of Y established		11.124646
R squared		0.3556382
Number of observations		10
Degrees of freedom		8
X coefficient(s)	19.834413	
Standard error of coefficient	9.4391972	

All three constituencies are recognized by the ANSI/ISO/ASQ Q9001-2000 standard. And an argument can easily be made that unless all three of these constituencies receive some report from the findings of your satisfaction process, it will be underutilized and will probably eventually die. Reasons to support giving feedback to each group include these:

- Management has obviously funded your project, and constituent managers must sanction and act on the improvements necessary to fix the problems you identify.

- Employees need and deserve feedback because they're the ones who will have to implement the changes you identify. Without a report of your findings they may fail to understand why changes are necessary to your products and processes. Without that understanding, they may resist or even sabotage improvement efforts.

- Customers require feedback to assure them that your project is legitimate and worthy of their involvement. Even with resulting improvements visible, it will still be advantageous for you to acknowledge customers who have participated, assuring them that it was their opinions and needs that triggered the improvements.

STEP 8.3 REPORTS TO MANAGEMENT AND EMPLOYEES

The focus of chapter 7 was on how to create useful reports for management. Without repeating the entire contents of the chapter, it may be useful to reiterate the value of organization and summary in your reports. It has been said that to properly communicate you should tell your audience what you're going to tell them; and tell it to them; and finally, remind them of what you've told them. And most of all, don't attempt to communicate too many points. You may need to prioritize and select your improvement targets strategically. Don't be reluctant to do so. Sometimes information overload can derail the most sincere of efforts.

Not only must you communicate your findings to management, but you must also facilitate their appropriate reaction. This will generally be their authorization (to the organization) to:

1. Modify product designs or manufacturing defects

2. Fix the most serious of the malfunctioning systems or processes

Sometimes we seem to feel, "if management knows what's wrong, it'll get fixed." Nothing is probably further from the truth. Knowing your problems is one thing; knowing what has caused them and how to fix them are different issues. And motivating those who work in the problem areas or who cause the process breakdowns to modify their activities or behaviors so as to improve or alleviate the problems can be quite difficult. We're creatures of habit; we don't like to change our ways. We're also self-defensive. We don't like to be thought of as the problem. Avoidance or denial mitigates the success of far too many reengineering programs. People simply can't be expected to understand their culpability and to therefore instantly embrace change.

Without fully understanding the process by which you've collected your information and exactly what you've discovered, it's only natural for employees to be reluctant to accept your recommendations. On the other hand, if they understand your process and feel involved in it, then they can't help but give support to your improvement initiatives. That's where communicating with employees comes in. It creates understanding and builds involvement and support.

Checkpoint 8.3

1. Employees are the people who need to accept changes in processes or modify their conduct of existing processes. To facilitate change they need to be accepting of it. By describing your survey process and disseminating your findings, you'll make them more willing agents of change.

2. Do you plan to report your findings to your fellow employees? If so, how do you envision conducting the report?

STEP 8.4 REPORTS TO CUSTOMERS

Too many of us have participated in satisfaction programs that enjoy the same apparent attention as my suggestions to my health club (see sidebar). As we dutifully complete the questionnaire or submit to a 15-minute telephone interview, we are hopeful that someone really cares about us. Our expectations are raised and we eagerly anticipate changes, improvements, or modifications that will help eliminate the issues we have identified as troublesome. *The problem is that most CSM studies are conducted only as information collection procedures.* People with survey research or opinion-polling training may administer them. These individuals may believe it is unnecessary or even unethical to show an individual survey participant that the survey sponsor knows the participant's identity and what troubled him or her. And so they fail to acknowledge customers' participation and customers' problems and fail to identify anything that their organization may be contemplating to

---

There's a suggestion box on the reception desk of my health club. Forms nearby ask for members' suggestions and also ask for the member's name, address, telephone number, and membership number. My fellow members and I (who have completed forms and deposited them in the suggestion box) are convinced that the box is a vortex to a black hole in the cosmos! This is because once a suggestion is deposited there, it appears never to be seen or attended to, but rather is whisked off into the abyss of outer space far from the concerns of management of this particular club!

alleviate a problem or problems. Worse yet, either because the suggestions aren't addressed or because improvements made will take time to be noticed, we, as customers, feel ignored and devalued.

After numerous instances of not being acknowledged, most of us become uninterested in investing any more of our time or effort in complying with satisfaction surveys. We become cynical about all satisfaction measurement programs. The aggregated impact of this cynicism has fostered a significant decline in cooperation and response rates with all satisfaction surveys. And, unfortunately, even though business-to-business surveys tend to be more responsive to their participants, the cynicism nevertheless overlaps from our customers' experiences as retail customers to surveys conducted in our industries and professional associations.

A refreshing response to the often ignored customer is Section 7.2.3 of ANSI/ISO/ASQ Q9001-2000. This section addresses the value of communicating with customers.

7.2.3 Customer Communication

The organization shall identify and implement arrangements for communication with customers relating to:

a) Product information;

b) Inquiries, contracts or order handling, including amendments;

c) Customer feedback, including customer complaints.

Source: ANSI/ISO/ASQ Q9001-2000

The revised ANSI/ISO/ASQ Q9001-2000 standard and your author are in total agreement as to the importance of providing participating customers feedback and some sort of closure to their survey participation.[1] (Sometimes, it will even be beneficial to provide feedback to nonparticipating customers. You will build credibility for your program and may even predispose them to participate the next time you attempt to interview them.) Communication with your customers can be accomplished in a variety of ways.

---

[1] Consider reporting back to all of your customers, even those who didn't participate in your survey. You might explain to nonparticipants what you learned from customers who did participate. Your message could be subtle or overt: "If you want your needs incorporated in future findings, you must participate to have them heard!"

Participation Acknowledgment

The most modest (and minimal) closure you should offer is a simple acknowledgment to participating customers that you have received their questionnaire or interview results, that you appreciate their committing their time to the data collection process, and that you are reviewing their suggestions with those of other customers and will formulate process improvements and action plans accordingly.

While acknowledgments will add substantial expense to your field costs, they can be accomplished in a number of ways:

1. A simple postcard acknowledging a customer's participation is far better than no response at all. See Figure 8.3 for a sample card.

2. A more formal letter may be sent from your process champion or another organizational officer thanking the customer for his or her participation. This letter can be rather universal, but it should, if possible, bear a real signature. It is even more satisfying to customers if a specific action plan or timetable is also provided.

3. A more responsive form of a thank-you letter is to personalize each letter you send. You can mention specific items that your customer has requested, or you may respond to concerns that your customer has expressed. Such an acknowledgment is, of course, labor intensive but some would argue no more so than what is warranted by the participation of an organization's customers.

Thank you for your response to the AARP Investment Program satisfaction survey. Your feedback regarding the materials and services is important in helping guide continual improvement.

Please remember that you can always reach the Program with any questions or comments by:

- Writing to us at: AARP Investment Program from Scudder Investments, P.O. Box 219735, Kansas City, MO 64121-9735
- Calling one of our representatives (Mon.–Fri., 8am to 8pm E.T., and Sat., 9am to 4pm E.T.) at: 1-800-253-2277
- Accessing us on the Internet at www.aarp.scudder.com

Regards,

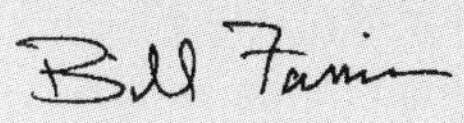

Bill Farris

Bill Farris
Director, Financial Products

Figure 8.3   A postcard acknowledgment.

Report on Adopting Customers' Suggestions

A response mechanism that combines the aforementioned elements is a newsletter or satisfaction process bulletin. This report can consist of a sanitized summary of your survey findings to show customers that you have, in fact, listened. (You will probably wish to be selective in what you publicly acknowledge; so identify some issues that you already may have under control.) The formality and wide distribution of a newsletter or bulletin provides evidence that your organization sincerely wants to hear from customers and will attempt to address their concerns. With such a public document you will generally have to establish a rather formal timetable for making improvements.

Red Flag Reports

Immediate and direct response, where required, is the element missing in most customer satisfaction programs.

In every business-to-business satisfaction program the author has helped design, a provision has always been made to issue *red flag reports* for specific customers who ought to be contacted. The purpose of such reports is to pass along a specific customer's problem to a field or marketing person who can follow up with the customer in hopes of providing him

---

A friend complied with his automobile manufacturer's request for information on his satisfaction with the manufacturer's automobile. In addition to answering all the requested questions, he added an urgent message regarding a malfunction he had been experiencing. He was never contacted, as he had requested. Again, with the next survey he issued the same plea for assistance—again, no response. He finally concluded that although the manufacturer's survey was well presented and possibly well intentioned, it lacked any mechanism for reviewing individual customer's comments and requests. His unread notes had simply been ignored as the accompanying ratings data were entered.

or her some relief. These red flag reports should contain a summary of all the information the customer has furnished along with the specific response triggering issuance of the report. See Figure 8.4. When you're processing large numbers of questionnaires, you'll need to institute some automatic decision rules that trigger the issuance of a red flag report. These may take the form of one or more of the following conditions:

- An overall satisfaction rating that falls below a threshold value. (You may decide to follow up with any customer so dissatisfied that he awards you only a 3 or less on your 0-to-10 overall satisfaction scale.)

- A performance rating on one or more key performance (require-ment) questions that falls below a similar rating threshold.

- A request for help or assistance noted anywhere on the customer's questionnaire.

- A response to an open-ended question that is so bitter or threaten-ing as to identify the customer as in real need of assistance and/or communication.

As you institute a red flag process, especially if you have a large num-ber of customers (any number greater than that which you could be expected to personally know), you'll be rewarded with lots of praise and reinforcement from the customers you touch. You'll hear back from them in the form of reactions such as these:

I didn't think you guys really cared!

Finally, someone listened to me, thanks!

*I never thought anyone read these questionnaires! I'm glad
I took the time to fill it out! You've made a believer out
of me.*

Red flag reports are generally issued as quickly as possible after you receive a customer's questionnaire (or completion of the customer's inter-view). Contact should be goaled to occur within a reasonably short time (24 to 72 hours seems the average).

Red flag, or contact-critical, reports are usually created as an elec-tronic summary of the customer's questionnaire with the triggering crite-ria clearly indicated. Figure 8.4 shows a typical contact-critical report. This one is formatted for easy distribution to the appropriate field employee by e-mail.

Toys "R" Us
Red Flag Report

Region: Central
Case # 123456789

STORE # 5555   **DATE** 3/5/2001   **REGISTER:** 1   **TRANSACTION #** 1234

Please rate your overall shopping experience: Average

What, in particular, causes you to rate Toys "R" Us this way?
TOYS "R" US DIDN'T HAVE WHAT I WAS LOOKING FOR YESTERDAY. THEY
DIDN'T HAVE THE LEGOS I WAS LOOKING FOR. I WAS LOOKING FOR ROCK
RAIDER AND SPECIAL STAR WARS LEGOS AND IT WASN'T IN STOCK.

Please rate the following:

Keeps merchandise in stock	Average
Knowledgeable associates that can assist you	Among the Best
Shelves, displays, and aisles are neat and clean	Among the Best
Cashier friendliness	Among the Best
Check-out speed	Average
Associates are readily available to assist you	Among the Best

**Were there any items that you were unable to purchase on your visit to
Toys "R" Us?**
ROCK RAIDERS LEGOS STAR WARS LEGOS

**The next time you are shopping for children's merchandise, how likely
are you to shop for it at Toys "R" Us?**
__ 100% Likely _X_ 80% Likely __ 60% Likely
__ 40% Likely __ 20% Likely __ Not Likely

NAME: JANE DOE
ADDRESS: 1234 ANY STREET
CITY: ANY TOWN   **STATE:** ANY STATE   **ZIP:** 12345
PHONE: (800) 555-1234

Figure 8.4   A red flag report.
Used with permission of Toys "R" Us, Inc.

 Checkpoint 8.4

1. Can you think of a way to help your management understand the importance of reporting back to customers?
   Review ANSI/ISO/ASQ Q9001-2000, Section 7.2 with them.

2. How do you plan to acknowledge your customers' participation in your survey?

3. Will you consider creating a red flag process? If so, flowchart how you envision implementing this process.
   Consider ways of documenting its value to your customers and ultimately to your organization.

STEP 8.5 ORGANIZE FOR IMPROVEMENT

Your customer satisfaction survey will be one initiative whose results are pertinent to virtually every department and area in your organization. The pervasiveness of the issues identified by your program will often foster a reluctance by individual departments to own up to their responsibility to fix things. A formalized procedure for acting on findings is necessary. Without such a process, your findings probably will not be widely used. That's because no *one* department owns (or could act on) all the findings of a customer satisfaction survey. Without an implementation process in place, the naive organization (that simply fields a survey of its customers) will find the results of a survey to be overwhelming. There simply will be too many different departments implicated and too many different processes to modify or to influence. Even if your satisfaction process reports directly to your organization's chief operating officer, fashioning the improvement plans and allocating responsibilities will still be difficult.

But in organizations where an implementation process has been considered *before* the customer survey is fielded, the results will not be so overwhelming. You should consider sponsoring or encouraging the formation of a task force (a quality improvement team) to receive and to act on your findings. This team should be composed of representatives of each of the many departments and processes in your organization that may need to be altered. Each representative will be responsible ultimately for taking information back to his or her area and prompting remedial actions to improve overall satisfaction.

A secondary benefit of having an implementation program in place is the continuity and continuous focus the task force creates for your customer satisfaction process. Rather than being a once-a-year, on-the-bookshelf project, your customer satisfaction process is given an ongoing life.

 Checkpoint 8.5

1. Do you currently have a quality improvement team with cross-departmental membership whose assistance you could enlist to help create positive reactions to your survey's findings? If not, can you create such a task force or enlist your manager to assist in creating a task force?

2. List the departments or areas in your organization you believe should participate on this team.

STEP 8.6 INTERPRETING CUSTOMERS' EVALUATIONS . . . A WARNING

It should be obvious that customers' ratings won't always be accurate, but their feelings nevertheless control their decisions. Your strategic reactions to your customers' perceptions must, therefore, be well thought out. As you prepare to react to your customers' judgments you face the situation illustrated in Figure 8.5. Here, two states of customer *perception* are depicted: customers perceive a problem; customers don't perceive a problem. Coupled with those two perceptions are the parallel states of your business: you have a problem; you don't have a problem. Knowing whether you have a product/process problem or a communication problem is critical to efficiently resolving the trouble. A product problem requires you to make a fundamental change in product or procedures. You can address a communication problem more directly—through what the author calls *management of evidence* (Vavra 1995).

 Checkpoint 8.6

1. Make sure you know the true nature of the "problems" your customers enumerate. List each perceived problem according to whether it's a real or a communication problem. Try to approach each with an open mind.

STEP 8.7 QUALITY FUNCTION DEPLOYMENT GRID

In the management of technology there is a generally evolving belief that cooperation and communication among the often disparate departments of engineering, R&D, manufacturing, and marketing leads to better product improvements and more acceptable new products (Griffin and Hauser 1992). Evidence shows that if engineering, manufacturing, and R&D fully understand customer needs and if marketing has explored how customer needs can be fulfilled by product or service changes, the resulting product or service is more likely to be profitable (Cooper 1984; Souder 1988; Pinto and Pinto 1990).

A technique developed at Mitsubishi's Kobe shipyards in Japan in 1972, the *house of quality*, was the first application of a quality function deployment (QFD) grid. Because of its apparent benefits, the process was adopted by Toyota in the late 1970s, and by Xerox and Ford in the United States in 1986. Griffin and Hauser (1992) reported its use by more than one hundred U.S. firms by 1991.

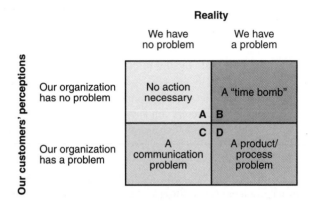

Figure 8.5 Determining the type of problem to solve.

The house of quality process is actually a series of four "houses," with each house relating (or connecting) two of the four input areas (*customer needs, design attributes, R&D actions,* and *manufacturing implementation*). The most widely used and discussed (in a customer satisfaction context) is the first house which links customer needs to design attributes (engineering's measures of product performance). This linkage essentially answers how customer satisfaction can be engineered into your products or services. The first house is diagrammed in Figure 8.6.

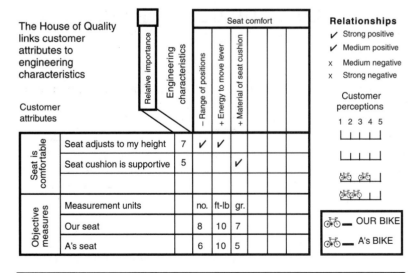

Figure 8.6 The house of quality.

The major benefit of a QFD grid and process is the facilitation and encouragement of communication and cooperation among departments that in most organizations have traditionally been isolated. In addition, the technique structures customer satisfaction information in such a way that it can be productively acted upon by all. QFD helps interpret how product characteristics and servicing policies affect customer preference, satisfaction, and ultimately sales. One discrete advantage QFD has over other similar processes is its visual format, which is easy to understand and communicates very well.

A simple QFD solution is shown in Figure 8.7. The grid is constructed with customer needs as rows and operating areas or departments as columns. Then, in each cell of the grid the relationship between the need and the department is graded, from *no relationship* to a *strong relationship*. Rating the relationship can be done numerically or in two or three steps or grades (the most common format). In Figure 8.7, the absence of a symbol in a cell indicates no relationship, a circle in the cell represents a weak relationship, and a square suggests a strong relationship between the need and the department. This is a simple way of allocating ownership of problems to operational areas in the organization.

Obviously, QFD grids can vary in their complexity. Some people speak of their modest QFD grids as "condos of quality," while other initiatives fully capitalize on the complexity of the original "house of quality." But, however simple or complex your grid, a QFD process allows you to align causes of customer dissatisfaction with those departments most likely to improve things.[2]

 Checkpoint 8.7

1. Consider how you will introduce the QFD grid to your improvement team. What sort of training will you necessarily give them so that they both use and accept the indications of a QFD analysis?

---

[2] The QFD process is an involved topic. The interested reader is referred to the many books devoted to the process. The author's 1997 book contains a much more thorough discussion.

Customer requirements/needs	Imp.	Responsibility							Customers' perceptions				Action	
		Engineering	Design team	Grooming staff	Base mgmt	Lodge mgmt	Housekeeping	Marketing	Our rating	Comp A	Comp B	Comp gap	Import gap	Priority
Trail signage	0.04		○	○					4.0	7.8	8.8	–4.8	–0.19	1
Cost of week package	0.10				○	○		■	6.3	7.5	8.0	–1.7	–0.17	2
Upkeep/condition of base station	0.20				■			○	6.9	7.7	7.5	–0.8	–0.16	3
Quality of lodge restaurants	0.07					○			6.7	8.8	7.1	–2.1	–0.15	4
Number of trails	0.18		■						7.5	7.7	6.9	–0.2	–0.04	5
Quality of food at base station	0.04				■				7.8	8.4	5.0	–0.6	–0.02	6
Spaciousness/comfort base station	0.01				○				7.1	7.9	6.7	–0.8	–0.01	7
Spaciousness/comfort of lodge	0.02					○		○	8.9	6.6	7.3	1.6	0.03	8
Lift lines and capacity	0.09	■							8.6	8.1	5.9	0.5	0.05	9
Comfort of lodge rooms	0.04								8.8	6.3	7.6	1.2	0.05	10
Condition of trails	0.13		○	■					8.3	7.1	6.4	1.2	0.16	11
Cleanliness of lodge rooms	0.08						■		9.0	4.9	7.0	2.0	0.16	12
	1.00													

Key: ■ Strong Relationship
○ Weak Relationship

Figure 8.7 A quality function deployment grid for a ski resort.

Step-by-Step: The Answers for Communicating Your Results

8.1 To succeed, your satisfaction program needs a champion, someone who both believes in the value of the information produced and has enough organizational influence to help others in your organization attend to that information. You need to get to know this individual's vision of your process. You can attempt to influence it, to steer it in slightly different directions, but you must be ready to support it. See pages 253–56.

8.2 Even though you believe in the value of the information you are collecting, not everyone in your organization will equally understand and trust it. You may wish to validate your process by showing its relationship to actual customer behaviors. You can document that association using either your attitudinal data or a combination of your attitudinal data and actual sales or purchase data. Your proof can be at an aggregate level (all customers) or at a disaggregated level (individual customer). See pages 256–62.

8.3 Consider how you will report results not just to your management but also to your employees and your customers. It's important for your employees to understand your process and what you've learned because they'll have to "believe" to willingly make the improvements your survey identifies. See page 262.

8.4 Customers require some feedback to keep them involved in the process and willing to participate in future waves. Your process may also uncover customers who need immediate assistance or attention. Design a *red flag report* process to see that their condition is brought to the attention of the right people in your organization who can act immediately to remedy the customer's problem. They'll be eternally grateful and will truly believe in the value of your satisfaction survey process! See pages 263–68.

8.5 You'll need to create a *quality improvement team* or a *satisfaction task force* to help stimulate the improvements you've identified. All functions or departments in your organization should be represented. See pages 268–69.

8.6 As you encounter what your customers cite as "problems" be careful to recognize that while your customers see such issues as shortcomings of your organization, solutions for some may actually exist! Customers' lists of problems identify for us two types of problems: *actual problems* and *problems of communication*. For the actual problems you'll need to fix or amend a product or process. But for issues that customers perceive as problems but that have already been solved, an opportunity exists for your organization to more visibly communicate its actions so that your customers appreciate its remedial efforts. See page 270.

8.7 You'll need to establish a *quality function deployment* grid as a tool to help you and your quality improvement team implement change. The QFD grid helps assign ownership of problems to specific operating areas. A problem acknowledged by everyone but owned by no one rarely gets fixed. Your QFD grid will focus energies from the relevant departments on the problems. See pages 270–73.

Chapter 8 Deliverables

Your work in this chapter will have produced these deliverables:

1. A vision statement describing how your survey results will be used in your organization to help improve customer satisfaction. Use information from sections 8.1, 8.3, and 8.4.

2. A statistical proof documenting the value of your satisfaction measures by showing that they correlate with the actual behavior (repeat purchases, amount of purchases, willingness to recommend) of your customers.

3. A report plan that shows what information you plan to offer your three audiences: management, employees, and customers. This plan should also describe how you intend to distribute the information.

4. Possibly a format for red flag, or contact-critical, reports to be used to get immediate assistance to customers you have discovered are in need of help or assistance.

5. An organization chart for your quality improvement team, showing representation from all departments in your organization.

6. A quality function deployment grid uniting departments with customer needs. The needs are prioritized; then problem ownership can be easily directed.

Appendix A
Worksheets

Worksheet 1.1   Your definition of customer satisfaction

Customer satisfaction is/occurs . . .

_____

_____

_____

_____

_____

_____

_____

_____

_____

_____

Worksheet 1.2   A profile of the use of customer
satisfaction by other organizations in your industry/category.

Competitor	Visibility of customer satisfaction program	How implemented? (format, coverage, responsiveness)

Worksheet 1.3   Determining the value of satisfied customers.

	A Our most satisfied customers	B Our least satisfied customers
How defined:		
1. Average purchase/order size of basic product		
2. Number of purchases per year		
3. Sales revenue (row 1 × row 2)		
4. Number of new customers referred to us		
5. Value of new customers (row 4 × row 3)		
6. Sales revenue from additional products purchased ("cross-sell")		
7. Total value (row 3 + row 5 + row 6)		
8. Value of satisfied customers (cell 7A – cell 7B)		

Worksheet 2.1 A decision-mapping sequence.

Customer:				
Decision maker	**Title**	**Department**	**Role**	**Amount of influence**
			[ ] Initiates the decision to buy [ ] Gathers information [ ] Evaluates alternative suppliers [ ] Influences the decision [ ] Makes the decision to buy [ ] Ratifies the decision to buy	
			[ ] Initiates the decision to buy [ ] Gathers information [ ] Evaluates alternative suppliers [ ] Influences the decision [ ] Makes the decision to buy [ ] Ratifies the decision to buy	
			[ ] Initiates the decision to buy [ ] Gathers information [ ] Evaluates alternative suppliers [ ] Influences the decision [ ] Makes the decision to buy [ ] Ratifies the decision to buy	
			[ ] Initiates the decision to buy [ ] Gathers information [ ] Evaluates alternative suppliers [ ] Influences the decision [ ] Makes the decision to buy [ ] Ratifies the decision to buy	
			[ ] Initiates the decision to buy [ ] Gathers information [ ] Evaluates alternative suppliers [ ] Influences the decision [ ] Makes the decision to buy [ ] Ratifies the decision to buy	

Worksheet 2.2   Your intended structure for
your customerbase.

Table: Main Namebase

Field position	Description of the contents of the field	Format	Width (no. of characters)
1.			
2.			
3.			
4.			
5.			
6.			
7.			
8.			
9.			
10.			
11.			
12.			
13.			
14.			
15.			
16.			
17.			
18.			
19.			
20.			

What field or contents will serve as your key if you need to relate another
table to this, your Main Name table? _____

Worksheet 4.1   Survey logistics summary sheet.

1. **Customer representation**		Census
		Survey
2. **Periodicity of measurement**		Continuously: weekly
		Continuously: monthly
		Continuously: quarterly
		Annually: when:
3. **Type of administration**		Interviewer
		Machine
		Self
4. **Modality for distribution**		Mail/courier
		Telephone
		Fax
		Computer
5. **Modality for return**		Mail/courier
		Telephone
		Fax
		Computer
6. **Sponsorship**		Identified, organization sponsored
		Anonymous
7. **Coding**		Open-ended questions:
		Closed-ended questions:
8. **Data entry**		Machine-entered (CATI, CAPI, Internet)
		Manually entered by data entry staff
		Customer self-enters

Appendix B

Questionnaires

3. How likely are you to repurchase from us (allocating to us approximately the same or better share of your needs in this category) in the future? Please circle a number on the scale below to indicate your likelihood.

Definitely will not
repurchase

Definitely will
repurchase

| 0 | 1 | 2 | 3 | 4 | 5 | 6 | 7 | 8 | 9 | 10 |

4. If asked by a colleague within your company, how willing would you be to recommend *company name* as a supplier of quality products? Please circle a number on the scale below to indicate your willingness.

Definitely will not
recommend

Definitely will
recommend

| 0 | 1 | 2 | 3 | 4 | 5 | 6 | 7 | 8 | 9 | 10 |

5. How much do you agree with the statement, "*company name's* products represent a very good value for their price?" Please circle a number on the scale below to indicate your agreement.

Completely
disagree

Completely
agree

| 0 | 1 | 2 | 3 | 4 | 5 | 6 | 7 | 8 | 9 | 10 |

6. How accessible (able to be reached in person or by electronic media) would you say we are to you, our customer? Please circle a number on the scale below to indicate our accessibility.

Not at all
accessible

Highly
accessible

| 0 | 1 | 2 | 3 | 4 | 5 | 6 | 7 | 8 | 9 | 10 |

7. If contacted, how responsive (solving problems in a timely way) would you say we are to you, our customer? Please circle a number on the scale below to indicate our responsiveness.

Not at all
responsive

Highly
responsive

| 0 | 1 | 2 | 3 | 4 | 5 | 6 | 7 | 8 | 9 | 10 |

Some Process-Specific Ratings

For each of the following issues, please rate your satisfaction with our hardware by circling a number on the adjoining scale. (If you have no experience with an issue relative to our product, please check the "no experience" box to the right of the numbered scale.)

8. The basic functionality of our products

Completely
dissatisfied

Completely
satisfied

0 1 2 3 4 5 6 7 8 9 10   No exp [ ]

9. Features offered

Completely
dissatisfied

Completely
satisfied

0 1 2 3 4 5 6 7 8 9 10   No exp [ ]

10. Reliability of our products/equipment

Completely
dissatisfied

Completely
satisfied

0 1 2 3 4 5 6 7 8 9 10   No exp [ ]

11. Conformance (meeting your specs)

Completely
dissatisfied

Completely
satisfied

0 1 2 3 4 5 6 7 8 9 10   No exp [ ]

12. Durability

Completely
dissatisfied

Completely
satisfied

0 1 2 3 4 5 6 7 8 9 10   No exp [ ]

13. Serviceability

Completely
dissatisfied

Completely
satisfied

0 1 2 3 4 5 6 7 8 9 10   No exp [ ]

14. Documentation

Completely
dissatisfied

Completely
satisfied

0 1 2 3 4 5 6 7 8 9 10   No exp [ ]

Final Thoughts

15. Please rate your satisfaction with our **delivery**. Please circle a
number below to indicate your satisfaction.

Not at all
satisfied

Completely
satisfied

0 1 2 3 4 5 6 7 8 9 10   Doesn't apply [ ]

(continued)

16. Please rate your satisfaction with our **installation** (if applicable). Please circle a number below to indicate your satisfaction.

Not at all satisfied   Completely satisfied

0 1 2 3 4 5 6 7 8 9 10   Doesn't apply [ ]

17. Please rate your satisfaction with our **qualification** (if applicable). Please circle a number below to indicate your satisfaction.

Not at all satisfied   Completely satisfied

0 1 2 3 4 5 6 7 8 9 10   Doesn't apply [ ]

18. Overall, how satisfied are you with the servicing you have received from our *company name* organization? Please circle a number below to indicate your satisfaction.

Not at all satisfied   Completely satisfied

0 1 2 3 4 5 6 7 8 9 10   Doesn't apply [ ]

19. Do you have any unmet needs that we are currently not addressing?

_____

_____

_____

20. Do you have any comments, complaints, compliments, or concerns you care to offer us?

_____

_____

_____

21. Unless you check here, we will share your ratings and comments with our department managers and supervisors.

[ ] Please **do not share** my *individual* ratings and comments with your managers and supervisors.

Thank you very much for your time and the information you have provided us. We look forward to continuing to provide you the utmost in satisfaction.

Questionnaire 2: Software Manufacturers

Thank you for your interest in helping *company name* better understand the quality of our performance for you, our customer.

Our Overall Conduct

1. Overall, how satisfied are you with *company name?* Please circle a number on the scale below to indicate your satisfaction.

Completely   Completely
dissatisfied   satisfied

0   1   2   3   4   5   6   7   8   9   10

2. Please help us understand this rating by describing (in your own words) why you rated us as you did in question 1. (Please be as specific as possible.)

_____

_____

_____

3. How likely are you to repurchase from us (allocating to us approximately the same or better share of your needs in this category) in the future? Please circle a number on the scale below to indicate your likelihood.

Definitely will not   Definitely will
repurchase   repurchase

0   1   2   3   4   5   6   7   8   9   10

4. If asked by a colleague within your company, how willing would you be to recommend *company name* as a supplier of quality software? Please circle a number on the scale below to indicate your willingness.

Definitely will not   Definitely will
recommend   recommend

0   1   2   3   4   5   6   7   8   9   10

5. How much do you agree with the statement, "*company name's* software represents a very good value for the price?" Please circle a number on the scale below to indicate your agreement.

Completely   Completely
disagree   agree

0   1   2   3   4   5   6   7   8   9   10

(continued)

6. How accessible (able to be reached in person or by electronic media) would you say we are to you, our customer? Please circle a number on the scale below to indicate our accessibility.

Not at all   Highly
accessible   accessible

0   1   2   3   4   5   6   7   8   9   10

7. If contacted, how responsive (solving problems in a timely way) would you say we are to you, our customer? Please circle a number on the scale below to indicate our responsiveness.

Not at all   Highly
responsive   responsive

0   1   2   3   4   5   6   7   8   9   10

Some Process-Specific Ratings

For each of the following issues, please rate your satisfaction with our software by circling a number on the adjoining scale. (If you have no experience with an issue relative to our product, please check the "No experience" box to the right of the numbered scale.)

8. The basic functionality of our software

Completely   Completely
dissatisfied   satisfied

0   1   2   3   4   5   6   7   8   9   10   No exp [ ]

9. Features offered

Completely   Completely
dissatisfied   satisfied

0   1   2   3   4   5   6   7   8   9   10   No exp [ ]

10. Reliability of our software

Completely   Completely
dissatisfied   satisfied

0   1   2   3   4   5   6   7   8   9   10   No exp [ ]

11. Conformance (meeting your specs)

Completely   Completely
dissatisfied   satisfied

0   1   2   3   4   5   6   7   8   9   10   No exp [ ]

12. Durability

Completely   Completely
dissatisfied   satisfied

0   1   2   3   4   5   6   7   8   9   10   No exp [ ]

13. Serviceability

Completely   Completely
dissatisfied   satisfied

0   1   2   3   4   5   6   7   8   9   10   No exp [ ]

14. Documentation

Completely   Completely
dissatisfied   satisfied

0   1   2   3   4   5   6   7   8   9   10   No exp [ ]

Final Thoughts

15. Please rate your satisfaction with our **delivery**. Please circle a number below to indicate your satisfaction.

Not at all   Completely
satisfied   satisfied

0   1   2   3   4   5   6   7   8   9   10   Doesn't apply [ ]

16. Please rate your satisfaction with our **installation** (if applicable). Please circle a number below to indicate your satisfaction.

Not at all   Completely
satisfied   satisfied

0   1   2   3   4   5   6   7   8   9   10   Doesn't apply [ ]

17. Please rate your satisfaction with our **qualification** (if applicable). Please circle a number below to indicate your satisfaction.

Not at all   Completely
satisfied   satisfied

0   1   2   3   4   5   6   7   8   9   10   Doesn't apply [ ]

18. Overall, how satisfied are you with the servicing you have received from our *company name* organization? Please circle a number below to indicate your satisfaction.

Not at all   Completely
satisfied   satisfied

0   1   2   3   4   5   6   7   8   9   10   Doesn't apply [ ]

19. Do you have any unmet needs that we are currently not addressing?

_____

_____

_____

(continued)

20. Do you have any comments, complaints, compliments, or concerns you care to offer us?

_____

_____

_____

21. Unless you check here, we will share your ratings and comments with our department managers and supervisors

[ ] Please **do not share** my *individual* ratings and comments with your managers and supervisors.

Thank you very much for your time and the information you have provided us. We look forward to continuing to provide you the utmost in satisfaction.

Questionnaire 3: Service Providers

Thank you for your interest in helping *company name* better understand the quality of our performance for you, our customer.

Our Overall Conduct

1. Overall, how satisfied are you with *company name?* Please circle a number on the scale below to indicate your satisfaction.

Completely   Completely
dissatisfied   satisfied

0   1   2   3   4   5   6   7   8   9   10

2. Please help us understand this rating by describing (in your own words) why you rated us as you did in question 1. (Please be as specific as possible.)

_____

_____

_____

3. How likely are you to repurchase from us (allocating to us approximately the same or better share of your needs in this category) in the future? Please circle a number on the scale below to indicate your satisfaction.

Definitely will not repurchase   Definitely will repurchase

0   1   2   3   4   5   6   7   8   9   10

4. If asked by a colleague within your company, how willing would you be to recommend *company name* as a supplier of quality services? Please circle a number on the scale below to indicate your willingness.

Definitely will not recommend   Definitely will recommend

0   1   2   3   4   5   6   7   8   9   10

5. How much do you agree with the statement, "*company name's* services represent a very good value for their price?" Please circle a number on the scale below to indicate your agreement.

Completely disagree   Completely agree

0   1   2   3   4   5   6   7   8   9   10

6. How accessible (able to be reached in person or by electronic media) would you say we are to you, our customer? Please circle a number on the scale below to indicate our accessibility.

Not at all accessible   Highly accessible

0   1   2   3   4   5   6   7   8   9   10

7. If contacted, how responsive (solving problems in a timely way) would you say we are to you, our customer? Please circle a number on the scale below to indicate our responsiveness.

Not at all responsive   Highly responsive

0   1   2   3   4   5   6   7   8   9   10

Some Process-Specific Ratings

For each of the following issues, please rate your satisfaction with us by circling a number on the adjoining scale. (If you have no experience with an issue relative to our product, please check the "No experience" box to the right of the numbered scale.)

(continued)

8. The reliability of our service

Completely
dissatisfied

Completely
satisfied

0   1   2   3   4   5   6   7   8   9   10   No exp [ ]

9. The competence of our staff

Completely
dissatisfied

Completely
satisfied

0   1   2   3   4   5   6   7   8   9   10   No exp [ ]

10. Our courtesy in working with you

Completely
dissatisfied

Completely
satisfied

0   1   2   3   4   5   6   7   8   9   10   No exp [ ]

11. Our credibility

Completely
dissatisfied

Completely
satisfied

0   1   2   3   4   5   6   7   8   9   10   No exp [ ]

12. The security your work receives

Completely
dissatisfied

Completely
satisfied

0   1   2   3   4   5   6   7   8   9   10   No exp [ ]

13. Our empathy to your needs

Completely
dissatisfied

Completely
satisfied

0   1   2   3   4   5   6   7   8   9   10   No exp [ ]

14. Our communication skills

Completely
dissatisfied

Completely
satisfied

0   1   2   3   4   5   6   7   8   9   10   No exp [ ]

Final Thoughts

15. Please rate your satisfaction with our **delivery**. Please circle a number below to indicate your satisfaction.

Not at all
satisfied

Completely
satisfied

0   1   2   3   4   5   6   7   8   9   10   Doesn't apply [ ]

16. Please rate your satisfaction with our **configuration and alignment** (if applicable). Please circle a number below to indicate your satisfaction.

Not at all
satisfied

Completely
satisfied

0   1   2   3   4   5   6   7   8   9   10   Doesn't apply [ ]

17. Please rate your satisfaction with our **qualification** (if applicable). Please circle a number below to indicate your satisfaction.

Not at all
satisfied

Completely
satisfied

0   1   2   3   4   5   6   7   8   9   10   Doesn't apply [ ]

18. Overall, how satisfied are you with the **servicing** you have received from our *company name* organization? Please circle a number below to indicate your satisfaction.

Not at all
satisfied

Completely
satisfied

0   1   2   3   4   5   6   7   8   9   10   Doesn't apply [ ]

19. Do you have any unmet needs that we are currently not addressing?

_____

_____

_____

20. Do you have any comments, complaints, compliments, or concerns you care to offer us?

_____

_____

_____

21. Unless you check here, we will share your ratings and comments with our department managers and supervisors

[ ] Please **do not share** my *individual* ratings and comments with your managers and supervisors.

Thank you very much for your time and the information you have provided us. We look forward to continuing to provide you the utmost in satisfaction.

Appendix C

Recommended Resources

CUSTOMER SATISFACTION THEORY AND MEASUREMENT

Hayes, Bob E. *Measuring Customer Satisfaction: Survey Design, Use, and Statistical Analysis Methods.* Milwaukee: ASQ Quality Press, 1998.

Kessler, Sheila. *Measuring and Managing Customer Satisfaction: Going for the Gold.* Milwaukee: ASQC Quality Press, 1996.

Myers, James H. *Measuring Customer Satisfaction: Hot Buttons and Other Measurement Issues,* Chicago: American Marketing Association, 2001.

Naumann, Earl and Kathleen Giel. *Customer Satisfaction Measurement and Management: Using the Voice of the Customer.* Cincinnati, OH: Thomson Executive Press, 1995.

Oliver, Richard L. *Satisfaction: A Behavioral Perspective on the Consumer.* Burr Ridge, IL: Irwin McGraw-Hill, 1997.

Vavra, Terry G. *Improving Your Measurement of Customer Satisfaction: A Guide to Creating, Conducting, Analyzing and Reporting Customer Satisfaction Measurement Programs.* Milwaukee: ASQ Quality Press, 1997.

SURVEY RESEARCH AND QUESTIONNAIRE CONSTRUCTION

Alreck, Pamela L. and Robert B. Settle. *The Survey Research Handbook*, Burr Ridge, IL: Irwin McGraw-Hill, 1995.

Fowler, Floyd J., Jr. *Improving Survey Questions: Design and Evaluation.* Thousand Oaks, CA: Sage Publications, 1995.

Payne, Stanley L.. *The Art of Asking Questions.* Princeton, NJ: Princeton University Press, 1951.

Schuman, Howard and Stanley Presser. *Questions & Answers in Attitude Surveys: Experiments on Question Form, Wording, and Context.* Thousand Oaks, CA: Sage Publications, 1996.

Sudman, Seymour and Norman M. Bradburn. *Asking Questions: A Practical Guide to Questionnaire Design.* San Francisco: Jossey-Bass Publishers, 1982.

STATISTICAL ANALYSIS

Allen, Derek R. and Tanniru R. Rao. *Analysis of Customer Satisfaction Data: A Comprehensive Guide to Multivariate Statistical Analysis in Customer Satisfaction, Loyalty, and Service Quality Research.* Milwaukee: ASQ Quality Press, 2000.

Bruning, James L. and B. L. Kintz. *Computational Handbook of Statistics*, Third Edition. Glenview, IL: Scott Foresman and Company, 2000.

Churchill, Gilbert A. *Marketing Research Method Foundations*, Seventh Edition. Fort Worth, TX: Harcourt College Publishers, 1999.

Hair, Joseph F., Jr., Rolph E. Anderson, and Ronald L. Tatham. *Multivariate Data Analysis with Readings*, Second Edition. New York: Macmillan Publishing Company, 1987.

Nunnally, Jum. *Psychometric Theory*, Second Edition. New York: McGraw-Hill, 1985.

Works Cited

INTRODUCTION

Deming, W. Edwards. *Out of the Crisis*. Cambridge, MA: Massachusetts Institute of Technology, Center for Advanced Engineering Study, 1986.

CHAPTER ONE

Buzzell, Robert D. and Bradley T. Gale. *The PIMS Principles*. New York: Free Press, 1987.

Cianfrani, Charles A., Joseph J. Tsiakals, and John E. West. *ISO 9001:2000 Explained*, Second Edition. Milwaukee: ASQ Quality Press, 2001.

Cohen, M. J. and J. M. Cohen. *The Penguin Dictionary of Modern Quotations*, Second Edition. London: Penguin Books, 1980.

Fay, Christopher. "Royalties from Loyalties." *Journal of Business Strategy* 15, no. 2 (March/April 1994): 47–51.

Fierman, Jaclyn. "Americans Can't Get No Satisfaction." *Fortune* (December 11, 1995): 186–93.

Fornell, Claes and Birger Wernerfelt. "Defensive Marketing Strategy by Customer Complaint Management: A Theoretical Analysis." *Journal of Marketing Research* 24, no. 4 (November 1987): 337–46.

Gieszl, Yale. EVP Toyota Motor Sales, USA, Chairman of the Customer Satisfaction Committee. 1995.

Juran, Joseph M. "Made in USA: A Renaissance of Quality." *Harvard Business Review* (July/August 1993): 42–50.

Kotler, Philip. *Managerial Marketing, Planning, Analysis, and Control.* Englewood Cliffs, NJ: Prentice-Hall Inc., 1967.

McCarthy, E. Jerome, and William D. Perreault. *Basic Marketing: A Managerial Approach.* Homewood, IL: Richard D. Irwin, 1960.

Mentzer, John T., Carol C. Bienstock, and Kenneth B. Kahn. "Benchmarking Satisfaction: Market Leaders Use Sophisticated Processes to Measure and Manage Their Customers' Perceptions," *Marketing Management* 4, no. 1 (Summer 1995): 41–46.

Reicheld, Frederick, and W. Earl Sasser. "Zero Defections: Quality Comes to Services." *Harvard Business Review* 68 (Sept–Oct. 1990): 105–11.

Rokeach, Milton. *Understanding Human Values.* New York: Free Press, 1979.

Rust, Roland and Anthony J. Zahorik. "Customer Satisfaction, Customer Retention and Market Share," *Journal of Retailing* 69, no. 2 (Summer 1993): 193–215.

Schlesinger, L. A., and J. L. Heskitt. "Breaking the Cycle of Failure in Services." *Sloan Management Review* (Spring 1991): 17–28.

Schneider, Ben. Presentation at Frontiers of Service Marketing Conference. Nashville, TN: Vanderbilt University, October 2000.

Yi, Youjae. "A Critical Review of Consumer Satisfaction," *Review of Marketing*, edited by Valerie Zeithaml. Chicago: American Marketing Association, 1989.

CHAPTER THREE

Bitner, Mary Jo, Bernard C. Booms, and Mary Stanfield Tretault. "The Service Encounter: Diagnosing Favorable and Unfavorable Incidents." *Journal of Marketing* 54, no. 1 (January 1990): 71–84.

Carlzon, Jan. *Moments of Truth.* Cambridge, MA: Ballinger, 1987.

Flanagan, John C. "The Critical Incident Technique." *Psychological Bulletin* 51, (July 1954): 327–57.

Garvin, David A. *Managing Quality.* New York: Free Press, 1988.

Hayes, Bob E. *Measuring Customer Satisfaction: Survey Design, Use, and Statistical Analysis Methods,* Second Edition. Milwaukee: ASQC Quality Press, 1998.

Juran, J. M. *Juran on Planning for Quality.* New York: Free Press, 1988.

Juran, J. M. *Juran on Quality by Design.* Milwaukee: ASQC Quality Press, 1992.

Kelly, George, A. *The Psychology of Personal Constructs.* New York: Norton, 1955.

Reynolds, Thomas J., and Jonathan Gutman. "Laddering Theory, Method, Analysis, and Interpretation." *Journal of Advertising Research* (February–March 1988): 11–31.

Rokeach, Milton. *Understanding Human Values.* New York: Free Press, 1979.

Shostack, G. Lynn. "Breaking Free From Product Marketing." *Journal of Marketing* 41, no. 2 (April 1977): 73–80.

Vavra, Terry G. *Aftermarketing: How to Keep Customers for Life through Relationship Marketing.* New York: McGraw Hill, 1995.

Zeithaml, Valerie A., A. Parasuraman, and Leonard L. Berry. *Delivering Quality Service: Balancing Customer Perceptions and Expectations.* New York: Free Press, 1990.

CHAPTER FIVE

Garvin, David. *Managing Quality.* New York: Free Press, 1988.

Zeithaml, Valerie A., A. Parasuraman, and Leonard L. Berry. *Delivering Quality Service: Balancing Customer Perceptions and Expectations.* New York: Free Press, 1990.

CHAPTER SIX

Bruning, James L., and B. L. Kintz, *Computational Handbook of Statistics*, Fourth Edition. Glenview, IL: Scott, Foresman and Company, 1996.

Dandrade, Robert. "Loyaltizing: A White Paper." Digital Equipment Corporation, 1994.

Keiningham, Timothy and Terry G. Vavra. *The Customer Delight Principle: Exceeding Customer's Expectations for Bottom-Line Success.* New York: American Marketing Association and Contemporary Press McGraw-Hill, 2001.

Kessler, Sheila. *Measuring and Managing Customer Satisfaction Going for the Gold.* Milwaukee: ASQC Quality Press, 1996.

Vavra, Terry G. *Improving Your Measurement of Customer Satisfaction: A Guide to Creating, Conducting, Analyzing, and Reporting Customer Satisfaction.* Milwaukee: ASQ Quality Press, 1997.

CHAPTER SEVEN

Martilla, John A., and John C. James. "Importance-Performance Analysis," *Journal of Marketing* 41, no. 1 (January 1977): 77–79.

Rust, Roland T. and Navenne Donthu, "Combatting Multicollinearity in Customer Satisfaction Survey Analysis," Draft. Center for Service Marketing. Nashville, TN: Vanderbilt University, 1999.

Smith, Scott M. "PC-MDS Multidimensional Statistics Package," Institute of Business Management. Provo, UT: Brigham Young University, 1996.

Vavra, Terry G. *Aftermarketing: How to Keep Customers for Life through Relationship Marketing.* New York: McGraw-Hill, 1995.

Vavra, Terry G. *Improving Your Measurement of Customer Satisfaction: A Guide to Creating, Conducting, Analyzing, and Reporting Customer Satisfaction.* Milwaukee: ASQ Quality Press, 1997.

CHAPTER EIGHT

Cooper, Robert G. "New Product Strategies: What Distinguishes the Top
Performers?" *The Journal of Product Innovation Management* 2 (1984):
151–64.

Griffin, Abbie, and John Hauser. *The Voice of the Customer.* Report no. 92–106.
Cambridge, MA: The Marketing Science Institute, 1992.

Keiningham, Timothy Goddard, Vavra, T. and Iaci, A. "Customer Delight and the
Bottom Line," *Marketing Management* (Fall 1999): 57–63.

Pinto, Mary Beth and Jeffrey K. Pinto. "Project Team Communication and
Cross-Functional Cooperation in New Program Development." *Journal of
Product Innovation Management* 7 (1990): 200–212.

Souder, William E. "Managing Relations Between R&D and Marketing in
New Product Development Projects." *Journal of Product Innovation
Management* 5 (1988): 6–19.

Vavra, Terry G. *Aftermarketing: How to Keep Customers for Life through
Relationship Marketing.* New York: McGraw Hill, 1995.

Index